Strategic Risk Management Practice

At a time when corporate scandals and major financial failures dominate newspaper headlines, the importance of good risk management practices has never been more obvious. The absence or mismanagement of such practices can have devastating effects on exposed organizations and the wider economy (the stories of Barings Bank, Enron, Lehman Brothers, Northern Rock, to name but a few, illustrate this very fact). Today's organizations and corporate leaders must learn the lessons of such failures by developing practices to deal effectively with risk. This book is an important step towards this end. Written from a European perspective, it brings together ideas, concepts and practices developed in various risk markets and academic fields to provide a much-needed overview of different approaches to risk management. It critiques prevailing enterprise risk management frameworks (ERM) and proposes a suitable alternative. Combining academic rigour and practical experience, this is an important resource for graduate students and professionals concerned with strategic risk management.

TORBEN JUUL ANDERSEN is Professor at the Copenhagen Business School. He has taught financial economics and strategy at George Mason University and Johns Hopkins University. He previously held positions as Senior Consultant at PHB Hagler Bailly, Arlington; Senior Vice President at Unibank A/S; Managing Director at SDS Securities A/S, Copenhagen; and Vice President at Citibank/Citicorp Investment Bank, London. He is the author of numerous articles and books on strategy and risk management, including *Global Derivatives* (2005) and *Currency and Interest Rate Hedging* (1993).

PETER WINTHER SCHRØDER is a director at Saxo Bank A/S, Copenhagen where he is responsible for all risk management within the group. He has held various executive risk management positions in the banking, insurance and management services industries over the past twenty years where he gained comprehensive practical experience in all aspects of financial and operational risk management. He is also a part-time associate professor at the Copenhagen Business School.

Strategic Risk Management Practice

How to Deal Effectively with Major
Corporate Exposures

Torben Juul Andersen
and
Peter Winther Schrøder

CAMBRIDGE
UNIVERSITY PRESS

CAMBRIDGE UNIVERSITY PRESS
Cambridge, New York, Melbourne, Madrid, Cape Town, Singapore,
São Paulo, Delhi, Dubai, Tokyo, Mexico City

Cambridge University Press
The Edinburgh Building, Cambridge CB2 8RU, UK

Published in the United States of America by Cambridge University Press, New York

www.cambridge.org
Information on this title: www.cambridge.org/9780521132152

First published 2010
Reprinted 2011

Printed in the United Kingdom at the University Press, Cambridge

A catalogue record for this publication is available from the British Library

Library of Congress Cataloguing in Publication data
Andersen, Torben Juul.
Strategic risk management practice : how to deal effectively with major corporate exposures / Torben
Juul Andersen, Peter Winther Schrøder.
    p.   cm.
Includes index.
ISBN 978-0-521-11424-0 (hardback)
1. Risk management.   2. Strategic planning.   I. Schrøder, Peter Winther.   II. Title.
HD61.A528   2010
658.15′5 – dc22   2009040255

ISBN 978-0-521-11424-0 Hardback
ISBN 978-0-521-13215-2 Paperback

Contents

Appendices

Abbreviations

ASIC	application-specific integrated circuit
BIS	Bank for International Settlements
BU	business unit
CAIB	Columbia Accident Investigation Board
CATEX	Catastrophe Risk Exchange
CD	certificate of deposit
CEO	Chief Executive Officer
COSO	Committee of Sponsoring Organizations of the Treadway Commission
CPI	Consumer Price Index
CRO	Chief Risk Officer
CSR	corporate social responsibility
DEM	Deutschmark
ERM	enterprise risk management
FERMA	Federation of European Risk Management Associations
FTSE	Financial Times Stock Exchange
GKA	glucokinase activator
GNP	gross national product
HR	human resources
HRO	high reliability organization
ICT	information and communication technologies
IF	If P&C Insurance
IPO	initial public offering
IT	information technology
KPI	key performance indicator
KRI	key risk indicator
LIBOR	London interbank offered rate
LTCM	Long-Term Capital Management
MSCI	Morgan Stanley Capital International
MV	market value
NASA	National Aeronautics and Space Administration
NASDAQ	National Association of Securities Dealers Automated Quotation (system)
NPV	net present value
NZ	New Zealand

OECD	Organisation for Economic Cooperation and Development
OTC	over-the-counter
p.a.	per annum
PDCA	Plan-Do-Check-Act
PEST	political, economic, socio-economic, technological
PESTEL	political, economic, socio-economic, technological, environmental and legal
PPP	Purchasing Power Parity
R&D	research and development
REMIC	Real Estate Mortgage Investment Conduit
RM	risk management
RME	risk management effectiveness
ROA	return on assets
S&Ls	savings and loan institutions
S&P	Standard & Poor's
SARS	severe acute respiratory syndrome
SE	Stora Enso
SEC	US Securities and Exchange Commission
SEK	Swedish krona
SIC	Standard Industry Code
SOI	silicon-on-insulator
SOX	Sarbanes–Oxley Act
SP	strategic planning
SRM	strategic risk management
SWOT	strengths, weaknesses, opportunities and threats
TQM	total quality management
TTP	TransTech Pharma Inc.
UK	United Kingdom
US	United States
VaR	value-at-risk
VRIO	value, rarity, imitibility and organization
WACC	weighted average cost of capital

Figures

Tables

Boxes

Preface

Today's institutions and the executives who lead them must be able to demonstrate an ability to deal with frequent and often abrupt changes fuelled by new market developments, political events, technological inventions and different environmental hazards that confront their activities across the global economy. These risks affect the activities of large, multinational corporations, medium-sized enterprises and small commercial entities alike and thereby also affect public institutions and the very communities they operate in. In short, the underlying risk management concerns have wide ramifications and consequently apply to a wide constituency, including both private and public institutions as well as policy makers who care about the wider consequences of risk. Accordingly, there has been a tremendous increase in the public focus on 'corporate risk' in recent years. A predominant reason for the increased recognition of risk undoubtedly lies in the higher frequency of major risk events over the past decade, some of which have had severe repercussions for exposed organizations, with a potential to affect severely economic activity at large. Many corporate incidents have hit the newspaper headlines. These include scandals like the diversion of funds from the Maxwell companies in the early 1990s; the rogue trader, Nick Leeson, who brought the Barings Bank to extinction in the mid-1990s; Bernie Ebbers, the former Chief Executive Officer, who committed major accounting frauds in his company WorldCom from the late 1990s; and Kenneth Lay, Chairman, and Jeffrey Skilling, the CEO of Enron, who submitted misleading annual reports that preceded the company's eventual collapse in the early 2000s. And these types of incidents with mindboggling economic consequences continue to unfold as evidenced by Société Générale's trading losses in Europe and Bernard Madoff's Ponzi scheme in the United States.[1] The underlying causes of these events are often related to the quality of internal controls, and historically implicated several of the major auditing firms as partial accomplices. The events have

---

[1] Société Générale reportedly lost an amount of around US$7 billion (close to €5 billion) in January 2008 as they allegedly closed unauthorized positions in European stock futures contracts created by Jérôme Kerviel, a trader with the bank. In December 2008, Bernard Madoff was charged with investor fraud conducted through his Wall Street firm, Bernard L. Madoff Investment Securities LLC. The prior chairman of the NASDAQ stock exchange was accused of engaging in a giant Ponzi scheme whereby he paid returns to current investors with the proceeds from new investors. As the economy aggravated and customers asked for release of their investments, the funds were not there. The associated losses (which also involve some European banks) are suggested to be around US$50 billion, although the exact amount is yet to be determined.

also focused attention on the integrity and personal accountability of corporate executives.

In addition to spectacular corporate scandals, there has been a steady increase in man-made disasters around the world, some of which include wilful human actions. These include the infamous attack on the World Trade Center on 11 September 2001. The surreal unfolding of events that morning hit society and the business community with surprise and utter disbelief and, yet, the financial markets showed an impressive resilience by being back in action within weeks of the devastating event. However, the dramatic loss of productive assets and intellectual capital imposed significant direct economic costs on businesses, as these resources had to be replaced and reconstructed. The business disruption caused by the event had immediate repercussions for the level of economic activity. Furthermore, the perpetrators' total disregard for human life engendered a level of anxiety and loss of business confidence that could have longer-term indirect effects on new investment activities and general economic activity. The international character of many terrorist events also points to a potential resurgence of political and country risk issues that at times appear to have been somewhat underplayed in the urge to engage in a globalized market economy.

Obviously, these events have induced intense political concerns about the societal impact of corporate risks and generated further scrutiny of prevailing business practices. As a consequence, new regulatory frameworks have been introduced in national markets. These include, for example, the Cadbury Code on Corporate Governance (1992) and the Turnbull Report (1999) with subsequent updates in the United Kingdom, and the Sarbanes–Oxley legislation (2002) in the United States. Similarly, the European Union is planning to impose new directives intended to strengthen internal risk assessment, compliance and corporate governance practices across member countries. These developments have been rather universal among the major industrialized countries as epitomized by the issuance of Principles of Corporate Governance by the OECD (1998). Likewise, the COSO enterprise risk management framework, released by the Committee of Sponsoring Organizations (2004), proposed a new set of corporate principles in managing the corporate risk environment. Similarly, the new regulatory framework (Basel II) introduced by the Bank for International Settlements (2002) incorporated self-monitoring and internal control systems as focal elements to regulate institutions in the international financial markets.

In the wake of these regulatory trends, risk management has been imposed on public affairs in general and on the business community in particular to extend corporate accountability for the consequences of potential risks and institute internal control frameworks to circumvent their occurrence. This surge in regulatory activity and corporate policy development has largely focused on operational risk elements, including opportunities for fraud and infrastructural breakdown. Hence, we have seen a greater recognition of the necessity for risk management processes, with a predominant focus on routine system errors, operational malfunctions, uncontrolled employees and personal accountability of corporate executives.[2]

Yet, one may question the virtue of checklists and formal internal controls that frequently serve merely as convenient tools to demonstrate that the executive board has acted in good faith and has done what it could should a scandal inadvertently catch the attention of the media. The pressure to introduce formal practices of internal controls and personal accountability has clearly led to greater scrutiny of internal processes and reporting systems. However, these practices often promote a defensive corporate mentality, where internal controls may inhibit rather than create a proactive organizational environment that encourages innovative responses to environmental challenges in an uncertain world. What is more, the various risk management frameworks typically propose the implementation of a uniform and integrated structure across the organization to manage all types of risks often institutionalized around a central corporate risk management function.[3] Such a simplified approach is, in our opinion, questionable as a means of handling the multifaceted corporate risk landscape, which requires more complex combinations of specialized risk expertise, timely decentralized responses and central coordination mechanisms.

The aim of this book is to uncover shortcomings in current risk management practices, which are, to a great extent, synonymous with enterprise risk management (ERM). Given that risk can be analyzed from many different perspectives, we do this by combining various elements from traditional risk management areas with elements from the strategic management field, brought keenly to life with theoretical insights and our own practical experiences. We have no illusion that this book will arrive at a definitive recipe for a single 'correct' risk management approach, if such a construct exists. Nonetheless, it is our hope that the book will provide the reader with a more nuanced picture of the risk management challenge in both public and private enterprise.

The book covers various risk management subjects structured around nine major chapters. Chapter 1 provides an overview, outlining the various approaches to exposure assessments and risk management and discusses the diverse dynamics and strategic nature of the corporate risk management challenge.

Chapter 2 outlines more conventional concerns about financial and longer-term economic exposures faced by corporations engaged in international business activities and looks at recent methodologies developed to assess aggregate exposures in all-encompassing value-at-risk measures.

---

[2] For an excellent account of this, see, e.g. Michael Power (2007). *Organized Uncertainty: Designing a World of Risk Management*. Oxford University Press: London.

[3] In this context, it is quite thought provoking that Société Générale was fully compliant with the requirements imposed by the Sarbanes–Oxley legislation and yet experienced a loss of around US$7 billion presumably caused by shortcomings in internal controls and reporting procedures around their financial trading activities.

Chapter 3 presents some of the modern diversification techniques used to hedge and cover against conventional hazards, financial risks and economic exposures and gives an update on recent interfaces between instruments traded in the financial, insurance and capital markets.

Chapter 4 challenges traditional risk management rationales and extends the risk perspective to include important competitive exposures, arguing that a wider range of risk practices is required to deal with current operational and strategic risks. Financial hedging techniques are transposed to the introduction of real options, suggesting that an options logic may alleviate the handling of commercial exposures that are beyond the reach of conventional hedging techniques.

Chapter 5 introduces a more integrated view of the corporate risk landscape and challenges the silo orientation often adopted in existing risk management practices. The shortcomings of existing approaches are highlighted, and we argue that management should consider all risks and possible interactions between them while pursuing a strategy-oriented approach. The chapter discusses the practical challenges associated with the myriad of risks faced by the modern corporation, stressing the simultaneous need for specialized risk expertise and an integrated treatment of corporate exposures.

Chapter 6 introduces a 'new' risk approach – enterprise-wide risk management – aimed at an integrated assessment of important corporate exposures in a systematic manner. We examine whether this approach constitutes a framework that can manage risks appropriately in dynamic business environments where companies face increasing uncertainty and lower ability to forecast events. This leads to a critique of the ERM framework and argues for much-needed amendments.

Chapter 7 illustrates how different conventional strategic and risk management tools can be combined and applied to perform extended analyses of the corporate risk landscape. Further, we illustrate how these rather static tools can be complemented by extended techniques to deal with uncertainties and hard-to-forecast developments. Finally, the importance of establishing a strong culture of risk awareness and mindfulness, enabling the organization to sense, observe and react to environmental changes in a timely manner, is discussed.

Chapter 8 extends our critique of the ERM framework provided in Chapter 6. We demonstrate that a centralized and uniform structure across the organization, as proposed by various ERM frameworks, is unsuited to dealing with the uncertainty that surrounds contemporary business environments and that a more balanced organization of corporate risk management activities is required. Amendments to the ERM framework are proposed in view of the need for improved responsiveness and better coordination of risk responses in line with corporate strategy.

Chapter 9 concludes by describing how effective risk management practices may be integrated with the corporate strategy process and how specialized risk management expertise, decentralized functional insights and responsive initiatives to emerging threats may be facilitated by a central risk management function. A case example of an organization that seems to have succeeded in shaping its own version of such a well-functioning integrated risk management system is used to illustrate how this can be accomplished.

The structure and framing of the book has been inspired by a course in strategic risk management co-developed by the two authors at the Copenhagen Business School and taught to graduate students attending the acclaimed international CEMS programme. However, in view of the high profile of the topic of risk management among executive leaders in public and private enterprises, we believe the book should have wide appeal among an audience of practising managers as well. For this purpose, the book has been written with clarity and accessibility in mind so as to reduce the time it takes to get to important points and facts. Hence, the main sections of Chapters 1 through 9 can be read in conjunction with considerable speed. We provide examples and more detailed insights of interest to management scholars in boxed inserts that can be omitted without loss of continuity. It is our hope that our good intentions will materialize and we welcome readers to gauge this through the ensuing nine chapters – bon appétit!

Frederiksberg, December 2008   *Torben Juul Andersen*
                                                               Peter Winther Schrøder

1 The strategic nature of corporate risk management

Contemporary institutions are exposed to a variety of risks ranging from natural catastrophes and uncontrolled human behaviours to different strategic exposures that may hit the organization in unexpected ways. This chapter describes, partially by illustrative examples, the diverse nature of the corporate risk landscape and how related exposures seem to increase. The chapter discusses how different approaches to risk management may enable corporate executives to deal more effectively with these important challenges. The relationship between positive risk management outcomes and performance is explored and the question about uncovering an effective risk management model is developed.

1.1 The nature of risk management

Risks are everywhere, as evidenced by many corporate events reported in the popular press, including major corporate scandals around once venerable companies like the Maxwell group, Baring Brothers, WorldCom, Enron, Parmalat and so on. We also witness a steady increase in man-made disasters around the world and even the emergence of mega-catastrophes caused by wilful human actions that have both direct and indirect economic effects. These developments have intensified our focus on corporate and public risks and the risk management processes that may be needed to circumvent the adverse economic impacts from such events. All the while, we have seen a public risk perception aimed at reducing system errors, operational malfunctions and uncontrolled human behaviours that affect the way in which we try to deal with corporate risks.[1]

Hence, corporate risk management has become an essential topic and arguably constitutes a new lens through which we may conceive corporate strategy development – because poor risk management may lead to bankruptcy, whereas good risk management practices can excel corporate performance outcomes. Hence, risk management may be seen as a process that lets the organization achieve its full potential and gain optimal economic returns, or to use strategy jargon, effective risk management may be seen as a way in which to create sustainable competitive

---

[1] See, e.g. J. Adams (1995). *Risk*. Ruthledge: Abingdon, Oxon; and M. Power (2004). *The Risk Management of Everything: Rethinking the Politics of Uncertainty*. Demos: London.

advantage. Yet, we do not fully comprehend how the many complex managerial processes relate to strategic risk management practices. We have seen the introduction of formal enterprise-wide risk management frameworks that may help us contain specific exposures, but these approaches do not necessarily constitute sufficient conditions for effective risk management outcomes. Indeed, the invention of operational risk as a concept may be trying to frame the unframeable.[2] Hence, there may be too many aspects of risk that cannot be contained within simple formalized control systems. That is, the importance of risks and the importance of strategic risk factors and related corporate responsiveness in increasingly turbulent market environments point to a need for an extended view of the risk management process.

Where risk events typically are conceived as hazards and dangers caused by identifiable triggers, such as accidents, human error, natural phenomena, etc., conventional risk management seeks to reduce the potential for downside losses derived from such events. However, risk can also be interpreted as the volatility of performance outcomes, in which case the risk management task is seen as the ability to remove possibilities for underperformance while being cognizant of the upside gains associated with emerging business opportunities. Hence, there is a strategic element to the risk management concept that should also consider the potential for new opportunities arising from dramatic changes in the business environment and these may actually constitute some of the most important risk management concerns.[3]

While the nature of common downside risk events is well defined and accounted for in statistical records, many of the emerging operational and strategic risks are less precise and thus much harder to describe and predict. Much of the contemporary risk management literature is supported by calculable odds for identifiable risk events determined by analysis of objective historical records. However, true uncertainty arises when one is unable to determine the odds or even foresee the future risk events.[4] There seems to be a trend towards higher uncertainty due to the emergence of new risks caused by terrorist acts, natural catastrophes, political events, path breaking technologies and continuous innovation.

1.2   The significance of potential risk effects

Risk management as a professional discipline is nothing new. The insurance industry has operated for centuries on the basis of practices that allowed economic entities with specified risks to obtain cover by diversifying the

[2] M. Power (2005). 'The Invention of Operational Risk'. *Review of International Political Economy* 12(4), pp. 577–99.

[3] See, e.g. A. J. Slywotzky and J. Drzik (2005). 'Countering the Biggest Risk of All'. *Harvard Business Review* 82(4), pp. 78–88.

[4] See F. Knight (2006). *Risk, Uncertainty, and Profit*. Dover Publications: Mineola, New York for an early discussion of the distinctions between the concepts of risk and uncertainty.

exposures across many insured parties through the intermediation of professional insurance companies. Similarly, there is really nothing new to the various risk events we see play out today as they affect individuals, institutions and societies. The history is replete with examples of accidents, operational disruptions, fraud cases, political unrest and market collapses, which all constitute incidents with adverse effects on business and economic activity. However, there may have been a change in the underlying causes of adverse risk events with increasing importance in new areas like technology risk, computer hacking, hypercompetitive disruptions, mega-terrorism, etc. The impact of these incidents has been further aggravated by increasing dependence on communication and information technologies and the chase for economic efficiencies in more tightly connected multinational business structures.

The sheer magnitude of potential economic repercussions has brought risk management to a new level of attention as the public has witnessed the (sometimes) exorbitant personal gains derived from corporate fraud and excessive losses from extreme weather conditions, terrorist events and so forth. As populations grow and business activities expand, the accumulation of economic assets also increases, while the coupling between international economies intensifies. As a consequence, the potential losses on economic assets caused by disruptive events also increase as an inevitable outcome of economic growth. All the while, there seems to be a general increase in the risk consciousness of modern society where economic and human losses experienced in yesteryear appear excessive under the current day. In other words, the public risk perception has become increasingly sensitized to the adverse consequences of potential exposures. The increased risk alertness has also affected politicians and lawmakers in their capacity to impose new legislation and rules that public companies must abide by as witnessed by the growth in regulatory frameworks and corporate governance guidelines.

In practice, the risk management initiatives are overwhelmingly concerned with the elimination of potential losses with a focus on cost reduction. The principle of insurance carries with it an idea that exposures beyond individual control can be covered by sharing these risks over a larger diversified portfolio of insurance takers that are unlikely to be hit by accidents at the same time. That is, some accidents cannot be avoided, but it is possible to cover against their adverse economic effects in advance by engaging in insurance contracts. On the other hand, the very size of loss effects is also influenced by human intervention and timely risk mitigation efforts. Indeed, the history of risk management is arguably one of human ingenuity and effort that against the odds of nature have improved the living conditions for mankind over time.[5] Hence, large risk effects are increasingly seen as, at least partially, caused by human error that could be prevented through advance precaution, timely actions, appropriate mitigation efforts and installation of early warning systems to increase general

---

[5] See P. Bernstein (1996). *Against the Gods: The Remarkable Story of Risk*. John Wiley & Sons: New York.

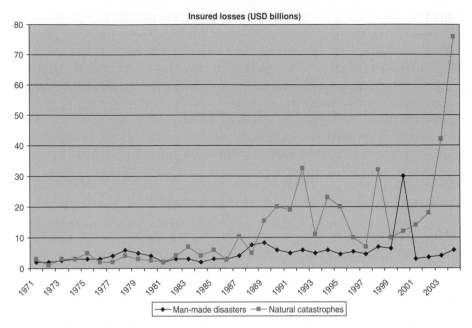

Figure 1.1 *Environmental hazards: exponential growth in insured disaster losses*
Source: Sigma No. 2/2007, Natural Catastrophes and Man-Made Disasters in 2006, Swiss Re.

preparedness and improved responses in the face of major incidents. This view of risk management is supported by the events frequently reported in the press where institutional losses typically arise from negligence, economic fraud and insufficient internal controls.

Yet, many things may be going on that are beyond direct human influence and managerial control. While economic exposures are rising due to a general expansion of the economic infrastructure and placement of productive assets in exposed areas, they also increase due to the higher connections between international markets and through tighter integration of multinational operations. For example, an earthquake in Taiwan may have severe effects on the global sourcing of major corporations because such an incidence can break Internet connections between major production units where manufacturing processes are integrated by information technology. The frequency of earthquake events per se does not seem to increase, but the exposed economic infrastructure is extended. However, there seem to be other climatic changes that increase economic losses in exposed areas due to wind storms, hurricanes and flooding events. The overwhelming consequence of these developments is that the insured losses from man-made disasters and natural catastrophes have been increasing dramatically (Figure 1.1).

Table 1.1 lists the most costly insurance losses caused by man-made disasters and natural catastrophes over the past thirty-five years.[6] It appears that most of the

---

[6] It is worth noting that the insured losses predominantly relate to developed economies where insurance penetration generally speaking is quite high, whereas economic assets in less-developed

Table 1.1 *The 40 most costly insurance losses over the past decades (1970–2006)*

Loss (US$ million)	Victims	Date	Events	Countries
66,311	1,836	08.2005	Hurricane Katrina; floods, damage to oil rigs	US, Gulf of Mexico
22,987	43	08.1992	Hurricane Andrew; flooding	US, Bahamas
21,379	2,982	09.2001	Terror attack on the World Trade Center	US
19,040	61	01.1994	Northridge earthquake	US
13,651	124	09.2004	Hurricane Ivan; damage to oil rigs	US, Barbados
12,953	35	10.2005	Hurricane Wilma; torrential rain, floods	US, Mexico, Jamaica
10,382	34	09.2005	Hurricane Rita; damage to oil rigs	US, Mexican Gulf
8,590	24	08.2004	Hurricane Charley	US, Cuba, Jamaica
8,357	51	09.1991	Typhoon Mireille	Japan
7,434	71	09.1989	Hurricane Hugo	US, Puerto Rico
7,204	95	01.1990	Winter storm Daria	Benelux, France, UK
7,019	110	12.1999	Winter storm Lothar	France, Switzerland, UK
5,500	22	10.1987	Storm and floods	France, Netherlands, UK
5,485	38	08.2004	Hurricane Frances	US, Bahamas
4,923	64	02.1990	Winter storm Vivian	Europe
4,889	26	09.1999	Typhoon Bart	Japan
4,366	600	09.1998	Hurricane George; flooding	US, Caribbean
4,100	41	06.2001	Tropical storm Alison; heavy rain, flooding	US
4,022	3,034	09.2004	Hurricane Jeanne; flooding, landslides	US, Caribbean
3,826	45	09.2004	Typhoon Songda	Japan, South Korea
3,512	45	05.2003	Thunderstorms, tornadoes, hail	US
3,415	70	09.1999	Hurricane Floyd	US, Bahamas, Colombia
3,409	167	07.1988	Explosion on platform Piper Alpha	UK
3,315	59	10.1995	Hurricane Opal; flooding	US, Mexico
3,270	6,425	01.1995	Great Hanshin earthquake in Kobe	Japan
2,905	45	12.1999	Winter storm Martin	France, Spain, Switzerland
2,736	246	03.1993	Blizzard, tornadoes, flooding	US, Canada, Mexico
2,587	38	08.2002	Several floods	Austria, Germany, Spain, UK
2,516	26	10.1991	Forest fires, draught	US
2,505	–	04.2001	Hail, floods, tornadoes	US

(cont.)

Table 1.1 *(cont.)*

Loss (US$ million)	Victims	Date	Events	Countries
2,364	30	09.2003	Hurricane Isabel	US, Canada
2,331	39	09.1996	Hurricane Fran	US
2,305	20	12.1999	Winter storm Anatol	Scandinavia, UK
2,299	4	09.1992	Hurricane Iniki	US, North Pacific
2,217	–	08.1979	Hurricane Frederic	US
2,155	23	10.1989	Explosion in petrochemical plant	US
2,134	220,000	12.2004	Earthquake, tsunami in the Indian Ocean	Indonesia, Thailand
2,091	49	08.2005	Rain, floods, landslides	Germany, Switzerland
2,044	2,000	09.1974	Tropical cyclone Fifi	Honduras
2,009	100	07.1997	Heavy rain, flooding	Czech Republic, Poland

Source: Sigma No. 2/2007, Natural Catastrophes and Man-Made Disasters in 2006, Swiss Re.

significant losses relate to natural catastrophes like hurricanes, storms and earthquakes that may have significant adverse effects on the level of economic activity (see Box 1.1 *The Hyogo-Ken Nanbu earthquake (Kobe)*, Box 1.2 *The Hengchun earthquake (Taiwan)* and Box 1.3 *Global supply chain risks*).[7] However, we also note that the terrorist attack on the World Trade Center in September 2001 emerges as the second largest insured catastrophe loss, while two other man-made disasters figure in the list of the forty most costly insurance losses, namely the explosion on the oil rig Piper Alpha in 1988 and the explosion in a petrochemical plant in 1989. The list of man-made disasters includes other events like fires, plane crashes, boats capsizing, trains derailing, collisions, etc.

Box 1.1 The Hyogo-Ken Nanbu earthquake (Kobe)

One of the worst earthquake catastrophes for years occurred on 17 January 1995 on the western Honshu Island in southern Hyogo. As a consequence of this event, more than 6,000 people perished in and around the city of Kobe, which is Japan's most important port, disrupting the international commercial traffic to and from Japan. An earthquake may show direct

---

countries often are uninsured. On average, around half of the direct economic losses suffered in OECD countries are covered by insurance contracts, whereas only around 5 per cent of direct economic losses in emerging markets have insurance cover. See, e.g. T. J. Andersen (2005). 'Applications of Risk Financing Techniques to Managing Economic Exposures to Natural Hazards'. Technical Paper Series, Inter-American Development Bank: Washington, DC.

[7] These illustrative inserts present well-publicized risk events discussed in many public news media and the information contained in these inserts derive from multiple sources and are not ascribable to a single origin.

physical effects around fault ruptures where the surface is displaced, while secondary effects arise from seismic waves from the fault lines that may cause various aftershocks. In Kobe, most of the devastation was caused by aftershocks as building structures collapsed and fires started around broken gas lines, etc. The direct economic effects relate to the damage imposed on the economic infrastructure that requires substantial resources to reinstall. However, there may also be significant secondary economic effects associated with the disruption of economic activity, displacement of human capital and negative influences on business confidence.

Box 1.2 The Hengchun earthquake (Taiwan)

The Hengchun earthquake occurred around the southwest coast of Taiwan on 26 December 2006 off Hengchun in the Luzon Strait that connects the South China Sea and the Philippine Sea. The earthquake caused some injuries and a few deaths as nearby structures collapsed and the earthquake could be felt in Taipei some 450 km north of Hengchun as well as in Hong Kong and China. A nuclear power plant was on high alert due to serious vibrations. However, the major economic effects were related to the direct and indirect damages caused to several under-sea cables that interrupted telecommunication services to other parts of Asia. The associated disruption of Internet services had serious effects on financial market transactions and broke the connections between multinational business entities and seriously affected their global sourcing networks.

Box 1.3 Global supply chain risks

Numerous catastrophes from the Kobe earthquake in 1995 to Hurricane Katrina in 2005 illustrate that we routinely underestimate the potential business disruption caused by these events. The Kobe earthquake killed more than 6,400 people, destroyed 100,000 buildings causing an estimated US$100 billion in total damages and closed Japan's largest port for two months, thereby disrupting the production and transportation structure of major multinationals, including Toyota. Prior to Hurricane Katrina, many companies diversified their transportation risks by contracting with multiple shippers. However, Katrina closed all traffic through New Orleans, thereby disrupting the business flow of companies that relied on international access via the Mississippi River. Similarly, over-dependence on business activities in a single geographical location may increase disruption exposures to extreme events like the unexpected Hengchun earthquake in 2006.

Some of the major corporate risk events that have hit the newspaper headlines over the past decades include numerous incidents that are closely linked with excessive financial market activities gone awry, while another group of incidents mainly relates to situations of economic fraud and misreporting (see Box 1.4 *Baring Brothers – wild trading*, Box 1.5 *Orange County – exotic instruments*, Box 1.6 *Maxwell Group – diversion of funds*, Box 1.7 *Parmalat – forgeries and fraud* and Box 1.8 *Enron – misleading accounting*). The major part of these intensely reported incidents points towards failed corporate governance as a major culprit in these developments, since a major role of the executive board is to control corporate activities. The events also raised issues regarding the integrity of the CEOs and their responsibility for corporate accounting practices.

Box 1.4 Baring Brothers – wild trading

Baring Brothers was the oldest merchant bank in the UK, but went bankrupt in 1995 when Nick Leeson, a derivatives trader in their Singapore branch, took unauthorized positions in various futures contracts and kept them hidden by booking the transactions on an unused error account. When the accumulated losses from these positions were eventually uncovered, they amounted to the staggering sum of £827 million, enough to erase the entire capital reserve of this venerable and highly esteemed institution.

Box 1.5 Orange County – exotic instruments

Orange County, located in Southern California around Santa Ana with a population of around 2.8 million people, had to declare bankruptcy in 1994 due to losses from investment in interest rate instruments speculating in a positive yield curve with lower short-term rates. As the Federal Reserves Bank against expectations increased the interest rate level, these geared transactions became unprofitable and resulted in total losses of around US$1.5 billion.

Box 1.6 Maxwell Group – diversion of funds

When Robert Maxwell fell from his yacht in 1991, a neat sum of £550 million was missing from his companies. This looting of the companies and their pension funds within the Maxwell Group may have reflected inadequacies of the existing accounting standards as well as the auditing practices adopted by Coopers & Lybrand Deloitte, the long-term accountant for most of the Maxwell companies. A key failing in this case may have been the extraordinary power wielded by Robert Maxwell himself, who was a very dominant person with no intention to share management responsibility. Hence, the highly centralized management style with power concentrated around a single involved executive spelled trouble.

Box 1.7 Parmalat – forgeries and fraud

In 2004 we saw the unravelling of Italy's food giant Parmalat, producer of popular dairy products, biscuits and beverages. The company founder Calisto Tanzi was formally charged for siphoning at least €500 million to a family-owned subsidiary where numerous companies were set up to generate fake profits for the Parmalat subsidiaries, including document forgery to verify a deposit account of $4.98 billion. This was finally revealed after Tanzi met with the Blackstone Group to discuss the sale of the 51 per cent family stake where subsequent scrutiny by the US Securities and Exchange Commission (SEC) indicated that there were hardly any liquid assets, but rather a debt position of €10 billion. The fraudulent activities allegedly took off after the stock went public in the early 1990s due to pressures to meet expectations of global investors.

Box 1.8 Enron – misleading accounting

Enron engaged in a number of complex tax schemes which shifted debt into a series of almost non-existent companies set up by Enron executives and thereby reported more than $2 billion in profits over a long period of time when the company was actually losing money. Enron appeared to be profitable, but in fact was rather engaged in transactions with no true business purpose other than to appear profitable. In other words, the company's management seemed to inflate deliberately the short-term earnings of the company and in the process enriched several of the senior executives, while the eventual collapse of the company in 2002 caused serious financial harm to investors, employees and other stakeholders.

It is hardly surprising that these events spurred a significant increase in the business volume among institutional sellers of compliance services, much of which was further induced by formal regulatory requirements. Yet, one may question the virtue of check lists and formal internal controls that too often serve as tools to let the executive board show that it has acted in good faith and has done nothing wrong in case potential scandals inadvertently arise in the press. The increased requirements for formal control systems and personal accountability have clearly led to increased scrutiny of internal processes and formalized reporting practices. However, it may also at the same time have created a defensive corporate mentality of imposing inhibiting internal controls rather than instituting a proactive organizational environment to encourage innovative responses in the face of environmental challenges and new risks. The importance of remaining vigilant and responsive may be illustrated by reported technology and public policy developments that have affected companies like Eastman Kodak and Coloplast among many others (see Box 1.9 *Eastman Kodak – reshaping the photographic industry* and Box 1.10 *Coloplast – vulnerability to political developments*).

Box 1.9 Eastman Kodak – reshaping the photographic industry[8]

Until the 1980s, Eastman Kodak had for more than 100 years been the most successful company within the photographic industry due to its ongoing efforts utilizing incremental technology improvements to enhance internal capabilities, innovate processes and expand product offerings. This ability made Kodak outstanding within the area of photographic film making.

However, the introduction of digital imaging in the late 1980s changed the competitive landscape fundamentally, with the result that Kodak's chemically based business model became obsolete. An attempt to develop expertise in computer-based digital photography was relatively unsuccessful and, consequently, the change in technology was the onset to Kodak's decline.

As a consequence, the baton was passed on to Sony in 1989 when the company launched a camera based on electronic digital technology, where the image could be viewed immediately on the screen without any need for further processing – a radical departure from the chemical tradition pursued by Kodak.

Box 1.10 Coloplast – vulnerability to political developments[9]

The Danish medico company Coloplast is one of the leading suppliers of ostomy care products in Europe. Forty per cent of the company's turnover is within this product category, while products within urology and continence care and wound and skin care make up the rest. Most of the company's products are sold to public sector institutions and reimbursed by national healthcare authorities. Consequently, the company is vulnerable to developments in the political environment and changes in public healthcare policies.

This risk actually materialized when the German Government announced in 2004 that a new healthcare reform was under way that among other things would cut reimbursement prices for ostomy products by 13 per cent, effective from January 2005. Since Germany was Coloplast's biggest market for ostomy products, this constituted a major risk exposure. The German healthcare reform meant that the company's profit margin for the year 2004/2005 was reduced by 1.5 percentage points, leading to a reduction in operating profits for the year of around 9 per cent.

---

[8] Based on J. M. Utterback (1995). 'Developing Technologies: The Eastman'. *The McKinsey Quarterly* 1, pp. 130–44. For an interesting account of many other failures to adapt new technologies, see C. M. Christensen (1997). *The Innovator's Dilemma: When New Technologies Cause Great Firms to Fail.* Harvard Business School Press: Boston, Massachusetts.

[9] Based on information from company annual reports and various newspaper articles.

Similarly, in October 2005, the British healthcare authorities put forward a proposal to change reimbursement for the supply of wound care products, continence products and ostomy products, with the aim of reducing public healthcare expenditures. While the proposal has not been adopted at the time of writing, and it remains uncertain if and when changes might be adopted, it is sure that Coloplast will be affected by the proposed reforms.

All in all, there is virtually no end to potential sources for economic disruption. A conventional risk management focus has been concentrated on volatile financial markets, insurable casualties and macroeconomic conditions. However, these risks have been extended to include many other factors beyond managerial control, including systemic disruptions, industry paradigm changes, competitive initiatives, technological shifts, political incidents, mega-terrorist events and the like, many of which are hard to foresee and predict (Figure 1.2).

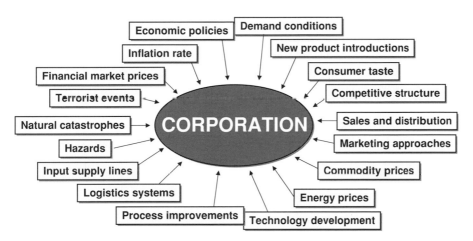

Figure 1.2 *The wide scope of corporate risk exposures*

1.3   Different approaches to risk management

The risk management challenge has been approached in many different ways depending on the assumed professional perspective. The insurance profession looks upon risk management as a technique adopted to cover identifiable risks by diversifying exposures among many insurance takers through the active intermediation of insurance companies. The insurers charge a risk premium reflecting the expected risk of the events based on actuarial calculations plus a margin to cover administration and capital costs. While this approach works for many accidents and casualties where events are independent of each other, it becomes more complicated when risk events are related because the natural diversification across different insurance takers falls short. That is, if the hurricane runs through a certain region, all of the insurance company's customers in the vicinity are hit at the same time and the drain on capital reserves of local insurance companies becomes too large. Therefore, cover for these types of catastrophe risks requires more comprehensive risk-transfer solutions involving the global reinsurance and capital market intermediaries.

The finance discipline has been preoccupied with various market-related risks as institutional investors and borrowers are affected by changes in the interest rates, foreign exchange rates and the associated volatility of financial asset prices. This has led to various approaches from rather mundane cash management techniques of leading and lagging to the development of more sophisticated financial instruments with the purpose of hedging these exposures, including instruments like financial futures, options, swaps and other exotic derivatives.[10] The underlying rationales of these market practices have been to develop mechanisms for pricing different market-related risks and creating effective vehicles to spread these exposures among investors that trade in the underlying financial instruments.

Assuming a multinational financial management perspective, the emphasis changes more towards the foreign exchange rate exposures imposed on companies engaged in international trade and foreign direct investment. These exposures extend from short-term transactions to longer-term economic risks arising from volatile foreign exchange markets, while also considering the potential adverse effects from different political risks that arise in connection with overseas operations. As all of these risks relate to exposures that can be identified, quantified and assessed, they fit quite well with the cyclical activities described in the formal risk management process (see Box 1.11 *The formal risk management cycle*).

Box 1.11 The formal risk management cycle

The conventional risk management process is often presented as an ongoing process comprising four consecutive activities that continue over time. First, the major risks that expose the corporation must be identified. Once this is done, various techniques are adopted to analyze event frequencies and the potential economic effects of the identified exposures. Based on assessments of potential exposures, corporate management decides whether these exposures are acceptable in view of prevailing organizational responses. Finally, the exposures are modified through risk mitigation efforts

---

[10] For a representative account of these risk management instruments in multinational financial management, see, e.g. T. J. Andersen (1993). *Currency and Interest Rate Hedging* (2nd edn). Prentice Hall: Upper Saddle River, New Jersey.

and adoption of various risk-transfer activities, so the corporation retains a risk level that is acceptable within the overall corporate risk policy.

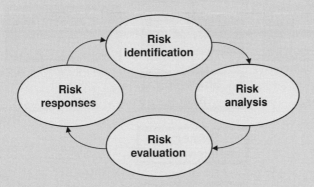

As risk factors and the associated economic exposures may change dynamically over time, the described elements of the formal risk management process should be repeated within regular time intervals.

With the emerging emphasis on various operational risks, there has also been an increased focus on the potential for human errors and misconduct as well as technological breakdowns. Managing these types of exposures depends on effective corporate accounting systems to identify and measure the relevant exposures as well as internal control processes adopted to check whether exposures are kept within bounds and whether processes remain in line. All together, these perspectives on possible risk events are commensurate with the practices promoted by enterprise-wide risk management approaches that assume the formal elements of the risk management process. They also resonate with contemporary public policy concerns where various legislative initiatives, regulation and supervision are imposed to reduce the adverse societal consequences of human error.[11]

Other disciplines seem to take slightly varied views on the risk phenomenon. While total quality management, six-sigma and lean management principles seem focused on improving operational efficiencies, they ideally also pay attention to emerging customer needs and process improvements through continuous learning. Similarly, risk assessments in project management see a need to balance advance planning with adaptive solutions that arise as the projects are implemented.[12] We may even extend this perspective to corporate strategy

[11] Adams (1995).
[12] See, e.g. C. Chapman and S. Ward (2003). *Project Risk Management: Processes, Techniques, and Insights* (2nd edn). John Wiley & Sons: Chichester, West Sussex; and C. H. Loach, A. DeMeyer and M. T. Pich (2006). *Managing the Unknown: A New Approach to Managing High Uncertainty and Risk in Projects*. John Wiley & Sons: Hoboken, New Jersey.

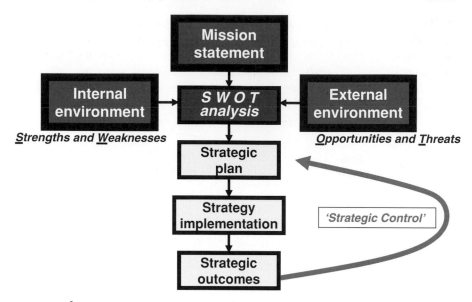

Figure 1.3 *Risk assessments in the strategic management process*

formulation, which can be seen as the execution of a string of projects or strategic actions where the upside potential for improvements and uncovered opportunities should be exploited during implementation. Although the strategy-making process is rarely conceived this way, one might argue that strategic management, which incorporates analyses of institutional strengths, weaknesses, opportunities and threats (often epitomized as SWOT analysis), is de facto engaged in explicit analysis of strategic risks (Figure 1.3).

The formal strategy process resembles the risk management process by including a strategic control element whereby corporate management is supposed to monitor performance outcomes against intended strategic goals to ensure that corporate activities remain on track and correspond to the set course without major discrepancies.[13] What seems to be sometimes forgotten in this context is that some digression from the beaten track also can hold the key for generating innovative ideas and adaptive responses to changing environmental conditions.

The risk perspective embedded in the strategic management process is not commonly recognized in the broad strategy literature. Hence, predominant strategy-related frameworks, such as the balanced scorecard and strategy mapping, retain a risk focus that is largely confined to the consideration of internal process errors

---

[13] See, e.g. R. Simons (2000). *Performance Measurement and Control Systems for Implementing Strategy*. Prentice Hall: Upper Saddle River, New Jersey ('Managing Strategic Risk', Ch. 13, pp. 275–300). To a large extent this is the strategic planning model adopted in the various ERM frameworks as they try to monitor and control outcomes in accordance with predetermined goals.

and potential adverse effects of poor market reputation.[14] Only a few contemporary strategy textbooks take a more explicit view on the significance of a formal risk management focus.[15] Nonetheless, there is general recognition that the ability to respond to changing environmental conditions is an important strategic concern variously referred to as dynamic capabilities, strategic response capabilities or strategic responsiveness.

1.4 Integrating risk management approaches

A firm that is unable to manage its exposures to various financial market volatilities will experience significant variances in corporate earnings over time as global economic conditions change. In the case of foreign exchange rates, interest rates, commodity prices, etc., there are a number of hedging tools available in the financial markets that may allow the firm to hedge these short- to medium-term exposures and thereby reduce the impact on earnings variability over time. However, in the case of longer-term trends in the market rates, hedging can only serve to minimize erratic movements in corporate earnings, but it cannot permanently avoid an unfavourable development of the foreign exchange rates. Under these circumstances there is a requirement for structural modifications to the organization's real assets that can provide general diversification of economic exposures across different currency areas. It may also in some cases provide production flexibilities so the level of business activities can be switched between different economic regions, thus allowing for potential exploitation of factor cost advantages, price arbitrage opportunities and general economic optimization of multinational business activities.

The exposure to environmental hazards and corporate catastrophe events can have a significant effect on the earnings variation from one accounting period to the next and may in extreme situations jeopardize the survival of the firm as an independent entity. It is possible to obtain covers for many of these economic exposures through conventional insurance contracts and various risk-transfer arrangements in the reinsurance and capital markets. Other risk management precautions include diversification of productive assets, backup arrangements for essential processes, systems and resources, imposition of various internal control systems to reduce the likelihood of adverse events, etc. Yet, we also realize that the

---

[14] R. S. Kaplan and D. P. Norton (2004). *Strategy Maps: Converting Intangible Assets into Tangible Outcomes*. Harvard Business School Press: Boston, Massachusetts as an influential strategy book makes reference to two kinds of risk: operational risks, such as credit operations, interest rate and currency fluctuations in financial institutions; and environmental risks, such as environmental incidents leading to clean-up costs, litigation costs, consumer boycotts and loss of reputation (p. 179).

[15] See J. McGee, H. Thomas and D. Wilson (2005). *Strategy Analysis and Practice*. McGraw-Hill: London ('Risk, Uncertainty, and Strategy', Ch. 14, pp. 529–52).

ability to recover and rein in the extreme effects of catastrophic events and major operational disruptions is highly dependent on the risk management capabilities of corporate managers. Hence, where conventional insurance covers may reverse the direct economic losses, the ability to circumvent adverse secondary economic effects depends on managerial competencies that are more important in the long run.

Finally, the hard-to-quantify strategic risks seem to arise in abundance under the turbulence of global markets and may eventually constitute some of the most significant corporate exposures that exceed the potential adverse effects of financial and economic risks. The handling of these exposures is more delicate because they often represent a higher level of uncertainty that make them difficult to describe and even foresee and as a consequence require different organizational features to facilitate appropriate responses. These may include involvement, observance, openness, internal communication, flexible information exchange, autonomous experimentation, and combinations of central monitoring and coordination with decentralized responses enabled close to the locations where new risks arise.

Hence, we have briefly discussed different approaches to manage a diversity of risks, ranging from very specialized and measurable exposures to more general and indicative risks associated with highly uncertain environmental contexts. We further argue that the ability to adopt different risk management approaches to deal effectively with these diverse exposures will serve to minimize the variability in the development of corporate earnings as circumstances change over time. While this may serve to reduce bankruptcy risk and create stability around important stakeholder relationships, there are few empirical studies that provide conclusive evidence about the eventual pay-offs of the underlying risk management efforts.

1.5   Does risk management pay?

A common perception associated with the evaluation of alternative business propositions is that since new ventures are often risky, where the estimated value of the potential future cash flows can vary considerably, they also require a higher rate of return. The rationale behind this approach is to impose a certain degree of conservatism on resource commitments to engage in new risky ventures. Therefore, when the projected cash flows are assessed with a higher required rate of return to discount the future cash flows, it also means that the net present value of the project is reduced.[16] That is, according to this approach there is direct proportionality between the the venture's level of risk and the return to be

---

[16] It should be noted here that this constitutes an ex ante analysis, i.e. we seek to determine whether a certain future investment opportunity is economically viable before it is made. This is different

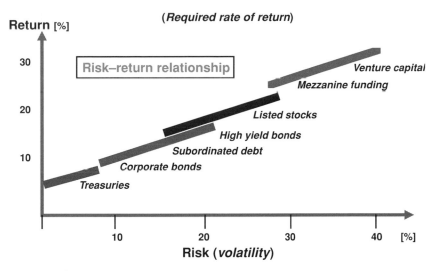

Figure 1.4 *The risk–return relationship of financial assets*

gained from it. This positive risk–return relationship is typically reflected in the average returns obtained from financial assets belonging to different risk classes and captured in the so-called capital asset pricing model, which is widely applied in modern portfolio theory. In short, the common perception from investment decisions in corporate finance and analyses of financial market returns is the notion of a positive relationship between risk and return (Figure 1.4). However, managers also take new initiatives and assume commercial risks with an inner sense that whatever obstacles may arise over the course of a new venture can be handled through managerial competencies, be they formal risk management practices or improvised adaptations.

The curious reader will probably ask whether these relationships also hold as companies realize their business propositions over time. That is, what does analysis of empirical corporate data reveal? To this end, we can conduct such an investigation by comparing the variability of reported corporate earnings over time to the average level of economic returns realized by these institutions during the same time period. If the common perception of the risk–return relationship is true, then we should expect to observe higher economic performance among corporations that display a more risky development in their earnings flows.[17]

from performing an ex post analysis of the realized returns and the variability of earnings after the business venture has been realized.

[17] We should note here that the determination of returns used in the capital asset pricing model is based on market returns, i.e. the sum of the interest payments received and the capital gains obtained from the development of quoted market prices. This measure can be different from the economic returns calculated on the reported earnings, although the market evaluations and realized corporate earnings should converge over longer periods of time.

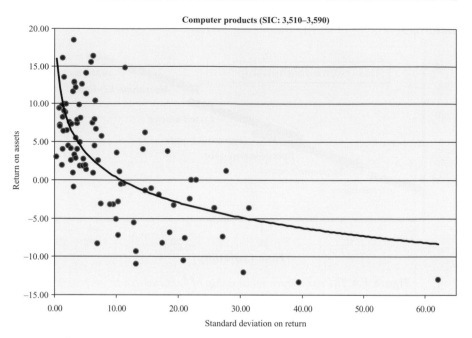

Figure 1.5 *The risk–return relationship in turbulent industries*

Conversely, if the promoted risk management effects have any bearing, we should observe the inverse relationships. That is, lower earnings variability reflecting good risk management should correspond to higher realized economic returns. Now, analyzing the data among firms operating within specific industry environments consistently shows a negative risk–return relationship, the size of which varies across environmental contexts.[18] That is, these analyses indicate that lower earnings variability generally is associated with higher reported earnings over the same time period. Hence, an analysis of companies in US-based computer products industries during the ten-year period 1991 to 2000 shows an inverse relationship between the standard deviation on returns (ROA) and the average returns over the same period (Figure 1.5).[19]

Comparable studies in other environmental contexts, such as the US-based food processing industries, over the same time period show a similar kind of inverse relationship between the standard deviation on returns and average returns (Figure 1.6). However, we notice that while the inverse risk–return relationship is reproduced, it is less pronounced in the food processing industries compared to the computer products industries. In other words, the positive economic effects of

---

[18] The comparisons should be made within industries to control for the potential moderating influences of industry-specific environmental contexts.

[19] The standard deviation on return is a commonly used risk measure, which is determined as the square root of the variance of the returns observed over the period.

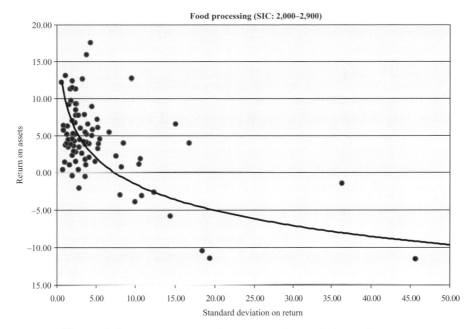

Figure 1.6 *The risk–return relationship in less turbulent industries*

effective risk management capabilities, as reflected in a less vulnerable earnings development, seem to be somewhat higher in turbulent industrial contexts like computer products that are more exposed to new innovations and face more frequent changes. This apparent relationship between risk management effectiveness and performance is not surprising in view of the preceding discussions of the many types of risk that expose corporations operating in the turbulent markets of global competition.

While the predominant managerial view projects a higher return on a higher level of risk, the empirical evidence from numerous analyses of corporate accounting returns indicates that higher levels of performance risk (measured as the standard deviation in returns) are associated with lower average returns. That is, the more stable the corporate earnings development is, which arguably is symptomatic for effective risk management practices, the higher a return will be earned from the corporate business activities. These somewhat controversial risk–return relationships can be explained by good risk management capabilities where the ability to respond effectively to changes in the environmental context of the corporation is essential. However, these results obviously do not provide us with an exact recipe for how to construe and implement effective risk management practices.

Risk transfer, financial hedging, operational controls and strategic responsiveness all seem to matter, but we have not uncovered the organization and the management processes necessary to achieve effective risk management outcomes. A number of practice-based risk management frameworks claim to furnish effective risk management, but at present there is little factual evidence to support these claims. Whereas existing risk management frameworks provide important attention to essential exposures and uncover ways in which to deal with associated losses, there are few concrete propositions as to how risk management practices may furnish initiatives that can exploit the upside potentials deriving from a turbulent environmental development.

There may be a number of potentially competing explanations for this phenomenon. It could arise from good risk management practices that allow the firm to observe environmental changes, interpret these observations and adapt corporate actions accordingly. Organizations practising such a managerial approach do not necessarily have to implement a formal ERM framework, although they could. However, this managerial perspective is consistent with the risk management propositions – that is, effective risk management capabilities provide the organization with the means to respond to environmental changes and thereby minimize the effect on corporate earnings. That is, effective risk management allows the firm to avoid large losses and at the same time develop a stream of new business opportunities that support a steady flow of corporate earnings. We could also interpret effective risk management as a complex integrative process that enables the corporation to obtain a better fit with current business conditions over time, which everything else equal should provide higher returns and lower variability in those returns.[20]

An alternative explanation could be that managerial decision-making and the risk perceptions of decision-makers are influenced by the current performance of the organization. That is, we may observe a circumstantial framing of decisions where high current performance increases risk aversion and thereby engages the organization in less risky ventures that tend to reduce earnings variability. Conversely, a receding earnings development or permanently poor performance levels may increase the pressures to accept risky ventures and thereby improve economic performance, which will increase earnings variability.[21] Another explanation could relate to the natural left-skewed performance outcomes associated with economic return ratios where the numerator and the denominator are partially related. Hence, when the profit and loss statement posts large losses, total assets are likely to contract in size, which leads to relatively higher negative return ratios. That is, when earnings are negative, total assets are also reduced, which will tend to overestimate the nominal value of negative return on asset ratios. Conversely,

---

[20] A better fit could relate to better fulfilment of changing customer needs, faster deployment of new relevant technologies, ongoing modifications to structural parameters in the organization, etc.

[21] This perspective is captured by the idea behind 'prospect theory': see, e.g. D. Kahneman and A. Tversky (1979). 'Prospect Theory: An Analysis of Decisions under Risk'. *Econometrica* 47, pp. 263–91. It also resembles organizational behaviour models where search processes (innovation) are induced by poor performance or situations of below target outcomes. See, e.g. J. March and Z. Shapira (1987). 'Managerial Perspectives on Risk and Risk Taking'. *Management Science* 33, pp. 1404–18.

positive earnings will tend to expand the asset base and thereby underestimate positive return on assets ratios. This technical aspect of the inverse risk–return relationship may play a role, but it does not constitute a full explanation of the observed phenomenon.[22]

Here we claim that *effective risk management* comprises all organizational practices that serve to improve the firm's ability to respond so as to avoid the adverse economic effects and to exploit the upside economic potential afforded by changes in environmental risk factors. That is, various risk management approaches, including insurance contracting, financial hedging, internal controls and strategic response capabilities, all contribute to the firm's ability to respond to environmental changes. When dealing with observable and quantifiable risks, the firm may adopt the practices proposed by the common risk management cycle of identifying, analyzing, evaluating and responding. When dealing with high uncertainty events that are difficult to foresee, more subtle processes might be required, allowing responses to take effect as and when environmental changes are observed to influence organizational activities. Hence, a firm that is able to respond effectively to all of the different types of environmental change to which it is exposed should generally experience improved earnings with lower variability in the earnings development. Therefore, such a comprehensive strategic risk management model can explain the inverse risk–return relationship and specify the observed differences in the risk–return dynamic across different industrial environments.[23] See Appendix 1 for a more detailed description of the underlying strategic responsiveness model.

1.6 Effective risk management

So far, we have discussed the general corporate ability to manage diverse risk exposures effectively in ways that will minimize the earnings development over time as reflected in a lower standard deviation in return on assets. In line with this thinking, we might be able to introduce a suitable measure of risk management effectiveness (RME). Since effective risk management arguably constitutes a corporate ability to reduce the earnings effects from exogenous changes in the environment, such a measure should capture the variability in corporate sales effects held against the development in corporate earnings. Hence, a measure determined as the standard deviation in sales divided by the standard deviation of returns over a specified time period would indicate the variability in sales as

---

[22] See T. J. Andersen, J. Denrell and R. A. Bettis (2007). 'Strategic Responsiveness and Bowman's Risk–Return Paradox'. *Strategic Management Journal* 28, pp. 407–29 for a discussion of alternative explanations.

[23] This model is analyzed in more detail in Andersen, Denrell and Bettis (2007).

affected by various market factors compared to the resulting variability in the earnings development.

Different risks are imposed on the organization from various market conditions that are beyond managerial control, such as environmental hazards, market prices, political events, changing demand, competitive moves, new technologies, etc. Changes in these risk factors are likely to affect corporate sales opportunities, for example, secondary economic effects, market disruption, new tastes, decreasing demand, supply chain and inventory management, etc. Hence, the effect of significant exogenous market risks should be reflected in the standard deviation of the corporate sales development over the period. That is, the higher the level of exogenous risks, the higher the variability in corporate sales. If the firm is able to deal effectively with these exogenous market risks by engaging in responsive actions, it should result in a more stable development in earnings. Such a development will then be reflected in a lower standard deviation of returns for the firm. Therefore, the standard deviation of corporate sales divided by the standard deviation in corporate returns over the period would constitute a rough indicator of the firm's RME.

$\textbf{RME}_{t,j} = sd(sales_{t,j})/sd(return_{t,j})$
$\textbf{RME}_{t,j} =$ firm j's risk management effectiveness over time period t
$\textbf{sd(sales}_{t,j}) =$ the standard deviation in firm j's sales over time period t
$\textbf{sd(return}_{t,j}) =$ the standard deviation in firm j's ROA over period t

In a 'sunshine' scenario, sales are increasing steadily in a volatile market, but the firm is able to manage its resources effectively to accommodate these market conditions. The cost base does not increase faster than the incremental sales and may even develop at a lower rate, reflecting continuous operational improvements and a constant increase in economic efficiencies. As a consequence, the earnings development shows less variance than the corresponding development in corporate sales, while corporate returns increase. That is, the RME measure should display higher relative values.

In a 'bad weather' scenario, there are pressures on market sales due to sluggish demand, political tensions, changing tastes, competing products, etc. As a consequence, corporate sales may be falling off and thus show significant variance from period to period. If there are substantial fixed costs associated with prior commitments to the operational structure, the sales force and the necessary administrative back office, it may be difficult to reduce these costs in conjunction with changes in the sales volume. This may lead to significant periodic losses where corporate performance becomes more volatile than the corporate sales development. That is, the RME measure would fall to dramatically lower levels. Hence, in its simplest form the ability to pursue sales and adapt the cost base accordingly is alpha and omega in risk management effectiveness (see Box 1.12 *The RME indicator*).

Box 1.12 The RME indicator

The RME indicator provides a basic measure of the firm's adaptive behaviour in the face of an erratic sales development. For many firms a first natural reaction in view of waning sales may be to pursue new market initiatives to try to accomplish the set sales targets and achieve budgeted revenue goals. Hence, the ability to engage in these adaptive measures depends on good external market insights and accessible management information systems. If the adaptive initiatives fail to reach the desired outcomes, the next best solution may be to try to reduce the cost base to salvage profitability in the face of adverse market conditions. Hence, a good risk manager as reflected in a high RME measure may also indicate a high ability to adjust corporate costs to prevailing market conditions through flexible manufacturing structures, retaining high levels of variable costs and engaging in reasonable outsourcing arrangements.

$$RME = \text{market risk/firm risk} = \text{sd(sales)}/\text{sd(return)}$$

When sales increase faster than costs, profitability and returns will increase. Conversely, when sales decrease faster than costs, profitability and returns will fall. Furthermore, sales expansion will frequently lead to higher assets, which will tend to reduce the relative return measure. Conversely, a drop in sales will typically be associated with lower assets, particularly if profits turn into losses, and this will tend to enhance the relative return measure. Hence, the denominator and the numerator in the RME indicator are interrelated and, therefore, we need to consider the implications of this relationship. Basically, the standard deviation of returns in the denominator is influenced by the development in sales and hence is related to the standard deviation in sales in the numerator. This relationship can be expressed mathematically and a simple derivation can tease out the relationship between the underlying variances.

$$\text{return} = f(\text{sales} - \text{costs}) \Rightarrow$$
$$\text{var(return)} = \text{var(sales)} + \text{var(costs)} - 2\text{cov(sales, costs)}$$

Consequently, the higher the covariance between sales and costs, the more we can reduce the variance in returns (and hence the standard deviation in returns) that will achieve high scores on the RME measure. Therefore, a company that is faced with waning sales can achieve a high RME by adjusting costs perfectly to match this development. Conversely, a firm that is faced with increasing costs may achieve a high RME by adjusting its sales upwards perfectly to match this increase.

The firm can be affected by different types of exogenous risks, including environmental hazards, economic risks and strategic risks. If the firm is hit by a hazard risk, say the operational structure is partially destroyed by an earthquake, there may be direct economic losses with regard to firm assets and secondary economic effects associated with disruptions to the normal business activities. If the firm has good insurance contracts in place, the direct economic losses are covered and there should be little impact on current economic performance. Furthermore, if the firm has diligent responsiveness skills, it should also be able to recover the indirect economic effects that may arise subsequently due to longer-term effects on demand conditions, customer relationships, etc. By comparison, a firm that has neither insurance coverage nor response capabilities will show more dramatic volatilities in the earnings development.

In the case of economic risks, firms with good financial risk management skills should be better shielded from serious short-term effects of erratic market prices and a flexible economic infrastructure will provide some room to allow manoeuvring that can circumvent major long-term effects of changing financial and economic conditions. By comparison, a firm that fails to identify and manage major financial and economic exposures should show a more volatile earnings development.[24]

Strategic risk factors can affect market sales, operational processes, business models, etc., and the ability to cope with these factors requires strong strategic response capabilities. Hence, the firms that can sense environmental change and adapt corporate activities accordingly are able to deflect the major consequences of changing conditions and retain high, relatively stable profit levels. In contrast, firms that lack these capabilities will suffer.

In summary, then, firms that are good at managing their hazard, economic and strategic risks should display high measures on the RME indicator. The truly good risk managers must be good at handling all of these risks to ensure that high RME measures materialize. Conversely, poor risk managers should display low measures on the RME indicator.

RME measures the effective handling of various exogenous risks that are associated with the many exposures assumed by companies operating in a complex global market context and exposing themselves to the uncertainty of turbulent environments. However, the RME measure should capture the ability to handle endogenous risks as well. That is, firms that are good at handling their operational risks by imposing effective control systems and auditing practices around attentive and risk-aware corporate cultures will only rarely suffer from disruptive operational events. Should those events occur nonetheless, the good risk managers are able to counteract and contain the adverse economic outcomes. The poor risk managers will be unable to achieve this: they will suffer the adverse consequence of major losses and thus display a volatile earnings development. Hence, the

---

[24] Hence, the use of currency derivatives is shown to enhance market value among non-financial firms: see G. Allayannis and J. Weston (2001). 'The Use of Foreign Currency Derivatives and Firm Market Value'. *Review of Financial Studies* 14, pp. 243–76. See also C. Smithson and B. J. Simkins (2005). 'Does Risk Management Add Value? A Survey of the Evidence'. *Journal of Applied Corporate Finance* 17(3), pp. 8–17 for a further discussion of the financial hedging effects.

RME indicator should also consistently reflect an organization's ability to handle different operational risks.

Effective risk management then constitutes an amalgam of capabilities ranging from specialized insurance and financial hedging practices, embedded structural flexibilities and strategic response capabilities that allow the firm to adapt to exogenous market changes and exploit proactively observed market opportunities.[25] It also comprises an ability to contain and manage various operational risks. This description of the risk management challenge constitutes a truly integrative and enterprise-wide perspective that in many ways goes beyond the scope of current ERM frameworks.

The RME measure is catering to an overarching risk management perspective. It has a direct focus on the hard-to-quantify strategic risks, but also captures the effects caused by the conventional risk factors, including changes in market prices, environmental hazards and operational disruptions. Therefore, when firms are unable to adapt and retain sales and when major losses occur, the variability in performance will exceed the variability in sales, and RME will drop correspondingly. Looking at empirical data, the variability in corporate sales and corporate earnings (measured by their standard deviation) is positively correlated and both measures have negative correlations to average performance expressed as return on assets. Nonetheless, when the two measures are combined in the RME ratio, this ratio appears to be positively correlated to corporate performance as indicated both by economic returns as well as increases in market values.[26]

A study of US-based firms operating in industrial machinery and computer products industries over the ten-year period 1991 to 2000 illustrates the positive relationship between effective risk management and corporate performance (Figure 1.7).

The positive relationships are reproduced in other industrial environments, although the shape and slope of the risk management effects will vary somewhat between different environmental contexts. A study of US-based firms operating in the pharmaceutical products industry, which is considered a knowledge- and research-intensive environment, shows a comparable positive relationship between risk management effectiveness and performance outcomes (Figure 1.8).

The more comprehensive view of the corporate risk landscape discussed here covers all aspects of the risk management processes. It incorporates environmental hazards, financial exposures and operational disruptions, all of which may cause excessive one-time losses if they get out of hand. In many ways these factors represent the conventional downside risks that can be covered through insurance arrangements or hedged through use of financial derivatives and the like, but also extend to limit operational flaws through internal controls, etc. Hence, risk management techniques of insurance, financial hedging and management

[25] John Chambers, the CEO of Cisco, refers to these phenomena as 'market transitions'. See J. Chambers (2008). 'Cisco Sees the Future – The HBR Interview, Interviewed by Bronwyn Fryer and Thomas A. Stewart'. *Harvard Business Review* 86(11), pp. 72–9.

[26] See T. J. Andersen (2008). 'The Performance Relationship of Effective Risk Management: Exploring the Firm-Specific Investment Rationale'. *Long Range Planning* 41, pp. 155–76.

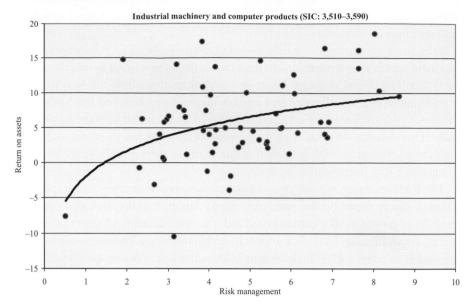

Figure 1.7 *The relationship between effective risk management and performance (I)*

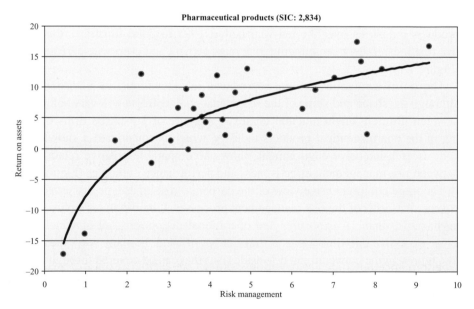

Figure 1.8 *The relationship between effective risk management and performance (II)*

accounting systems in many cases serve to reduce downside loss exposures that, in turn, may lead to process improvements through appropriate application of total quality management (TQM) and lean practices.

At the same time, the risk landscape also deals with longer-term economic exposures embedded in the complexity and dynamism of the global economy as well as strategic risks that increase corporate exposures under hypercompetitive market conditions. Dealing with economic exposures and various strategic risk factors requires a rather comprehensive understanding of the changing environmental conditions and potential interrelationships between different market parameters. It also entails intricate processes of identifying new emerging risks and business opportunities that are often outside the view of corporate executives. The eyes and ears of employees at the operational levels will, therefore, be very helpful in this context. In fact, the ability to engage lower-level managers in autonomous initiatives to explore new possibilities and responses could turn out to be crucial elements of effective risk management. Hence, we also have to deal with practices whereby the firm can identify, develop and exploit new business opportunities that may arise as a consequence of effective handling of emerging threats.

These aspects of effective risk management may illustrate a duality in the strategic risk management process where the handling of strategic risks is combined with the ability to reduce excessive losses (see Box 1.13 *The dual aims of strategic risk management*).

Box 1.13 The dual aims of strategic risk management

The profile of possible performance outcomes in the firm is often assumed to follow a normal distribution. This profiling is based on an assumption about the environment as constituting a series of random independent events, each one of which may affect firm performance in either negative or positive ways. When taken together, the aggregate effect of these events should lead to a normally distributed expected outcome profile (see Graphic 1 below).

A firm may be responsive to environmental changes – for example, management is alert and observant, encourages interpretive discussions and is able to instigate new initiatives that allow the firm to respond to observed changes. To the extent that this is the case, the firm is said to have strategic responsiveness, which in turn should allow the firm to engage in new responsive business ventures. This ability should increase the expected performance outcomes as new opportunities are exploited, but may also increase downside risk exposures as the firm enters into new territory (see Graphic 2 below).

However, by imposing conventional risk management processes that establish covers against different types of loss events and impose internal controls to avoid major operational disruptions may allow the firm to circumvent, maybe even 'cut off', the downside losses in the lower end of the expected performance distribution (see Graphics 3 and 4 below).

The combined effect of strategic responsiveness and conventional risk management

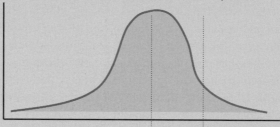

1. A normally distributed performance outcome profile

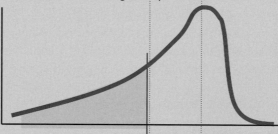

2. Performance enhancing strategic responsiveness

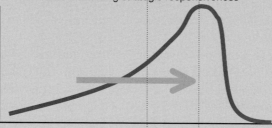

3. Conventional risk management processes

4. The performance outcome of combined approaches

The net effect of this type of effective strategic risk management practices might arguably be that management has been able to increase the expected returns from operations while at the same time reducing the variation in possible future outcomes (see graphic below).

Transforming the performance profile through strategic risk management

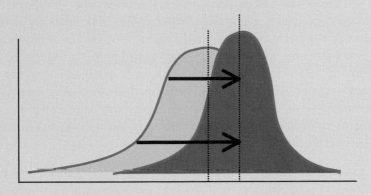

Since the previous argumentation relates to expected future returns for the individual firm, it is impossible to recreate and test these arguments empirically. Instead, the underlying reasoning can only serve as a way to conceptualize how the combination of different risk management approaches eventually may lead to effective risk management outcomes.

By comparison, historical performance data will typically indicate slightly skewed distributions. For illustrative purposes, the graphic below shows the average performance, measured as return on assets, for a large cross-sectional group of firms.

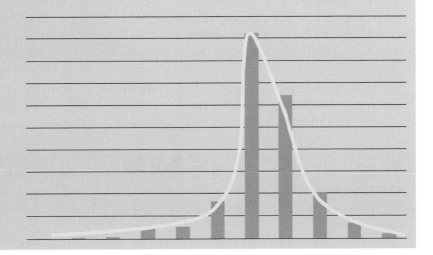

That is, a true enterprise-wide risk management approach must combine more conventional approaches to avoid downside loss effects with newer perspectives on responsive organizational structures to enhance the ability to exploit upside potential. Hence, a strategic risk management focus will also comprise an engaged strategy-making process with the ability to take decentralized initiatives that can search new risk areas and seek out related business opportunities. While this ideally will serve to expand the economic performance opportunities available to the firm, the engagement in new full-blown business initiatives may also extend the downside risks of the corporation. However, engaging in conventional risk management practices and various internal control processes can serve to limit the occurrence of excessive loss situations as the corporation engages to exploit new business opportunities. In effect, then, this dual perspective illustrates how an enhanced strategic approach seeking to exploit upside potential in a rapidly changing environment can be combined with more conventional risk management practices to fend off downside risk events.

1.7   Conclusion

The performance relationship of effective risk management capabilities seems to be consistently positive. This positive outcome may be partially related to an ability to identify, assess and manage risks so as to minimize potential downside losses, which corresponds to conventional views on risk management as practices of risk reduction and transfer of excess exposures. It complies with the formal risk management cycle comprising risk identification, measurement, mitigation, transfer, preparedness, monitoring and risk management as an ongoing analytical and control-based exercise. The underlying view of exposures is rooted in a risk conception driven by human error that somehow can be reduced and controlled. However, such a view by itself ignores proactive reasons for taking risks, namely to explore new opportunities under changing market conditions and to try out these ideas in new business initiatives that can increase corporate responsiveness.

Managing risks is not just about avoiding downside losses; it is also a process of developing and probing innovative and responsive ideas that can help the organization to gain insights about new opportunities under changing environmental conditions. In other words, there is a need for multiple conceptualizations of risk in effective risk management processes to both minimize downside losses and enhance upside business potentials. While this is often mentioned in passing in descriptions of various enterprise-wide risk management approaches, it is rarely outlined in any detail nor truly practised in the formal risk management frameworks.

In the following chapters, we will seek to address the concern for effective risk management with the hope of clarifying the multifaceted nature of this complex process. One should not expect final answers to this puzzle, but hopefully it will induce a movement towards a more comprehensive and meaningful risk management construct compared to the fragmented way in which we often seem to study risk management.

References

Adams, J., 1995. *Risk*. Ruthledge: Abingdon, Oxon.

Allayannis, G. and Weston, J., 2001. 'The Use of Foreign Currency Derivatives and Firm Market Value'. *Review of Financial Studies* 14, pp. 243–76.

Andersen, T. J., 1993. *Currency and Interest Rate Hedging* (2nd edn). Prentice Hall: Upper Saddle River, New Jersey.

2005. 'Applications of Risk Financing Techniques to Managing Economic Exposures to Natural Hazards'. Technical Paper Series, Inter-American Development Bank: Washington, DC.

2008. 'The Performance Relationship of Effective Risk Management: Exploring the Firm-Specific Investment Rationale'. *Long Range Planning* 41, pp. 155–76.

Andersen, T. J., Denrell, J., and Bettis, R. A. 2007. 'Strategic Responsiveness and Bowman's Risk–Return Paradox'. *Strategic Management Journal* 28, pp. 407–29.

Bernstein, P., 1996. *Against the Gods: The Remarkable Story of Risk*. John Wiley & Sons: New York.

Chambers, J., 2008. 'Cisco Sees the Future – The HBR Interview, Interviewed by Bronwyn Fryer and Thomas A. Stewart'. *Harvard Business Review* 86(11), pp. 72–9.

Chapman, C. and Ward, S., 2003. *Project Risk Management: Processes, Techniques, and Insights* (2nd edn). John Wiley & Sons: Chichester, West Sussex.

Christensen, C. M., 1997. *The Innovator's Dilemma: When New Technologies Cause Great Firms to Fail*. Harvard Business School Press: Boston, Massachusetts.

Kahneman, D. and Tversky, A., 1979. 'Prospect Theory: An Analysis of Decisions under Risk'. *Econometrica* 47, pp. 263–91.

Kaplan, R. S. and Norton, D. P., 2004. *Strategy Maps: Converting Intangible Assets into Tangible Outcomes*. Harvard Business School Press: Boston, Massachusetts.

Knight, F., 2006 (first published in 1921). *Risk, Uncertainty, and Profit*. Dover Publications: Mineola, New York.

Loach, C. H., DeMeyer, A. and Pich, M. T., 2006. *Managing the Unknown: A New Approach to Managing High Uncertainty and Risk in Projects*. John Wiley & Sons: Hoboken, New Jersey.

March, J. and Shapira, Z., 1987. 'Managerial Perspectives on Risk and Risk Taking'. *Management Science* 33, pp. 1404–18.

McGee, J., Thomas, H. and Wilson, D., 2005. *Strategy Analysis and Practice*. McGraw-Hill: London.

Power, M., 2004. *The Risk Management of Everything: Rethinking the Politics of Uncertainty*. Demos: London.

2005. 'The Invention of Operational Risk'. *Review of International Political Economy* 12(4), pp. 577–99.

Simons, R., 2000. *Performance Measurement and Control Systems for Implementing Strategy*. Prentice Hall: Upper Saddle River, New Jersey.

Slywotzky, A. J. and Drzik, J., 2005. 'Countering the Biggest Risk of All'. *Harvard Business Review* 82(4), pp. 78–88.

Smithson, C. and Simkins, B. J., 2005. 'Does Risk Management Add Value? A Survey of the Evidence'. *Journal of Applied Corporate Finance* 17(3), pp. 8–17.

Utterback, J. M., 1995. 'Developing Technologies: The Eastman'. *The McKinsey Quarterly* 1, pp. 130–44.

2 Economic exposures in corporate risk management

To begin the risk management discourse, this chapter outlines more conventional approaches to risk management. The starting point is common financial and market-related risks reflected in currency and interest rate exposures. The chapter provides an outline of common analytical approaches to monitor excess exposures. General measures of price sensitivities are presented and extended to assess the sensitivity of corporate equity positions to changing business conditions. The treatment of more complex market-related exposures in value-at-risk calculations is outlined and illustrated in multiple examples. The consequences of fat-tailed distributions that reflect a potential for rare but extreme events are discussed, as is the need for stress testing in corporate risk assessments.

2.1 Exposures to market risk

The overarching risk considerations in international business and multinational financial management has been the potential influence of changes in foreign exchange rates on future corporate cash flows and the related effects on long-term competitiveness. In addition to this, there have been frequent discussions of political, sovereign and country risks associated with international funds transfer and cross-border investments. Many historical events illustrate the potential effects of fluctuations in foreign exchange rates and volatile financial market prices in general. Some of these notable events include dramatic stories like those of Herstatt Bank, Franklin National and Metallgesellschaft (see Box 2.1 *Bankhaus Herstatt – foreign exchange settlements*, Box 2.2 *Franklin National – currency speculation* and Box 2.3 *Metallgesellschaft – position on petroleum prices*).[1]

---

[1] These case examples are included in the inserts for illustrative purposes and relate to events that have been widely publicized in various media and hence the information contained in the case descriptions derive from multiple public sources.

Box 2.1 Bankhaus Herstatt – foreign exchange settlements

Bankhaus Herstatt's banking licence was withdrawn on 26 June 1974, and it was ordered into liquidation at 3.30 p.m. in Frankfurt. Several of Herstatt's counterparties had irrevocably paid Deutschmark to Herstatt that day prior to the announcement of Herstatt's closure against anticipated receipts of US dollars later the same day in New York in respect of maturing spot and forward foreign exchange transactions. However, Herstatt's New York correspondent bank suspended outgoing US dollar payments from Herstatt's account upon the termination of Herstatt's business at 10.30 a.m. New York time. This action left Herstatt's counterparty banks exposed to the full value of the Deutschmark deliveries (credit risk and liquidity risk). Moreover, banks that had entered into forward trades with Herstatt not yet due for settlement lost money when the contracts had to be replaced in the market.

Box 2.2 Franklin National – currency speculation

Franklin National Bank (USA) lost more than US$80 million in the first five months of 1974 due to currency trading and was eventually declared insolvent as the largest bank failure in US history. The bank gambled on foreign exchange rate trends, buying and selling currencies – betting on their future prices rising or falling against the dollar. However, in May 1974 the bank reported concealed foreign exchange losses of US$45 million and later announced another US$38 million of losses in other departments. By October, the inevitable happened and the bank was declared insolvent. The unfortunate fate was instigated by the prior acquisition of a controlling interest by Italian financier Michele Sindona in 1972. He was charged and found guilty on 65 counts of fraud, falsification, bribery, perjury, embezzlement and misappropriation of Franklin funds, and sentenced to 25 years in federal prison.

Box 2.3 Metallgesellschaft – position on petroleum prices

Metallgesellschaft's US-based subsidiary, Metallgesellschaft Refining and Marketing, sold long-term petroleum forward contracts above current spot prices in the early 1990s and covered the positions by buying short-term petroleum futures. However, as the petroleum price continued to fall, the futures contracts had to be closed out at a loss at maturity well before the gains from the long-term futures could be realized. The consequential liquidity squeeze eventually gave the executives at corporate headquarters cold feet and the subsidiary was asked to reverse the entire position, thereby incurring losses in excess of US$1 billion.

While these examples illustrate conventional exposures to market risks associated with changes in foreign exchange rates, interest rates, petroleum prices and other commodity prices, they also incorporate other types of risk. For example, the case of Metallgesellschaft shows a situation where corporate management mishandled positions established in different derivative instruments. In view of prevailing trends in the energy markets, the subsidiary took reasonable positions by selling petroleum forward at higher prices in a falling market covered by futures contracts. However, they failed to consider the consequences of the different maturities between the long forward contracts and the short futures contracts. They also did not recognize the different mechanics of the forward and futures markets and therefore had to incur substantial cash drains as they closed out on the short-term futures contracts before they could cash in the profits gained on the long-term forwards. Corporate headquarters, in turn, got worried and consequently ordered the otherwise profitable net position to be liquidated at significant losses.

The cases of Herstatt Bank and Franklin National Bank share elements of operational shortcomings. Herstatt's counterparties neglected and mismanaged the credit risks involved in the settlement of foreign exchange contracts across different time zones and thereby inadvertently paid out significant amounts of money to counterparts without any security. The reasons for these events could be rooted in ignorance of potential counterparty risks and/or mistakes in the internal processing of credit lines. Franklin's hardships were triggered by excessive currency speculations, but also had deep roots in fraudulent management behaviours that failed the scrutiny of internal controls and sound corporate governance practices. The use of financial derivatives to manage market exposures is discussed further in Chapter 3 and the internal control aspects of risk management are addressed in subsequent chapters.

2.2   Economic exposures

When corporations borrow money to invest in commercial activities, they expose themselves to changes in the credit terms and conditions offered by financial market participants and at the same time fall victim to the changing returns and payback periods offered in turbulent business environments. These exposures are associated with the underlying volatility of various market prices. When corporations trade overseas and operate in the international financial markets, they become sensitive to changes in foreign exchange rates as receivables and payables are executed in other currencies than that of the home market that typically constitutes the company's currency of accounting. Changes in interest rates affect the value of corporate dues on accounts payable and various loan obligations and cause comparable changes in the real terms for receivables, loan extensions and commercial cash flows. Similarly, the development of commodity

Figure 2.1 *The volatile development of market prices – USD/GBP*

prices can have significant influences on earnings in corporations that depend on steady supplies of productive inputs and raw materials, including agricultural products, metals, energy, etc. Given the at times extreme variance in different market prices, these corporate exposures can be of high significance (Figure 2.1).

Many different market prices, including interest rates, foreign exchange rates, energy prices, commodity prices, consumer prices, etc., pertain to financial and commercial assets traded and exchanged between counterparts operating across numerous interacting national economies. Some of these price trends are obviously more important than others in specific corporate contexts. That is, it is necessary to determine the market price developments that exert the highest influence on operating profit and consider ways to manage fluctuations in these prices. When market prices vary in unpredictable directions over time, they can have significant influences on corporate earnings and may affect longer-term competitive conditions. The classical stories of Caterpillar and Volkswagen provide ample evidence of these risk factors (see Box 2.4 *Caterpillar – the dollar foreign exchange rate* and Box 2.5 *Volkswagen – the euro foreign exchange rate*).[2]

In the case of Caterpillar, major swings in the value of the US dollar during the 1980s affected the margins commanded by the company when selling its products in overseas markets, as most of the manufacturing took place in the domestic US market. Hence, a strong dollar during the early 1980s made the company's products relatively costly and hence less competitive overseas, whereas the subsequent weakening dollar had the opposite effect, while causing some conspicuous accounting losses and gains. This eventually urged the corporate

---

[2] See, e.g. R. Bender and K. Ward (2002). *Corporate Financial Strategy*. Butterworth-Heinemann: Boston, Massachusetts, p. 314; M. Crouchy, D. Galai and R. Mark (2006). *The Essentials of Risk Management*. McGraw-Hill: New York, p. 28; and many other public sources.

Box 2.4 Caterpillar – the dollar foreign exchange rate

Caterpillar, the long-time market leader in construction equipment, accounted for close to US$1 billion losses over the period 1982 to 1984 due to its foreign exchange rate exposures, particularly against the Japanese yen, and currency risk became a major focus of its corporate strategy. With the high value of the US dollar in the early 1980s, Caterpillar found itself at a distinct disadvantage when competing with Komatsu, a Japanese manufacturer of hydraulic excavators. Since Caterpillar maintained its manufacturing capacity in the United States, the equipment became too expensive in foreign currency denominated prices.

When the monetary policy was subsequently eased in the United States after a decline in the inflation rate, US interest rates fell as a consequence. This caused a fall in value of the US dollar as short-term foreign investors lost the incentives to invest in US-dollar-denominated financial assets. In the wake of these developments, Caterpillar eventually reported a US$100 million gain on foreign exchange in 1986 that turned its $24 million operating loss into a $76 million net profit for the year.

As a result of these experiences, Caterpillar established its special currency management group to deal with currency risk.

executives to establish a specialized group dedicated to the management of the company's currency exposures. Volkswagen gained quite comparable experiences as a consequence of periodic appreciations of the Deutschmark in the early 1990s and a decade later in connection with a surge in the value of the euro that caused corporate management to adopt more conservative hedging policies against major currency exposures.

Box 2.5 Volkswagen – the euro foreign exchange rate

The devaluation of the Italian, British and Spanish currencies after the European foreign exchange crisis in 1992 made German cars more expensive in those important markets. High manufacturing costs drove German auto manufacturers to establish production plants outside their home country, a move also aimed at reducing the currency exposures associated with the overseas sales of domestically produced automobiles. Yet, Volkswagen continued to manufacture most of its cars in Germany and earnings fell significantly during 1992 and 1993 due to the combined effects of increasing costs and a strong home currency.

The common European currency was introduced in 2000 and over the period 2002 to 2004, the euro appreciated considerably against the US dollar. Hence, Volkswagen reported a 95 per cent drop in its 2003 fourth-quarter profits due to sluggish demand and an unprecedented rise in the value of the euro combined with a decision to hedge only 30 per cent of the currency exposure. Sales continued to fall during the first quarter of 2004 and the blame was again ascribed to the rise of the euro against the dollar, which had an adverse impact on sales in the United States and other dollar-pegged markets. Yet, much of the pain was self-inflicted, as the company failed to hedge its currency exposures. This led to major cost-cutting exercises and plans to increase production in non-euro-denominated countries, like Brazil and Mexico. Finally, the company announced that it was going to increase hedging of its currency exposures because the majority of its operating costs, in particular a large portion of its labour costs, were denominated in euros, while a substantial share of its revenues were denominated in US dollars.

2.3   Foreign exchange rate exposures

Foreign exchange rate exposures arise when there is a mismatch between the currency denomination of corporate receivables and payables (Figure 2.2). To the extent that such a mismatch exists, there is a high degree of uncertainty as to what the resulting net future cash flows will be when converted to the home currency.

In terms of practical risk management considerations, it is important to identify, analyze and monitor the structure of the implied currency cash flows with different maturities to assess potential short- and long-term effects of changing foreign exchange rates. This can, for example, be accomplished by developing

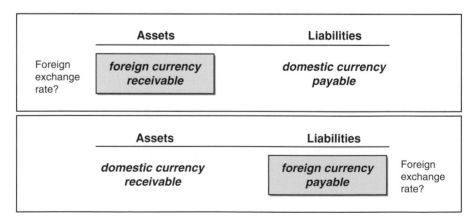

Figure 2.2 *Foreign exchange rate exposures*

periodic cash flow projections and calculating the currency mismatch for different future time intervals. This type of monitoring system provides the basis for evaluating the size of potential loss effects from particular foreign exchange rate developments and determines appropriate gapping positions in view of expected market uncertainties and the corporate ability to withstand potential losses.

Foreign exchange risk analyses distinguish between economic exposures and translation exposures. The analyses of *economic exposures* focus on the direct and indirect effects of changing foreign exchange rates on future corporate cash flows over different time horizons. Translation effects may occur when foreign-currency-denominated assets and liabilities are converted to the currency of accounting at year end according to specific accounting rules and may thereby influence corporate accounts and pro forma income statements. Translation exposures focus on the effects of changing foreign exchange rates on the future reported accounting income of the corporation, which in the short term may differ from the underlying effects on corporate cash flows. Hence, provided that managers and investors act rationally and see the differences between pro forma accounts and the true economic effects of currency swings, translation exposures should not constitute a major concern among professional market analysts.

Conventional analyses of economic exposures typically distinguish between assessments of transaction and operating exposures.[3] *Transaction exposures* relate to future commercial cross-border transactions that are agreed to and booked, but not yet effectuated. These transactions are typically of a short- to medium-term nature captured in accounts receivable and payables, contractual arrangements, loan commitments, etc. *Operating exposures* relate to future expected commercial cross-border transactions that have not yet been booked. These commercial transactions derive from expected continuation of certain overseas business activities, new international commercial ventures, downsizing of certain activities, etc. Since these transactions reflect future plans and expectations, they are typically of a medium- to longer-term nature and the actual effectuation of the underlying transactions is much more uncertain. Nonetheless, they do represent true exposures that will arise in the future and thereby affect corporate cash flows over time. Transaction as well as operating exposures will affect the future cash flows of the corporation and are, therefore, both referred to as economic exposures. The value of the firm is, in principle, determined as the net present value of discounted cash flows deriving from all expected future commercial activities converted into the home currency.

---

[3] For classical accounts of these approaches, see, e.g. D. K. Eitemann, A. I. Stonehill and M. H. Moffet (2004). *Multinational Business Finance* (10th edn). Pearson Education: Boston, Massachusetts (Part 3: 'Foreign Exchange Exposure'); A. C. Shapiro (2003). *Multinational Financial Management* (7th edn). John Wiley & Sons: New York (Part III: 'Foreign Exchange Risk Management'); and R. W. Click and J. D. Coval (2002). *The Theory and Practice of International Financial Management*. Prentice Hall: Upper Saddle River, New Jersey (Part III: 'Managing Foreign Exchange Risk').

2.4   Interest rate exposures

Interest rate exposures arise when there is a mismatch between the interest rate basis of corporate assets and liabilities (Figure 2.3). To the extent that such a mismatch exists, there is a high degree of uncertainty as to what the resulting future cash flows from interest payments will be. In principle, the interest rate mismatches should be considered for each of the currencies in which the corporation has major assets and liabilities.

In practice, the corporation may identify, analyze and monitor the implied periodic re-pricing gaps that exist between assets and liabilities in different currencies over alternating future time intervals. This allows corporate management to assess the potential effect of changes in the level of interest rates with different maturities. Interest rates may change across the board or there may be changes in the interest rate structure where changes in short- and long-term interest rates differ. The potential losses associated with changing interest rate scenarios can be evaluated in view of the corporate capacity to withstand external market shocks of this nature.

When interest rates change, the net present value of future cash flows will adapt accordingly – that is, when rates go up, the value of future cash flows goes down, and vice versa. Since the future cash flows of assets and liabilities with a variable rate structure are adapted more or less in accordance with changes in the interest rate level, floating-rate instruments are less price sensitive than fixed-rate instruments where future interest payments remain constant. Hence, the effect of changing interest rates in a given currency can be assessed in terms of their effects on the net present value of assets and liabilities. The concept of *duration* provides an indication of the relative price sensitivity of a given string of future cash flows, for example, of a security or commercial venture (see Box 2.6 *The concept of duration*).

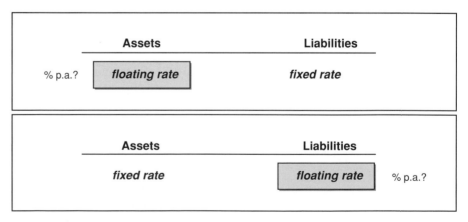

Figure 2.3 *Interest rate risk exposures*
Source: Adapted from Andersen (1993).

Box 2.6 The concept of duration

Duration is the weighted average maturity of the cash flows in an asset or liability where the weights are based on the relative size of periodic cash flows indicated by their present value discounted at the yield. This is expressed in the following formula:

$$D = \Sigma_t \times CF_t (1+y)^{-t}/P, \text{ where}$$

t = point in time CF_t = size of cash flow accruing at time t
y = yield-to-maturity P = market price of asset (bond value)

Example: Assume a three-year security with an annual coupon of 5 per cent and trading at a yield of 5.35 per cent. The following illustrates how the duration can be calculated in a standardized layout.

t	CF_t	V_{CF}	w_t	$t \times w_t$
1	5	$5/1.0535 = 4.75$	$4.75/99.06 = .0480$	$1 \times .0480 = .0480$
2	5	$5/1.0535^2 = 4.51$	$4.51/99.06 = .0455$	$2 \times .0455 = .0910$
3	105	$105/1.0535^3 = 89.80$	$89.80/99.06 = .9065$	$3 \times .9065 = 2.7195$
		$P = \Sigma = 99.06$	$\Sigma = 1.0000$	$D = \Sigma = 2.8585$

The modified duration, $D/(1+y)$, measures the relative change in the value of the asset or liability for a given change in the interest rate level.

Example: If the interest rate increases by 0.25 percentage points, then the price of the three-year bond will, given a current yield of 5.35 per cent, drop by $0.25 \times 2.8585/1.0535 = 0.68$ per cent from the current price of 99.06, i.e. 0.67 $[\Delta P = -2.8585/(1 + 0.0535) \times 0.0025 \times 99.06 = 0.67]$

The duration of a portfolio can be determined as the weighted average of the durations of the individual assets and liabilities in the portfolio weighted by the market values of each of the assets and liabilities.

Example: A portfolio of two assets with current market values (MV) of US$30 and 20 million and durations of two and three years respectively will have a duration of 2.4, determined as follows.

MV	D	$D_n \times MV_n$
30	2	60
20	3	60
Σ	50	120

$D_P = 120/50 = 2.4$

Since duration can be determined for both assets and liabilities, it is also possible to determine the overall sensitivity to changes in the interest rate level of the equity position of an institution as the weighted duration of assets and liabilities.

$$D_{Equity} = (MV_{Assets} \times D_{Assets} - MV_{Liabilities} \times D_{Liabilities}) / (MV_{Assets} - MV_{Liabilities})$$

If the interest rate level goes up, the value of assets – which reflect a string of expected future cash inflows – will go down, and when the interest rate level goes down, the value of assets will increase. Conversely, the value of liabilities – which reflect a string of expected future cash outflows – will go up and be more negative when the interest rate level goes down, and go down, that is, become less negative, when the interest rate level goes up. To the extent that the interest rate sensitivity of assets and liabilities differs, the corporation has an interest rate gap, and consequently the corporate equity position will be affected by changes in the interest rate level when assessed in terms of true market values.

The significance of interest rate gapping risk was illustrated by the crisis among US savings and loan institutions (S&Ls) during the 1980s. The S&Ls provided long-term property loans with maturities of up to twenty to thirty years, with the loans funded by relatively short-term deposits. As interest rates increased to double-digit levels during the high inflation period in the early 1980s, the S&Ls were caught in an interest rate trap as deposit rates increased quickly while the loans carried long-term fixed rates. As a consequence, many institutions went bankrupt and the entire industry had to be restructured.

Whereas this example relates to institutions that manage financial assets and liabilities, the same principles can be applied to corporate assets and liabilities and used to assess the sensitivity of corporate value to changes in the interest rate environment. Commercial assets in essence constitute business propositions that stipulate a string of expected future cash inflows from commercial activities. The market value of these commercial activities is affected by changes in interest rates, that is, if interest rates go up, the net present value of the future inflows goes down because the increase in time value makes the distant payments less valuable today. Similarly, the liabilities that provide the financing of the corporate business ventures will also be affected by interest rate changes (see Box 2.7 *Determining the interest rate sensitivity of corporate equity*). In other words, it is possible to use the same techniques to assess how sensitive the value of the corporate equity position is to changing interest rate conditions.

Box 2.7 Determining the interest rate sensitivity of corporate equity

$$D_{Equity} = (MV_{Assets} \times D_{Assets} - MV_{Liabilities} \times D_{Liabilities})/E$$

Where:

$$\Delta E = -(D_A - L/A \times D_L)/(1 + r) \times A \times \Delta r$$

ΔE = change in equity value D_A = duration of assets

D_L = duration of liabilities A = market value of assets

L = market value of liabilities E = equity position $(A - L)$

r = interest rate level (yield)

Looking upon corporate business activities as future earnings streams or cash in-flows and liabilities as sources of funding to be repaid makes it possible to assess the interest rate sensitivity of the corporate equity position under changing economic scenarios (see Box 2.8 *Calculating the corporate equity exposure*). Hence, the consequences of different business conditions reflecting alternating economic and financial environments could be assessed by relatively simple 'back-of-an-envelope' calculations. Part of this exercise would require an assessment of the future cash flow structure of corporate business activities and include considerations of changes in the underlying cash flow patterns.

Box 2.8 Calculating the corporate equity exposure

Example: A company has estimated that the duration of short-term assets (D_{STA}) is around 0.35, the duration of long-term assets (D_{LTA}) around 10.5, the duration of short-term debt (D_{STL}) around 0.5 and the duration of long-term debt (D_{LTL}) around 4.5. The market value of short-term assets (M_{STA}) is determined as US$250,000, the market value of long-term assets (M_{LTA}) at US$265,000, the market value of short-term debt (M_{STL}) at around US$90,000 and the market value of long-term debt (M_{LTL}) at around US$240,000.

With a total market value of assets amounting to US$515,000 and total liabilities to US$330,000, the implied equity position is calculated as US$185,000 ($= 515,000 - 330,000$).

We can then determine the weighted average duration of total assets and liabilities weighted by their market values. The average weighted duration of total assets is calculated as 5.57 ($= (250/515 \times 0.35) + (265/515 \times 10.5)$) and the average duration of liabilities as 3.41 ($= (90/330 \times 0.5) + (240/330 \times 4.5)$).

Thus, the expected value effect on the implied equity position from a 1 per cent increase in the interest rate level from an indicative current yield of 4.25 per cent can then be calculated as follows.

$$\Delta E = -(D_A - L/A \times D_L)/(1 + r) \times A \times \Delta r$$
$$= -(5.57 - 330/515 \times 3.41)/1.0425 \times 515,000 \times 0.01$$
$$= -16,721.81$$

That is, if the interest rate level increases by 1 per cent, the company will incur a loss of around US$16,700. The size of this loss can then be compared to the annual net income to assess whether or not this can be considered excessive.

The interest rate gap of a corporate business and funding position could be assessed further by considering the potential effects caused by changes in economic parameters, such as demand conditions that may change the maturity of future cash flows, inflation and interest rate developments. Hence, if the business cycle is heading towards a downturn, this may lead to an extended payback time on commercial assets, while renewed borrowing arrangements may assume shorter maturities caused by a credit slump. As a consequence, the duration of commercial assets might increase and the duration of liabilities decrease, thus causing the interest rate gap to go up, which indicates a more vulnerable corporate risk position (see Box 2.9 *Assessing the sensitivity of corporate value*). This way, an extended duration analysis of the corporate equity position might be used to assess the potential economic consequences of changing conditions in the business environment.

Box 2.9 Assessing the sensitivity of corporate value

A downturn in the business cycles is expected to increase the duration of short-term assets (D_{STA}) to around 0.50 and the duration of long-term assets (D_{LTA}) to around 15.0 because weakened demand conditions will tend to postpone sales and cash inflows. In contrast, the duration of short-term debt (D_{STL}) is expected to decrease to around 0.25 and the duration of long-term debt (D_{LTL}) to around 3.0 because credit conditions will become tighter.

Assuming unchanged market values of short-term assets (M_{STA}) at US\$250,000, long-term assets (M_{LTA}) at US\$265,000, short-term debt (M_{STL}) at US\$90,000 and long-term debt (M_{LTL}) at around US\$240,000, we can calculate the resulting duration of the equity position under the new economic scenario.

The average weighted duration of total assets is then calculated as 7.96 ($= (250/515 \times 0.50) + (265/515 \times 15.0)$) and the average duration of liabilities as 2.25 ($= (90/330 \times 0.25) + (240/330 \times 3.0)$).

Thus, the expected value effect on the implied equity position from a 1 per cent increase in the interest rate level from an indicative current yield of 4.25 per cent can then be calculated as follows.

$$\Delta E = -(D_A - L/A \times D_L)/(1 + r) \times A \times \Delta r$$
$$= -(7.96 - 330/515 \times 2.25)/1.0425 \times 515,000 \times 0.01$$
$$= -32,200.48$$

That is, the sensitivity of the corporate equity value to changing interest rate conditions in the expected adverse market situation will increase considerably, as indicated by a potential loss of around US\$32,200 for each percentage point increase in the interest rate level compared to a loss potential of US\$16,700 in the current market situation.

2.5   Interacting effects of market-related risks

The price relationships between different commercial markets are determined through a complex set of interacting supply and demand conditions across numerous intertwined industry value networks. Similarly, the relative prices between different countries are influenced by national economic policy variables as they affect economic conditions and commercial opportunities. The myriad of commercial transactions that take place among agents throughout the global economy shape the intricate relationships between different market prices as well as price relationships in one national economy affecting conditions in other economies through various cross-border transactions. Hence, the foreign exchange rates that determine the conversion between two currencies are related to the relative demand conditions, inflationary pressures and interest rate developments in the respective currency areas. Similarly, the price developments across different productive inputs, such as capital, labour, raw materials, energy, etc., and prices for different types of output, including semi-products, final goods and various services, interact in ways that link transnational price developments together. Therefore, when corporations consider the aggregate economic effects of these complex market developments, the underlying price relationships must be taken into account. However, the implied price risks should only be aggregated if they are completely independent of each other because the market-based price risk is reduced by diversification when the price changes are interrelated.

Different elements of the economic conditions are intertwined. For example, when demand is increasing, inflation goes up and interest rates increase to retain real returns. As nominal interest rates change between currency areas with different economic conditions, the foreign exchange rates that determine the exchange value between the two currencies will adapt accordingly.[4] Since these changes are interrelated, all of these effects should be taken into account when assessing the corporate economic exposures (Figure 2.4).

However, the analyses of transaction exposures treat both the quantity sold and the sales price as being independent of changes in foreign exchange rates.[5] While this may be the case over shorter periods of time, the likelihood of adjustment

---

[4] This is the essence of the so-called Purchasing Power Parity (PPP) paradigm, which suggests that with liberal financial and commercial flows between national economies and currency jurisdictions, there will be one set of real prices in global markets and consequently nominal interest rates in a given currency will compensate for inflation and foreign exchange rates will be based on the adjusted nominal interest rate levels in the two currency areas. See, e.g. A. M. Santomero and D. F. Babbel (2001). *Financial Markets, Instruments, and Institutions* (2nd edn). McGraw-Hill Irwin: Boston, Massachusetts (Ch. 10: 'Valuing Cash Flows in Foreign Currencies', pp. 191–221). Empirical evidence suggests that the PPP can be violated over shorter periods of time, whereas the proposed adjustments seem to occur over prolonged time periods of say five to ten years.

[5] L. Oxelheim and C. Wihlborg (2003). *Managing in the Turbulent World Economy: Corporate Performance and Risk Exposure*. John Wiley & Sons: Chichester, West Sussex.

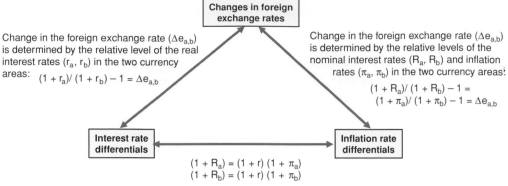

Figure 2.4 *The relationship between foreign exchange, interest and inflation rates*
Source: Adapted from Andersen (1993).

increases over time and thus becomes more important in the assessment of longer-term operational exposures that deal with extrapolations of future cash flows in foreign currencies.

One consequence of this may be that it only makes sense to hedge future foreign exchange positions over time periods where there is little transnational adaptation between economic conditions and financial market prices. It also means that when economic exposures are evaluated within a multinational corporate structure over longer time horizons, it is necessary to consider the interacting effects of all market-related risks at the same time.

2.6   Managing complex market exposures

The relatively simple currency and interest rate gapping positions can be managed by instituting position limits to keep the exposures within reasonable boundaries. Corporate risk policies, guidelines and controls can be adopted to formalize compliance within these limits. However, enforcing exposure limits on all financial instruments and commercial activities may be too cumbersome when dealing in many instruments and activities that are interrelated in complex ways. This is part of the reason why the banking industry developed the concept of value-at-risk to obtain a single measure of the aggregate exposure associated with dealings in multiple financial instruments while considering the interacting effects between the different market risks.[6]

---

[6] The value-at-risk measure was popularized by J. P. Morgan in 1994 when they introduced a service operated under the RiskMetrics name.

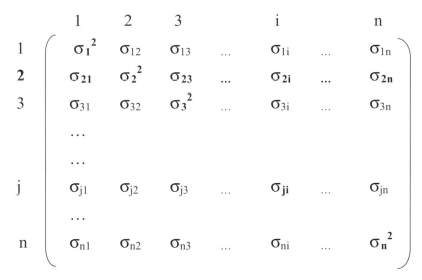

Figure 2.5 *Variance-covariance matrix – generic example*

The value-at-risk measure takes the interacting price relationship into account when assessing the overall market exposure from engagements in multiple financial instruments. The relationships between different price developments over time can be captured in covariance measures (σ_{ji}) indicating how the prices of two assets (j and i) co-vary over a certain period of time. These bivariate price relationships across n assets (1, 2, 3 ... n) are often expressed in the so-called variance-covariance matrix (see Figure 2.5). The co-variation between asset values observed over time reflects how changes in various market factors have affected asset prices in prevalent conjoint patterns within a given time period.

These measures of bivariate price relationships can be used to calculate the standard deviation of developments in the value of an aggregate portfolio made up by all of these assets.[7] The value-at-risk (VaR) then constitutes a single measure of the aggregate market exposure associated with a complex portfolio of interrelated assets (see Box 2.10 *Calculating the value-at-risk (VaR)*). In principle, the VaR indicates the potential loss in market value of the portfolio that may arise with a given probability, for example, a 5 per cent likelihood of occurrence, given that market prices continue to develop in the future as they have over the preceding period of observation.

---

[7] The standard deviation of a portfolio can be determined by the following general formula:
Standard deviation of portfolio $(\sigma_p) = (\sum \sum w_i \, w_j \, \rho_{ij} \, \sigma_i \, \sigma_j)^{-1/2}$.
w_i = the weight by market value by which asset i is included in the portfolio;
ρ_{ij} = the correlation coefficient between the returns of asset i and asset j;
σ_i = the standard deviation of the returns of asset i.

Box 2.10 Calculating the value-at-risk (VaR)

Example: An equally weighted three-asset portfolio consisting of a security (s), a currency position (c), and an equity investment (e) with a total current market value of $100 million.

This could, for example, reflect a company that has liquid securities, foreign exchange receivables and owns shares in a public firm.

Then the relative weight of each of these assets, as determined by their market values, is of equal size, i.e. $w_s = w_c = w_e = 1/3 = 0.33$

The standard deviations on the daily returns of each of the assets are determined as:

$$\sigma_s = 0.06\%, \sigma_c = 0.55\%, \sigma_e = 1.85\%$$

The correlation coefficients between returns of the assets have been determined as:

$$\rho_{sc} = -0.2, \rho_{ce} = 0.1, \rho_{se} = 0.4$$

Then, the standard deviation of the portfolio returns is determined as follows (a three-portfolio case):

$$
\begin{aligned}
\sigma_{portfolio} &= [(w_s\sigma_s)^2 + (w_c\sigma_c)^2 + (w_e\sigma_e)^2 + 2(\rho_{sc}w_sw_c\sigma_s\sigma_c) \\
&\quad + 2(\rho_{ce}w_cw_e\sigma_c\sigma_e) + 2(\rho_{se}w_sw_e\,\sigma_s\,\sigma_e)]^{-\frac{1}{2}} \\
&= [(0.33 \times 0.0006)^2 + (0.33 \times 0.0055)^2 + (0.33 \times 0.0185)^2 \\
&\quad + 2(-0.2 \times 0.33^2 \times 0.0006 \times 0.0055) \\
&\quad + 2(0.10 \times 0.33^2 \times 0.0055 \times 0.0185) \\
&\quad + 2(0.4 \times 0.33^2 \times 0.0006 \times 0.0185)]^{-\frac{1}{2}} \\
&= [0.00000004 + 0.00000329 + 0.00003727 \\
&\quad - 0.00000014 + 0.00000222 + 0.00000097]^{-\frac{1}{2}} \\
&= 0.00004365^{-\frac{1}{2}} \\
&= 0.006607
\end{aligned}
$$

Hence, the standard deviation in daily returns on the portfolio is around 0.66 per cent. This is less than the weighted average of the three standard deviations of 0.82 per cent ($=(0.06 + 0.55 + 1.85)/3$) due to diversification effects because the co-variations in returns of all of the assets are less than perfect ($\rho < 1$).

From this we can calculate the daily VaR associated with this portfolio at the 5 per cent level of confidence:

$$VaR = \$100,000,000 \times 1.645 \times 0.006607 = \$1,086,852$$

That is, there is a 5 per cent likelihood that this asset portfolio could drop in value by around $1.1 million from one day to the next.

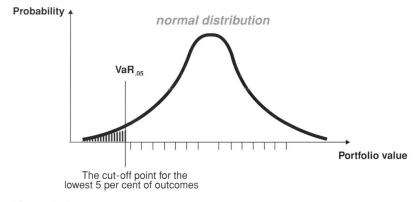

Figure 2.6 *The value-at-risk concept*

If the market value of the portfolio follows a normal distribution, we can use the standard deviation of the portfolio values ($\sigma_{portfolio}$) to determine the loss associated with 5 per cent likelihood because 90 per cent of all observations in a normal distribution fall within a range spanning from -1.645σ to $+1.645\sigma$ around the mean value. That is, the lower range indicator determines the loss reflecting a 5 per cent likelihood of occurrence (Figure 2.6). Once the standard deviation of the asset portfolio has been determined, we can calculate the value-at-risk as:[8] VaR = MV × 1.645 × standard deviation of portfolio.

However, it is important to keep in mind that the ability to set out these neat formulas builds on an underlying assumption that market price developments, and hence financial events, can be described adequately by a normal distribution (see Box 2.11 *Reliance on the Gaussian 'Bell Curve'*).[9] While this assumption for most market observation may hold true, it is challenged when it comes to the rare and extreme events that cause situations of market crisis. We revert to this issue in Chapter 7.

Box 2.11 Reliance on the Gaussian 'bell curve'

Techniques such as the standard VaR calculations discussed in this chapter rely on the 'law of large numbers' introduced by Bernoulli, which suggests that when a sufficient number of observations are collected, the frequency of outcomes will tend to move towards a normal distribution. As identified by Gauss, the normal distribution, often referred to as the 'bell curve', has a number of convenient features that can be used to assess the likelihood of

---

[8] This approach is based on the calculation of historical variance-covariance relationships and using this information to determine the standard deviation of the portfolio. The 5 per cent cut-off point could also be determined by listing all of the daily portfolio values over the past 250 trading days and then simply finding the market value corresponding to the twelfth lowest in the listing. The potential portfolio values could also be determined through Monte Carlo simulations based on random number generation and assuming that historical price co-variances prevail.

[9] For a critique of the widespread use of Gaussian statistics in economic and organizational research, see, e.g., J. A. C. Baum and B. McKelvey (2006). 'Analysis of Extremes in Management Studies'. *Research Methodology in Strategy and Management* 3, pp. 123–96.

extreme outcomes that exceed certain values as adopted in the VaR calculations. However, the normal distribution may not always constitute a valid description of outcomes in financial markets in distress or other types of catastrophe situations.

Bernoulli's law assumes that each of the underlying events is independent of the others. Hence, when that is not the case outcomes may follow other distributions possibly providing increased significance to the occurrence of events with more extreme outcomes. When individual events – such as the returns of different financial assets and losses imposed by natural disasters – are related, the aggregate outcomes can take on extreme values that refer to low-probability, high-loss catastrophe situations. The occurrence of such events may be captured by so-called 'leptokurtic' distributions where extreme outcomes lead to a more fat-tailed probability density function (see illustration below).

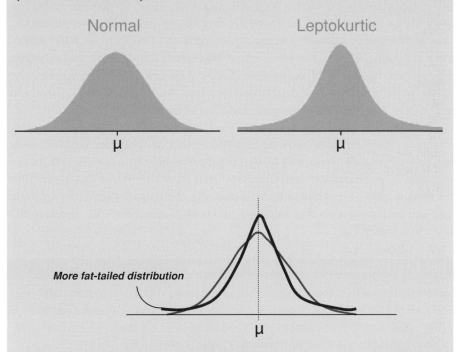

There are two types of probability density function:

To the extent that financial returns and catastrophe losses are better described as leptokurtic (and other probability density functions that allow for low-probability events with extreme outcomes), we should take these approaches into consideration when modelling the potential loss effects of various risk events.

A complementary approach is simply to consider the effects of extreme scenarios in various stress-testing exercises.

Hence, general experience seems to indicate that the real test of risk resilience happens when prevailing market conditions suddenly and unexpectedly go haywire, such as was the case with Long-Term Capital Management (LTCM) in the late 1990s (see Box 2.12 *Long-Term Capital Management (LTCM) – convergence trades*).[10] Therefore, it makes sense to perform so-called *stress testing* to see what happens to portfolio values and potential losses in market value when agent behaviour, economic conditions, interest rates, etc. all take a turn for the worse at the same time.

Box 2.12 Long-Term Capital Management (LTCM) – convergence trades

LTCM was a once-respected US-based 'hedge fund' started in 1994 by a highly reputed former bond trader from Salomon Brothers, John Meriweather, who even engaged the esteemed finance academics Robert Merton and Myron Scholes as strategic advisers. The fund used quantitative financial analysis to identify 'safe' convergence trades in government-backed securities with low credit risk. Hence, they took long positions in undervalued government securities and short positions in overvalued government securities and leveraged these transactions manifold to create larger returns from the small margin differentials. However, as the Russian Government unexpectedly declared a debt moratorium in August 1998, the rate structure in the market for sovereign debt went awry and caused the leveraged positions to lose money – and lots of it. The investment outfit was only saved through the intervention of the Federal Reserve Bank of New York and a cash injection of US$3.5 billion from a consortium of large investment and commercial banks.

2.7 Conclusion

Currency and interest rate gaps constitute some of the conventional corporate risks, together with exposures to other price volatilities. Interest rate gaps may in principle exist for all the major currency areas in which a corporation has activities. The concept of modified duration in major currencies can provide the basis for calculating relatively simple indicators of corporate exposures to changes in general business conditions. The value-at-risk concept has been developed primarily with financial assets in mind as the aggregate exposure must take the co-variation between different asset prices into account. However, the underlying idea to take the interrelatedness between risk factors into account has also been adopted in other types of risk as reflected in development of the influence matrix.[11] This approach tries to map how essential risks are assumed to

---

[10] This well-publicized event has been covered by many public sources. For an interesting academic account, see, e.g., D. MacKenzie (2003). 'Long-Term Capital Management and the Sociology of Arbitrage'. *Economy and Society* 32(3), pp. 349–80.

[11] This and other risk management techniques will be discussed further in Ch. 7.

affect other exposures and can serve to prioritize risk factors by their perceived influence on the aggregate corporate exposure. While these approaches constitute a priori evaluations, stress testing serves to assess the potential consequences if expectations fail and market conditions change in more extreme but not inconceivable directions. The practice of stress testing is usually adopted to evaluate value-at-risk calculations, but can also be applied to other areas from financial risks. Hence, a central idea behind scenario planning is to assess the consequences of extreme developments in important environmental factors that may constitute different commercial and strategic risks. We will pursue these issues further in subsequent chapters.

References

Andersen, T. J., 1993. *Currency and Interest Rate Hedging* (2nd edn). Prentice Hall: Upper Saddle River, New Jersey.

Baum, J. A. C. and McKelvey, B., 2006. 'Analysis of Extremes in Management Studies'. *Research Methodology in Strategy and Management* 3, pp. 123–96

Bender, R. and Ward, K., 2002. *Corporate Financial Strategy*. Butterworth-Heinemann: Boston, Massachusetts.

Click, R. W. and Coval, J. D., 2002. *The Theory and Practice of International Financial Management*. Prentice Hall: Upper Saddle River, New Jersey.

Crouchy, M., Galai, D. and Mark, R., 2006. *The Essentials of Risk Management*. McGraw-Hill: New York.

Eitemann, D. K., Stonehill, A. I. and Moffet, M. H., 2004. *Multinational Business Finance* (10th edn). Pearson Education: Boston, Massachusetts.

MacKenzie, D., 2003. 'Long-Term Capital Management and the Sociology of Arbitrage'. *Economy and Society* 32(3), pp. 349–80.

Oxelheim, L. and Wihlborg, C., 2003. *Managing in the Turbulent World Economy: Corporate Performance and Risk Exposure*. John Wiley & Sons: Chichester, West Sussex.

Santomero, A. M. and Babbel, D. F., 2001. *Financial Markets, Instruments, and Institutions* (2nd edn). McGraw-Hill Irwin: Boston, Massachusetts.

Shapiro, A. C., 2003. *Multinational Financial Management* (7th edn). John Wiley & Sons: New York.

3 Managing market-related business exposures

This chapter continues the discussion of predominant risk transfer markets and provides a general overview of various insurance and derivative instruments with more detailed explanations of the mechanics behind some of the most common corporate hedging techniques. The observed convergence between conventional insurance and capital market instruments is explained and the mechanisms driving the development of new alternative risk-transfer instruments are discussed further. The integrated use of different risk-transfer approaches to manage corporate exposures is outlined with examples of coordinated risk management practices.

3.1 Market-related risk exposures

A series of financial techniques have evolved that allow corporate management to deal with market-related exposures. By market-related risks we refer to events that are relatively well described and where event frequencies and associated losses are measured and documented on a regular basis. In other words, we are here dealing with measurable exposures that correspond to the traditional concept of risk as opposed to uncertainty that is impossible to measure because the unpredictable nature of events defeats measurability. In the case of hazards and casualties, the registration of events and associated losses is carried out by professionals in the insurance industry, often supported by industry-wide statistics and public databases. In the case of financial markets, the market prices of foreign currencies, interest rates and commodities are registered by individual market participants, stock exchanges, official statistics, etc. Price developments, trends and patterns derive from the analyses of defined price indices registered with regular time intervals, for example, minute-by-minute, hourly or daily.

The availability of historical evidence on risk events and market prices makes it possible to assess specific exposures and thereby provides a basis for evaluating the underlying risk phenomena. The ability to quantify risk effects and assign a value to an exposure makes it possible to exchange these exposures between different entities and in some cases establish formal exchanges to trade standardized exposures between interested counterparts. Hence, the availability of consistent data constitutes a necessary foundation for the development of professional markets for selective risks, which in turn constitutes possible hedging outlets for institutions with excess exposures.

3.2   Various hedging possibilities

Hedging practices have arisen from various sources and represent different traditions of professional development that have influenced the ways in which organizations deal with and think about risk management. The insurance markets evolved as investors saw an opportunity to place capital against expected future loss events. This could be organized in the form of individual professionals operating around consortia like the venerable Lloyds market in London, but also in the form of insurance businesses structured as mutual or limited companies that engage with each other to share the exposures of larger insurance portfolios. Futures and options markets were established as individual exchanges trading in standardized risk contracts that can be dealt with by investors, hedgers and arbitrageurs on official markets. Other contracts on many of the same risks were channelled via large open trading networks driven by professional market participants on an informal basis dealing in so-called over-the-counter transactions.

A common feature of these risk markets is that the underlying exposures are traded among various market participants so the risks can be diversified between these actors.[1] In the case of insurance, the insurance companies agglomerate large portfolios of insurance takers around the same risks, which allow them to determine reasonable premiums to charge against the cover they provide. Since the insurance takers rarely incur the loss events at the same time, the insurance arrangements de facto constitute diversification schemes, with the insurance companies acting as intermediaries in the process. In the case of futures exchanges, the exchanges act as platforms for trading where speculators, hedgers, intermediaries and arbitrageurs can trade the risks among them. Since all futures and options contracts in principle must have two counterparts, a buyer and a seller of the contract, the net effect is that the risk exposures are divided among market participants in accordance with their needs and views. The over-the-counter market works much in the same way, although contracts are less standardized and can be adapted to the specific needs of individual counterparts.

3.3   The insurance market

This constitutes the traditional market for dealing with adverse risk events that are beyond the control of individual households and commercial entities and provides financial cover against the downside loss effects of hazards and casualties. For the individual households this can provide economic surety and circumvents situations of extreme poverty that may arise out of bad luck.

---

[1] It is paradoxical of course that these instruments also provide the means to assemble excessive exposures. Corporate history is replete with examples of this happening (see, e.g. the story behind the demise of Baring Brothers).

In a similar manner, the insurance arrangements prevent private businesses from bankruptcy as a consequence of uncontrollable events caused by factors that are outside the influence of their normal management competencies (see Box 3.1 *Risk management and economic efficiency*).

Box 3.1 Risk management and economic efficiency

Optimal economic growth

Companies insure against risk to obtain financial cover for unfavourable developments that may jeopardize the livelihood of policyholders due to events beyond their control. Extreme economic vulnerabilities (catastrophic events) increase the insolvency risk of exposed entities and make it more difficult to obtain funding at economical rates. If funding gets scarce and the financial costs become prohibitive due to increased bankruptcy risk, investment activities may be curtailed, so economic activity will drop, and partnerships can suffer and affect long-term business development adversely. Hence, the absence of risk-transfer arrangements will everything else equal tend to reduce long-term economic growth.

Misallocation of resources

In the absence of appropriate risk-transfer arrangements, corporate investment considerations and financing decisions by financial institutions are influenced by uncontrollable risk exposures that may cause resources to be channelled into more rather than less exposed uses. Ignorance of major risk exposures may favour reckless agents and disfavour prudent economic agents and thereby furnish resource misallocation.

Capital market inefficiencies

Economic entities that avoid catastrophic exposures by pure luck as opposed to through managerial competence may receive more investment funding than the entities that are unlucky to be hit by disaster. Hence, in the absence of effective insurance and hedging markets, the availability of financial resources may not be determined by rational economic criteria.

The primary insurance companies determine the premiums to charge insurance buyers based on actuarial calculations, which basically utilizes the statistical normality that often applies to large portfolios of independent risk events. An insurance portfolio consisting of many policies in cover of a similar hazard, where events are independent of one another, is considered to be balanced. As a consequence, the loss ratio of this specific risk factor can be determined and future events predicted as the law of large numbers prevails and statistical analysis can

Unbalanced insurance portfolios and catastrophe risks are typically reinsured
(*the risk exposures are diversified across larger geographical regions*)

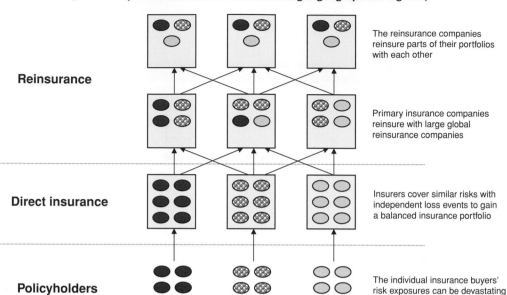

Figure 3.1 *Insurance and reinsurance techniques*

be applied to stipulate event frequencies and corresponding loss profiles. Hence, the collection of many independent exposures provides a basis for diversifying the risk impact across all of the insurance takers through the intermediation of agents in the insurance industry.

However, insurance companies may have risk portfolios that are less balanced, either because the portfolio retains a geographical bias or because there may be certain regional dependencies between events. In this case, a primary insurance company that collects premiums directly from the insurance buyers may reinsure part of the portfolio, say 50 per cent, with another insurance company, which in turn may want to reinsure 50 per cent of its portfolio with the first insurance company. Alternatively, the insurance companies may reinsure their excess exposures with reinsurance companies who only deal with primary insurance companies and other reinsurance companies. These practices serve to provide further risk diversification around global insurance markets (Figure 3.1). When risk events are highly dependent on each other, for example, as the hurricane sweeps over the entire city, primary insurers that retained the full insurance portfolio for own account would be badly hit, possibly to the extent of going bankrupt. These situations define catastrophe events and the only way to circumvent the adverse economic impact of these extreme hazards is to engage in global diversification through reinsurance arrangements.

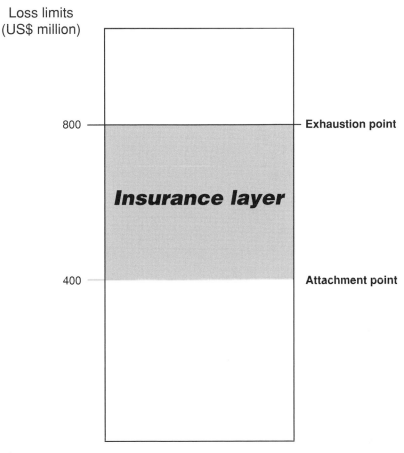

Figure 3.2 *Excess-of-loss reinsurance structure (insurance layers)*

In the case of high event dependencies that represent catastrophic loss outcomes, there may be a need for more advanced reinsurance techniques. In such cases, large economic exposures to specific hazards, such as hurricane events, may be structured as facultative facilities (i.e. focused on a specific risk). As total losses may be exorbitant (the upper limit is complete destruction of all economic assets), the facilities usually operate within certain loss ranges determined by an attachment point and an exhaustion point (Figure 3.2). This makes sense because large institutions are able to withstand losses below the attachment level, while losses above the exhaustion point are highly unlikely and very costly to cover and are, therefore, often retained. The insurance layers falling within the attachment and exhaustion thresholds can then be covered in the reinsurance market.

Since the global reinsurance market is of a relatively finite size limited by the aggregate reserves held by all of the reinsurance companies, there may be a need for alternative sources of risk transfer. With an increasing rate of catastrophe events, there have been a number of new market inventions that channel

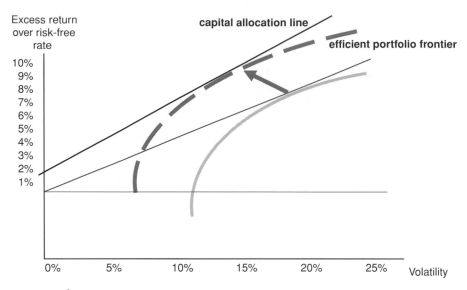

Figure 3.3 *Improving the investment possibilities*

insurance risks into the capital market where these instruments are assumed by large institutional investors. This transfer is enabled by securitization techniques, whereby the catastrophe risk exposures are converted into tradable securities in the form of risk-linked securities, catastrophe bonds (cat-bonds for short), etc. By incorporating these securitized investment instruments into their portfolios, institutional investors can improve their return characteristics. Since catastrophic risks are often uncorrelated with the economic exposures embedded in other financial assets, the risks can be diversified, while the premium offered on risk-linked instruments can enhance the average return to be gained on the invested portfolio. In other words, the 'efficient portfolio frontier' of the aggregate invest-ment is moved in a northwesterly direction and it is possible on average to earn a higher return for a given level of risk in the portfolio (Figure 3.3).

The basic insurance practices have in some instances been automated through the use of new communication and information technologies that can facilitate the interaction between institutional market players. Hence, online insurance market platforms have emerged where corporate insurance takers can specify their risk exposures in facultative structures and obtain bids from various insurance brokers and reinsurance companies affiliated with the online exchange.[2] Because insurable risks have carried significant weight in the corporate risk considerations, the initial corporate risk management functions have typically been organized in the form of 'insurance departments' focused on the handling of insurable risks. Their prime responsibility was to obtain insurance cover for the most important casualty risks in the corporation, which by itself requires a substantial amount

---

[2] See, e.g. the Catastrophe Risk Exchange (CATEX) established in 1996.

of coordination and market expertise. For large multinational corporations, this may often entail that a substantial part of their commercial assets are self-insured whenever the internal risk portfolio is sufficiently balanced[3] (see Box 3.2 *Self-insurance arrangements*). It may also be beneficial to engage in global multiple-line insurance facilities whereby the corporation is able to retain parts of the risk diversification benefits and thereby pay significantly lower premiums to the insurance companies. Hence, without a doubt, insurance covers remain an important feature of the corporate risk management practices.

Box 3.2 Self-insurance arrangements[4]

Pure self-insurance

Self-insurance is a decision by the company to retain certain exposures for own account. This may arise when insurance and alternative risk-transfer solutions are deemed too expensive, insurance capacity is limited, the company has a superior risk record or when the exposures are an ingrained element of the core business. The planned retention of risk is typically funded as the company invests money to obtain cover for future expected losses. This may be particularly important if credit conditions could be expected to worsen in case of loss events whereby pre-financing provisions become more economical. These risk-financing structures must be formalized to qualify for more favourable tax and accounting treatment as might apply to true insurance schemes.

Single-parent captives

To gain pure insurance treatment of reserves, it may be an advantage to organize the self-insurance in a separate licensed entity owned by the company as the sole parent. The wholly owned captive is usually located in tax- and captive-friendly locations (for example, Bermuda, Singapore, the Channel Islands, etc.) and provides insurance coverage for the company itself. Hence, the captive writes insurance to the sponsor (the parent company) on the risks the company wants to pre-fund in a formal insurance arrangement. These risks usually constitute high-frequency, low-risk events where expected loss frequencies are relatively easy to forecast. In many cases, local laws require that insurance coverage is obtained through local insurance companies. These situations require the engagement of a fronting (locally licensed) insurance company to write the primary insurance

---

[3] Self-insured global assets are often covered through corporate-owned captive insurance companies located in tax-efficient jurisdictions.

[4] See, e.g. P. Wöhrman and C. Bürer (2002). 'Captives' in M. Lane (ed.), *Alternative Risk Strategies*. Risk Books: London; and C. Culp (2005). 'Alternative Risk Transfer' in M. Frenkel, U. Hommel and M. Rudolf (eds.), *Risk Management: Challenge and Opportunity* (2nd edn). Springer: Berlin.

contracts with the company and in turn reinsure the entire insurance portfolio with the captive. The captive in turn may cede excess insurance exposures in various retrocession arrangements with international reinsurance companies. Furthermore, as the running of a licensed captive requires documented expertise, this is frequently outsourced to a professional service provider. The figure below shows a typical structure of such a single-parent reinsurance captive.

Typical structure of single-parent reinsurance captive

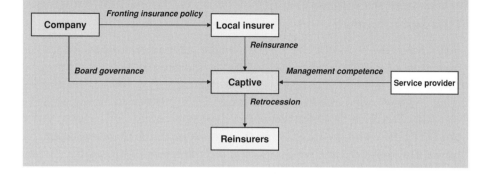

3.4   Derivative instruments

The insurance products discussed in the previous section represent the traditional risk-transfer market and constitute the conventional means of obtaining cover for the adverse economic effects of various risk events. However, moving towards the newer derivative security products introduced in the financial markets, we are faced with a string of market instruments that in many ways resemble the insurance products, at least in their ability to price risk and trade it among different market participants. The common derivative instruments comprise the standardized contracts traded on official stock exchanges and the tailored contracts traded in the over-the-counter (OTC) market among professional market makers (Figure 3.4). One may argue that a third type of derivative instruments is made up by the various securitized risk exposures traded in the capital market.

Hence, the financial derivatives are traded in two distinct market types, one where buyers and sellers transact through an official exchange mechanism and another where the instruments are exchanged through bid-offer quotes in dealer-markets. The exchange-traded derivatives are well-defined standardized contracts whereas OTC derivatives are non-standardized contracts often tailored to the specific needs of a corporate counterpart and traded in a network of interacting dealers (Figure 3.5).[5] The futures contracts and options contracts

---

[5] See, e.g. T. J. Andersen (2006). *Global Derivatives: A Strategic Risk Management Perspective.* Pearson Education: Harlow, UK (Part 2: 'Exchange Traded and OTC Derivatives').

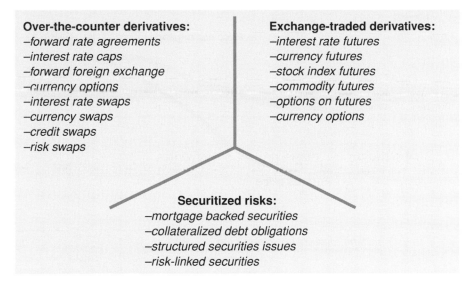

Over-the-counter derivatives:
–forward rate agreements
–interest rate caps
–forward foreign exchange
–currency options
–interest rate swaps
–currency swaps
–credit swaps
–risk swaps

Exchange-traded derivatives:
–interest rate futures
–currency futures
–stock index futures
–commodity futures
–options on futures
–currency options

Securitized risks:
–mortgage backed securities
–collateralized debt obligations
–structured securities issues
–risk-linked securities

Figure 3.4 *Three types of derivatives markets*

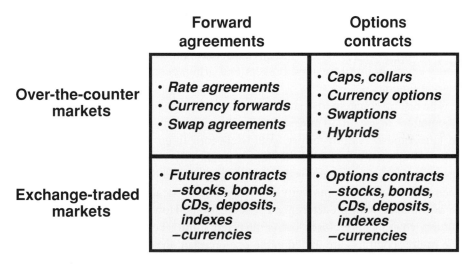

	Forward agreements	Options contracts
Over-the-counter markets	• *Rate agreements* • *Currency forwards* • *Swap agreements*	• *Caps, collars* • *Currency options* • *Swaptions* • *Hybrids*
Exchange-traded markets	• *Futures contracts* *–stocks, bonds,* *CDs, deposits,* *indexes* *–currencies*	• *Options contracts* *–stocks, bonds,* *CDs, deposits,* *indexes* *–currencies*

Figure 3.5 *Types of derivative instruments*

on futures were initially developed around the agricultural markets in the US Mid-West, where farmers and food processors traded instruments as natural counterparts to the underlying price risks. Corn farmers would like to know what prices they can receive on the harvest in late summer, whereas producers of corn flakes would like to know the future price they have to pay for these essential raw materials. Hence, the Chicago Board of Exchange and other futures exchanges offer contracts based on standard entities of corn and other agricultural commodities traded at specific future dates. Today, different types of financial futures are traded on a wide variety of exchanges around the world and contract

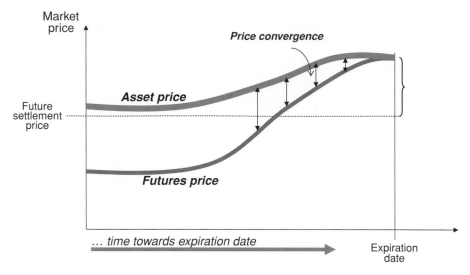

Figure 3.6 *Converging financial futures prices*

denominations have been extended to cover many market risks related to the development in different commodity and financial prices. These exchanges offer their instruments to counterparts with opposing interests, such as lenders and borrowers, buyers and sellers of foreign currencies, producers and users of energy, and so forth, while investors, brokers and arbitrageurs set prices and provide market liquidity.

The natural counterparts can use the financial futures contracts to hedge against fluctuations in the future prices of the underlying asset, such as the price on corn in late August. A corn farmer would sell corn futures for August delivery at a known quoted price, while Kellogg's might buy some of these contracts. If the contracts are executed in the form of physical delivery on the expiry date, then the underlying commodity is exchanged physically at contract expiration in accordance with predetermined specifications. However, in many cases, the futures contracts are closed out or reversed shortly before the expiry date. As the futures contracts are traded in the open market, the quoted futures price will converge towards the actual market price of the underlying asset when time moves towards the expiration date (Figure 3.6). Therefore, buying back or selling the contracts to close out a futures position will create financial gains or losses that counteract losses or gains incurred in the physical markets and thereby provide the means to hedge against future price fluctuations (see Box 3.3 *Hedging with financial futures – simple example*).[6]

---

[6] See, e.g. R. M. Stulz (2003). *Risk Management and Derivatives*. South-Western: Mason, Ohio (Part 2: 'Hedging with Forwards, Futures, and Options Contracts'); M. Grinblatt and S. Titman (1998). *Financial Markets and Corporate Strategy*. Irwin/McGraw-Hill: Boston, Massachusetts (Part IV: 'Risk Management'); and K. C. Butler (2004). *Multinational Finance* (3rd edn). South-Western: Mason, Ohio (Part 3: 'Derivative Securities for Currency Risk Management') for general discussions of hedging techniques.

Box 3.3 Hedging with financial futures – simple example

In early June, a farmer in the US Mid-West expects a record harvest of corn in the late summer, but worries about the price risk at the time he has to deliver the corn to his usual contractors. To reduce this risk, he sells a suitable number of *corn futures* on the Chicago Board of Trade. In line with expected delivery, he sells 100 contracts with September expiry and a size of 5,000 bushels per contract, i.e. he goes short on the futures contract. The current market price is 575 cents/bushel and the futures contracts are sold at a price of 585 cents/bushel, so the market currently expects a slight increase in the future market price of corn (see graphic below).

Nonetheless, by mid-September, a few days before the expiration date, the price of corn has dropped to 540 cents/bushel, i.e. the market price fell against initial expectations. Therefore, to hedge the corn farmer's underlying position, he 'closes out' the short futures position by buying back the 100 contracts previously sold on the futures exchange. Since the market price of corn has dropped and the futures price 'converges' towards the market price as we get closer to the expiration date, the futures contracts can be bought back at a price of around 540 cents/bushel. That is, the farmer can realize a profit from the closing trade. This profit pretty much corresponds to the loss he can expect to incur in the physical corn market when he has to sell the corn at the lower than expected market price.

The underlying calculations are as follows:

Price of corn future (10 June)	585 cents/bushel	– sell 100 contracts
Price of corn future (12 Sept.)	540 cents/bushel	– buy 100 contracts
Price gain per contract	45 cents/bushel	
Profit per contract sold	$2,250 (= 0.45 × 5,000)	
Loss in underlying corn market	$225,000 (= 500,000 × (5.85 − 5.40))	
Profit from closing the futures position	$225,000 (= 100 × 2,250)	

Falling market price scenario

This example is clearly 'idealized' to illustrate the basic mechanics behind the use of financial futures. However, for such a perfect hedge to occur assumes that the hedger, i.e. the farmer, is able to foresee the exact amount of corn he will have to sell in August. This is obviously not that easy to get exactly right because the outcome of the harvest will be affected by changing weather conditions and other practical issues associated with the farming operation. In other words, this type of hedge will rarely be as perfect as suggested by the example.[7]

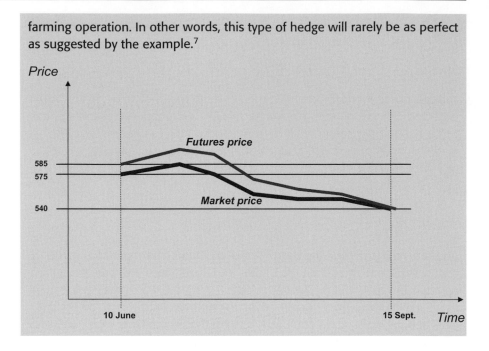

Buying call or put option contracts, either on a futures contract or directly on the underlying asset, creates more hedging flexibility because the option buyer can decide to exercise only the option if the market is favourable, i.e. when the option is *in-the-money*, and leave it if the market is unfavourable, i.e. when the option is *out-of-the-money*. Hence, where hedging by trading in futures contracts may attempt to lock in the future price of the underlying asset, the options contract allows the holder to capture the potential upside gains and avoid downside losses.[8] However, the hedger must pay a premium to acquire the options contract, which means that any realized gains will be net of this premium, whereas options contracts that expire out-of-the-money will incur an opportunity cost corresponding to the option premium paid up front.

Over-the-counter instruments are not traded as standardized contracts on exchanges, but are transacted between two counterparts, for example, a bank and a corporate hedger, in a form that may be tailored to specific requirements for amount and maturity. By engaging in forward agreements, a corporation may for example buy or sell a certain amount of foreign currency at a given future date at a predetermined foreign exchange rate and thereby eliminate a price risk by locking in the future price. Forward agreements resemble the financial futures contracts traded on exchanges and allow corporations to hedge the future prices of many different commodities and financial assets. The international financial

---

[7] For more detailed accounts of the intricacies that can apply to futures markets, see, e.g. J. J. Murphy (1986). *Technical Analysis of the Futures Market: A Comparative Guide to Trading Methods and Applications*. New York Institute of Finance: New York.

[8] See, e.g. R. L. McDonald (2003). *Derivatives Markets*. Addison-Wesley: Boston, Massachusetts (Part 1: 'Insurance, Hedging, and Simple Strategies').

institutions that make up the over-the-counter market also offer different types of options contracts that are tailored to the specific needs of corporations and other institutional counterparts. These instruments may comprise a wide variety of contracts, such as commodity options, energy options, currency options, interest rate options, bond options, stock index options, etc. Since over-the-counter transactions are arranged between two institutions, they incur counterparty risk, as is the case in the insurance market – i.e. the hedger (or insurance buyer) is dependent on the counterpart (or insurance provider) to fulfil the contractual obligations of the hedge (or cover). This is in contrast to financial futures where the exchange (or the associated clearing house) acts as counterpart to all transactions and uses margin payments to cover for potential losses.

Options contracts can be combined in different ways to create more opportune investment and hedging profiles for different types of market participants.[9] For example, double option strategies can be construed to establish covers for upside or downside price movements at lower all-in costs (see Box 3.4 *Double option strategies*). These positions can be established by buying and selling different call and put options quoted on futures exchanges, which provide the position taker with the flexibility of modifying the positions through subsequent trades in the highly liquid options contracts. In other cases, these types of positions are established by financial institutions and offered as packaged instruments in the over-the-counter market under special names like 'cylinder options', 'zero-cost cylinders', etc.

Box 3.4 Double option strategies

Assuming double option positions for hedging purposes may be based on bullish or bearish market views. A bullish option strategy is based on the expectation of an increase in the price of the underlying asset. Conversely, a bearish option strategy assumes a decrease in the price of the underlying asset.

In a vertical option strategy, the option contracts have the same expiration dates, but different strike prices. In a horizontal option strategy (also referred to as a calendar spread), the option contracts have the same strike price, but different expiration dates as the option holder tries to take advantage of changes in the option's time value.

A *vertical bull spread* can be established to hedge a short position in the underlying asset, such as a need to buy a foreign currency in the future. In a single option strategy, this exposure can be hedged by buying a call option on the currency. If we expect an increase in the price of the currency (a bullish view), the likelihood that a put contract with a lower strike price will be exercised is relatively low. Therefore, we might write a put option contract and receive an option premium at the same time as we buy the call option.

---

[9] For an authoritative treatment of possible option investment strategies, see, e.g. L. G. McMillan (1993). *Options as a Strategic Investment*. New York Institute of Finance: New York.

The premium received on the put option is then counted against the premium paid on the call option and this makes the up-front net premium of the combined position correspondingly lower. The resulting profit and loss profile of the vertical bull spread adds together the profiles of the put option and the call option.

Creating a profit and loss profile of a vertical bull spread

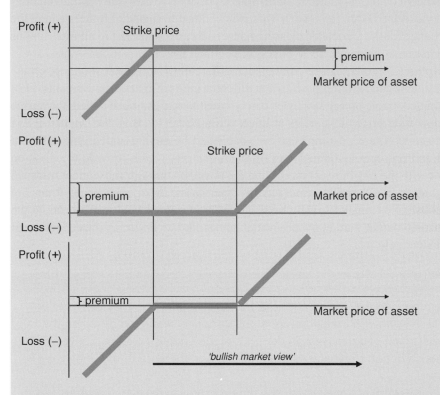

This position makes money when the market price of the underlying asset goes up.

Another type of financial derivative that has evolved over the past decades is the interest rate and currency swap that allows two (or multiple) counterparts to exchange fixed and floating interest rate bases in the same currency or across different currencies. In a basic interest rate swap, two counterparts, possibly intermediated by an international financial institution, exchange the basis for interest rate payments in the same currency (Figure 3.7). Today, the markets for interest rate swaps have become very liquid and it is quite common to receive two-way swap prices from financial intermediaries.[10]

[10] Two-way prices of an intermediary constitute a set of low-margin bid and offer quotes, e.g. where the bid price indicates the fixed rate amount paid to a seller (provider) of a floating rate (LIBOR) amount and the offer price indicates the fixed rate amount received from a buyer (acquirer) of a floating rate (LIBOR) amount.

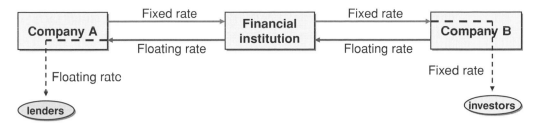

Figure 3.7 *Basic interest rate swap transaction*

The availability of financial futures and options contracts on interest-rate-sensitive financial assets, such as government bonds or treasuries and mortgage bonds, as well as interest rate swaps in the over-the-counter market makes it possible to adapt the interest rate sensitivity of an invested portfolio. In a similar manner, it is possible to use derivatives to modify the interest rate sensitivity of the equity position of a corporation (see Box 3.5 *Hedging interest rate exposures with financial derivatives*).

Box 3.5 Hedging interest rate exposures with financial derivatives

Futures contracts

An investor can sell futures contracts on treasuries to reduce the duration of a securities portfolio and buy futures on treasuries to increase the duration of a securities portfolio. Hence, by going short in futures, the price sensitivity of the combined securities and futures portfolio is reduced, whereas going long in futures increases the price sensitivity.

$$\text{Sell treasury futures contracts} \Rightarrow \text{Duration (D)} \downarrow$$
$$\text{Buy treasury futures contracts} \Rightarrow \text{Duration (D)} \uparrow$$

On this basis, it is possible to adapt and manage the duration of an invested portfolio and achieve targeted duration levels in line with prevailing views on market developments.

Options contracts

The delta of an options contract (Δ) indicates how much the option premium changes when the market price of the underlying asset changes. The delta of a put option on a fixed-coupon bond is negative ($\Delta_P < 0$), which means that an increase in the interest rate level that causes bond prices to drop will result in a higher put option premium. This change in the option price is opposite the change in the asset price. Hence, the interest rate sensitivity of the put option premium can be used for hedging purposes. By buying a suitable number of put options on a long-term interest rate futures contract, it is possible to hedge the price sensitivity of a securities portfolio or any other positive duration gap.

Interest rate swaps

The overall interest rate sensitivity of an organization is indicated by the combined durations of the assets and liabilities weighted at their respective market values, which is expressed in the duration of the equity position (duration of assets minus duration of liabilities).

$$D_E = D_A - L/A \times D_L$$

D_E = duration of equity position D_A = duration of total assets
D_L = duration of total liabilities   L = market value of total liabilities
A = market value of total assets

Therefore, we can engage in fixed-floating interest rate swaps to modify the interest rate sensitivity of the corporate equity position for each of the major currencies in which the multinational enterprise is engaged, for example, euro, US dollar, etc. Taken together, the interest rate gaps determined for each of the major currencies constitute the overall interest rate exposure of the organization.

Example: A multinational corporation has the following currency-denominated assets and liabilities:

Euro-denominated assets and liabilities (€1,000 (duration))

Total assets   125,000 (3.3)   Total liabilities   97,000 (2.4)

$$D_{E,€} = D_A - L/A \times D_L = 3.3 - (97/125 \times 2.4) = 1.44$$

US-dollar-denominated assets and liabilities ($1,000 (duration))

Total assets   100,000 (3.8)   Total liabilities   80,000 (3.0)

$$D_{E,\$} = D_A - L/A \times D_L = 3.8 - (80/100 \times 3.0) = 1.40$$

Hence, it is possible to reduce the duration gap on the corporate equity position in US dollars from 1.4 to, for example, 0.4 for, say, a two-year period. This can be accomplished by receiving floating rate payments against payment of fixed rates (going long, i.e. buying a fixed-floating-rate swap) in a nominal two-year swap (with duration 1.7) at an amount of US$58.8 million, which is determined in the following way.

$$0.4 = \{(D_A - L/A \times D_L) \times A + (D_{SWAP} \times N_{SWAP})\}/A \Rightarrow$$
$$N_{SWAP} = [0.4 - (D_A - L/A \times D_L)]A/D_{SWAP}$$
$$= [0.4 - (3.8 - 0.8 \times 3)]100/1.7$$
$$= -58.8$$

Note that the nominal amount of the interest rate swap derived from solving the equation is negative because the long swap position (buying floating rate for fixed) will reduce the duration.

3.5   Capital market instruments

As appears from the previous discussions, there are obvious similarities between insurance policies and options contracts. Insurance buyers must pay an actuarially determined premium up front to receive a policy that contractually commits the insurance company to provide economic compensation for losses caused by specified events. Similarly, a buyer of an option contract must pay a premium determined in accordance with expected price developments to receive a contract that obliges the seller to honour a specified transaction on predetermined conditions. In either case, it constitutes a form of cover, hedge or insurance against an adverse development in a specific risk factor, be it a fire hazard, a volatile market price or the like. It is noted that both insurance and reinsurance practices as well as trading in financial derivatives can serve as the means to diversify the risk exposures among many markets participants. We have even seen how certain environmental hazards can be securitized and placed among institutional investors because it has the potential to improve their risk–return characteristics through portfolio diversification. In short, there are indications of increasing interaction between insurance, financial and capital market activities, which implies that we may count securitized risk instruments among the list of possible derivative markets for hedging purposes.

The securitization technique has evolved from the initial development of mortgage-backed securities in the US market, where savings and loan institutions sold off large portfolios of long-term mortgage loans to separate legal entities that in turn issued securities to investors based on the future cash flows from the mortgage loans.[11] This way, the traditional savings and loan institutions were able to reduce their positive interest rate gaps, while skimming off some of the up-front arrangement fees charged on the mortgage loans. This securitization technique has since been extended to many other types of homogeneous debt obligations, such as car loans, credit card debt, commercial receivables, fixed asset investments, etc., which can be administered within a focused special purpose vehicle.[12]

---

[11] For the securitized US mortgage market to take off, it was necessary to take legislative measures that effectively exempted the pass-through entities, Real Estate Mortgage Investment Conduits (REMICs), from paying taxes on interest. See, e.g. F. J. Fabozzi (2000). *Bond Markets, Analysis and Strategies* (4th edn). Prentice Hall: Upper Saddle River, New Jersey. Without this exemption, the interest payments would be taxed twice and the pass-through structure would not be economically viable.

[12] The extreme example of this securitization exercise was the surging issuance of sub-prime mortgage loans in the US market, where financial institutions of many shapes assembled low-rate

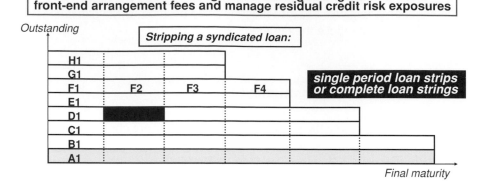

Figure 3.8 *Syndicated loan facilities and assets sales techniques*

The idea of converting longer-term illiquid bank loans into tradable capital market instruments through the adoption of the securitization technique has also been applied to the banking industry. Many syndicated loans have legal clauses that allow participants in lending consortia to sell their participations to interested third parties with or without recourse. In many cases, the managing banks established active markets to trade different parts of a syndicated loan facility, such as one-, two- or three-year loan strips, and even forward-forward arrangements like one-year loans in one, two and three years' time. Hence, a simple six-year syndicated loan with partial annual repayments, say after three, four and five years, can be split into, for example, one-year loan strips (A1, B1, ... H1), two-year loan strips (for example, F1 + F2), three-year loan strips (for example, F1 + F2 + F3), etc., up to a six-year loan strip (for example, the 'light blue' strip, including A1), as well as a one-year loan in one year (for example, the 'dark blue' strip after D1), a one-year loan in two years, a one-year loan in three years, etc. (see Figure 3.8).

For the managing banks, this provides origination fees. When the loans are arranged for the institutional borrowers, this provides servicing fees as the debt servicing payments are administered and executed, and it may incur additional fees when different loan strips are being traded. Finally, this ability to split up complicated longer-term loan structures into smaller parts that can be traded in a liquid OTC market provides the banks with increased flexibility to manage their cash, interest rate and credit exposures.

Other techniques have evolved that allow banks to change the credit characteristics of their loan portfolios by engaging in different types of credit derivatives. A simple credit swap constitutes a kind of insurance arrangement whereby the buyer pays a regular interest amount (or premium) in turn for a compensating payment

mortgage loans and sold them in securitized form to different institutional investors. Many of these instruments were also placed internationally with institutions located outside of the United States.

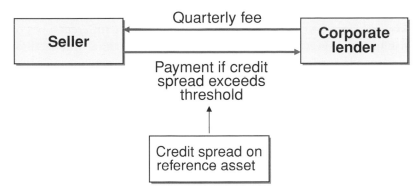

Figure 3.9 *A generic credit derivative contract*

in case a pre-defined credit event should occur. The credit event to trigger the derivative could be a simple default of an underlying loan asset, a widening credit spread (such as the difference between the yield on BBB-rated corporate bonds and treasuries with the same maturity) above a certain threshold or a widening of the credit spread on a reference credit portfolio above a predetermined threshold level. If the triggers in the credit swap are not activated before the final expiry date, the buyer will not receive any payments from the seller.

Credit swap triggers are as follows:

- events of default;
- excess of given credit spread; and
- excess of credit spread on reference loan portfolio.

In the case of a default event trigger, the regular premium payments are exchanged for a one-time payment to compensate for the credit loss incurred on the underlying loan asset. In the case of an excess credit spread trigger, the buyer will receive compensating payments corresponding to the interest amount of the excess above the threshold rate for each of the sub-periods over the duration of the swap arrangement (Figure 3.9).

Whether or not the credit swaps use simple default or excess of credit spreads as triggers, it is apparent that the credit swap arrangements incurred between different types of lenders as buyers and sellers of swaps provide opportunities to modify the contours of their credit exposures. For example, a southern European bank may buy a credit swap from a northern European bank that pays out a compensating interest amount if the credit spreads on a predetermined part of their local credit portfolio exceeds a certain level. Thereby, the bank has reduced its credit exposure to southern European borrowers. Similarly, the northern European bank may buy a credit swap from the southern European bank using their local loans as the reference assets. What the banks have then effectively done is to diversify their respective credit exposures without interfering with their close customer relationships in their respective markets.[13] The credit swaps are primarily geared to exchange credit exposures among different types of lending institutions. However, the exercise of credit swaps are also related to changes in economic conditions and, therefore, may allow corporations to consider such instruments as potential means to hedge their commercial exposures, such as accounts receivables, payments from business projects or future income from specific geographical regions (see Box 3.6 *Extending the use of swap arrangements*).

Box 3.6 Extending the use of swap arrangements

Technology risk

Consider an advanced computer products firm in the process of inventing a new process to build high-speed transistors for use in performance microchips as the technology can enhance the capacity to store information on the silicon-based chip structures. Such a technology leap might have strategic consequences as it enhances existing chip technologies towards smaller, more powerful and energy-efficient devices. An example of such a new process invention could be the 'silicon-on-insulator' (SOI) technology developed in the late 1990s.

However, the proposed advantages will only materialize if the new technology lives up to the initial promises and if alternative, more advanced technologies fail to emerge in the interim.

In other words, there are considerable risks associated with new technology development, for example, the inventing firm runs the risk that the technology fails to deliver, incumbent firms run the risk that they will be taken over by a superior technology and entrepreneurial inventors may threaten both of these firms, but under highly uncertain circumstances.

Yet, it seems like some of these parties have partially contravening exposures, for example, the new technology firm has a risk that the new process will not work, whereas the incumbent firm has an opposing risk that it will work.

Now we might think of ways in which the two parties could define a future event that serves as a trigger in a swap agreement between the two counterparts. One such trigger might be that the new technology works under pre-defined specifications by a certain date where the incumbent might be interested in paying a regular premium against a certain reimbursement in case the technological performance turns out to be favourable.

---

[13] While credit derivatives in principle are a type of insurance instrument that can provide risk diversification and hedging opportunities for different market participants, the paradox remains that they also constitute the means to assemble excessive credit exposures (recent examples include large exposures to securitized sub-prime loans and AIG's related commitments to a faltering US mortgage credit market).

This way, the research-and-development-intensive firm will receive periodic premium payments to cover part of the development expenses and the incumbent will receive compensation if it is brought into an adverse competitive position by the new technology that subsequently will be costly to implement.

It may be possible to think of many other scenarios where these kinds of hedging techniques developed as financial market instruments may be tailored to deal with different operational, commercial and strategic risks.

Other instruments, such as committed credit facilities and contingent capital, can make risk financing available when the corporation is faced with periodic cash shortfalls whatever their cause. While this guarantees availability of funding, these loan proceeds must be repaid in contrast to insurance arrangements that pay out compensations if events occur against receipt of regular premium payments. Committed credit facilities can take the form of bank overdrafts, commercial paper and medium-term note programmes, etc., supported by stand by and back-stop facilities. Contingent capital typically constitutes different types of option arrangements that allow, for example, an insurance company to issue different debt securities in the market on predetermined terms guaranteed by an investment bank or a consortium of financial institutions. Hence, these kinds of back-up financing arrangements can establish a general financial buffer for use if the corporation is unexpectedly faced with risk situations that cause major loss of revenue or impose large direct economic costs.

3.6   Coordinating risk management approaches

The presentation of different insurance, financial and capital market instruments illustrates the multitude of techniques that are available to adjust and manage the corporate risk profile as influenced by different market-related and commercial risk events. However, effective use of these often sophisticated instruments requires that specialized skills and market insights are available in focused risk entities. All the while, use of different risk-financing and risk-transfer instruments requires a degree of coordination to ensure that all major corporate exposures, including financial, insurance, operational and commercial risks, are taken into consideration. This means, for example, that corporate management must consider a minimum acceptable retention of risk exposures in view of existing capital and liquidity reserves as immediate buffers to withstand potential effects of unexpected losses. Above this level of exposure, corporate management must consider how to use the different techniques to cover different risk exposures above an acceptable retention level.

This kind of coordinated approach could imply the use of financial derivatives to provide covers for market-related risks, insurance to cover various hazards,

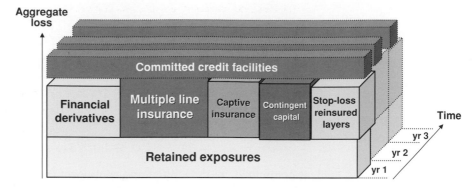

Figure 3.10 *Generic corporate risk coverage structure*

contingent capital to safeguard against different commercial risks and so forth (Figure 3.10). Realizing that it is impossible (and uneconomical) to cover all potential risks, there will always be an element of less likely residual risk levels that must be assumed or retained by the corporation. In view of this, corporate management could consider a certain level of flexible risk-financing arrangements, for example, in the form of committed credit facilities that would make financing available for the company to withstand the effects of unforeseeable events.

The previous discussion demonstrates a need for specialized expertise to assess particular types of risks and handle the specific risk-transfer techniques needed to cover these exposures by using advanced derivatives, insurance and alternative risk-transfer instruments. However, it also illustrates a conjoint need for overall corporate coordination and guidance of these activities in view of what appears to be a reasonable retention of aggregate exposures, use of multiple means to transfer excess risk levels and flexible facilities to cover for upper risk potentials. Together, this points to an ongoing challenge in corporate risk management of combining the need for technical expertise in functional risk units, while at the same time maintaining an integrative risk management function that can provide overall guidance to the specialist units.

3.7   Conclusion

The market-related risk exposures have historically been dealt with by relatively distinct professions, such as the insurance industry, derivatives exchanges, interbank dealer-traders, investment bankers, etc. However, the underlying instruments in these professions, such as insurance contracts and derivative securities including futures, options and swaps arrangements, all build upon the comparable idea of trading quantifiable risk exposures among market participants with the possibility of diversifying exposures or redistributing them in a more opportune manner. Due to these fundamental similarities, we have seen a certain convergence between the products offered in these conventional market segments where, for example, reinsurance contracts are executed as swap agreements and different loss exposures are transferred into different investment assets and derivative instruments. This development pinpoints the need to assess market-related exposures from an enterprise-wide perspective where the alternative risk management approaches are considered in an integrative manner. However, it also emphasizes the need for specialized expertise within these risk management disciplines to be able to act professionally and exploit opportunities in specific risk-transfer markets. The corporation must ensure that sufficient risk management expertise exists as internal competencies in the organization to deal with specific instruments and market practices that incorporate different market instruments and techniques in dealing with the corporate exposures.

References

Andersen, T. J., 2006. *Global Derivatives: A Strategic Risk Management Perspective.* Pearson Education: Harlow, UK.

Butler, K. C., 2004. *Multinational Finance* (3rd edn). South-Western: Mason, Ohio.

Culp, C., 2005. 'Alternative Risk Transfer' in Frenkel, M., Hommel, U. and Rudolf, M. (eds.), *Risk Management: Challenge and Opportunity* (2nd edn). Springer: Berlin.

Fabozzi, F. J., 2000. *Bond Markets, Analysis and Strategies* (4th edn). Prentice Hall: Upper Saddle River, New Jersey.

Grinblatt, M. and Titman, S., 1998. *Financial Markets and Corporate Strategy.* Irwin/McGraw-Hill: Boston, Massachusetts.

McDonald, R. L., 2003. *Derivatives Markets.* Addison-Wesley: Boston, Massachusetts.

McMillan, L. G., 1993. *Options as a Strategic Investment.* New York Institute of Finance: New York.

Murphy, J. J., 1986. *Technical Analysis of the Futures Market: A Comparative Guide to Trading Methods and Applications.* New York Institute of Finance: New York.

Stulz, R. M., 2003. *Risk Management & Derivatives.* South-Western: Mason, Ohio.

Wöhrman, P. and Bűrer, C., 2002. 'Captives' in Lane, M. (ed.), *Alternative Risk Strategies.* Risk Books: London.

4   Extending the risk management perspective

Now the focus moves beyond conventional risk management approaches and takes the wider spectrum of risks into consideration, including commercial and strategic exposures. The focus is also extended from insurance and derivative contracts to include alternative risk-transfer mechanisms and operational flexibilities needed to cope with longer-term systemic risks and firm-specific economic exposures. There is a focused discussion of the real options logic where financial options analysis is extended to the context of option structures framed by firm-specific asset positions, dynamic capabilities and external market conditions. A framework to analyze specific business opportunities as potential responsive actions in a turbulent environment is outlined and its potential use is discussed in more detail.

4.1   Risk management in all of its aspects

The range of exposures considered in conventional risk management thinking includes various insurable hazards as well as market-related, operational and commercial risks. Insurable risks comprise a range of casualties, accidents and man-made disasters, such as fire, collisions, explosions, etc., and natural disasters caused by, for example, windstorm, flooding and earthquake events that may destroy productive assets and disrupt the production flows. Market-related risks comprise the effects of changes in various market prices, such as commodity prices, energy prices, foreign exchanges rates, interest rates and so forth, all of which have the capacity to affect corporate performance. There has been an increased focus on operational risks in recent years comprising events like processing failures, technology breakdowns, human errors, misreporting, fraud and the like. Some commercial risk events may be resembled to operational mishaps as they constitute shortcomings with respect to stakeholder relationships inflicted by poor product quality, flawed after-sales service, harmful public press coverage, suboptimal input sourcing, etc. Hence, based on a philosophy that process flaws can be diminished or avoided, there has been a surge in control-driven frameworks to limit these exposures, including various enterprise-wide risk management approaches spurred by legal requirements to impose formal monitoring procedures.

The associated hazards and market exposures are typically handled through engagement in different insurance arrangements, financial hedging techniques and alternative risk-transfer solutions that at times may take rather sophisticated forms. The operational risk events are typically handled by implementing formalized control systems that may also consider the potential for process improvements while installing different monitoring, early warning and risk preparedness programmes. In this sense, the risk management efforts have been supported by many current management techniques, such as total quality management (TQM), six-sigma, lean, lean six-sigma, etc., all of which emphasize the need for customer-driven operational improvements.[1] These management techniques typically promote production efficiencies, while touting dynamic improvements in internal procedures and processing techniques often on the basis of a stronger customer-centred focus. In other words, the ideal is to achieve better customer fulfilment while using fewer economic resources than before.[2] However, this aim may also constitute a potential double-edged sword as economic efficiencies gained through tightly coupled processes, for example, in global sourcing networks, may increase sensitivity to disruptions in the value chain caused by exogenous environmental incidents including natural hazards, political events, civil unrest, etc.

In addition to the more traditional risk categories, there are a number of other risk factors associated with the strategic position of the corporation. The related exposures may represent some of the most significant effects on corporate earnings development. Accordingly, the ability to exploit the upside potential uncovered by strategic events constitutes an important aspect that is usually overlooked in conventional risk management practices.[3] The strategic risk factors may include major competitor moves, product innovations, process improvements, new business designs, technology leaps and the like, all of which constitute exposures that can be difficult to identify in advance and hence also hard to quantify. Therefore, a complete overview of significant corporate risks must include consideration of different strategic exposures, the treatment of which may require a closer look at risk management as an integral part of strategic decision-making, strategic planning and corporate management processes in general. This means that achieving effective risk management outcomes requires consideration of behavioural phenomena, organizational structure and alternative strategic actions in addition to formal risk management practices, as these may have a significant influence on the firm's ability to withstand emerging strategic risks. In this

---

[1] See, e.g. M. George, D. Rowlands and B. Kastle (2004). *What is Lean Six Sigma?* McGraw-Hill: New York; J. P. Womack and D. T. Jones (2005). *Lean Solutions: How Companies and Customers can Create Value and Wealth Together*. Simon & Schuster: London.

[2] While this expresses the idealized aim of the 'lean movement', it does not necessarily mean that proponents of the lean concept always live by these aims in practice, i.e. it is not uncommon to see corporations use 'lean' as a way to pursue simple cost-cutting exercises under a fancy heading that makes them more attractive to financial analysts.

[3] See, e.g. A. J. Slywozky (2007). *The Upside: How to Turn Your Greatest Threat into Your Biggest Growth Opportunity*. Capstone Publishing: Chichester, West Sussex.

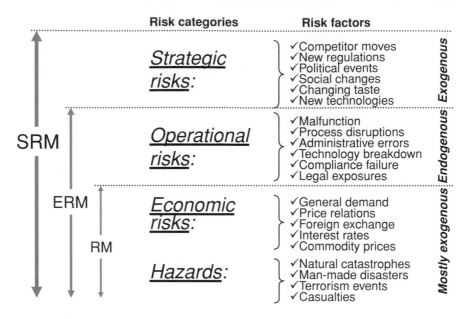

Figure 4.1 *The full range of corporate risk exposures*

context, one may deal with strategic exposures by extrapolating a financial hedging perspective to incorporate a real options lens in the analyses of corporate risk responsiveness opportunities.

4.2   An extended view on risk exposures

One way to conceive of the variety of corporate exposures is to look at their respective origins from *exogenous* environmental factors that are beyond managerial influence and *endogenous* factors related to the execution of activities within the organization. The exogenous risk factors comprise conventional insurable hazards where losses are inflicted by uncontrollable natural phenomena, casualties caused by third-party actions, etc. (Figure 4.1).

Another category of exogenous risks relates to economic exposures imposed by macro- and socio-economic developments across national markets and the global interaction between them. These risks include exposures to developments in different financial rates, commodity prices and inflation rates across economies both in terms of booked transactions and future business activities, as well as potential systemic risks in global institutional structures. The endogenous risk factors relate primarily to the operational risks associated with production processes and practices conducted by the corporation in pursuit of its business purpose. This is a relatively new focal area that has received increasing attention as illustrated by the inclusion of operational risks as part of the exposure management system proposed by the Bank for International Settlements (BIS).[4] These exposures can be associated with an organizational ability to carry out internal operations without major process disruptions, while avoiding occurrences of fraudulent activities. Another aspect relates to technology risks, which is not solely related to systems breakdown, but is as much associated with appropriate and timely adoption of new technologies to enable efficient operational procedures in data- and information-intensive business activities.[5]

It is relatively straightforward to extend the risk management perspective to include the consideration of other types of exogenous risks, such as strategic risks that can arise from rapid and abrupt changes taking place in increasingly turbulent high-velocity business environments.[6] The consequences of 'hypercompetitive' global market conditions driven by disruptive competition, continuous market innovations, new technological leaps, etc. have been addressed frequently in popular management books.[7] These strategic risk factors go beyond the conventional economic exposures as they consider potential consequences of competition from revolutionary business models, new demand characteristics and customer taste, adoption of path-breaking technologies, changes in industry and market structures, etc. Various techniques, approaches and frameworks have evolved to deal with more traditional hazards and financial, economic and operational risks, but the same cannot be said for the handling of strategic risks. However, given their relative importance, it is worth giving substantially more consideration to this essential concern.

The traditional risk management (RM) practices have typically adhered to risk mitigation and preparedness activities, while considering the need to engage in financial hedging arrangements, risk-transfer solutions and various financing contingencies to deal with excess risk levels. In some cases, the longer-term economic exposures have been considered in the context of investments in multinational sourcing and production facilities. In terms of corporate organization, these activities have typically been handled within specialized insurance units and finance departments in conformity with prevailing views on insurance contracting and financial hedging techniques in an optimal multinational enterprise structure (Figure 4.2).

---

[4] Bank for International Settlements (2006). *Basel II: International Convergence of Capital Measurement and Capital Standards: A Revised Framework – Comprehensive Version.* Available online from www.bis.org.

[5] See A. Saunders and M. M. Cornett (2003). *Financial Institutions Management: A Risk Management Approach.* McGraw-Hill Irwin: Boston, Massachusetts.

[6] This has been an ongoing discourse among management scholars, see, e.g. K. Eisenhardt (1989). 'Making Fast Strategic Decisions in High-Velocity Environments'. *Academy of Management Journal* 32(3), pp. 543–76; and L. G. Thomas III (1996). 'Dynamic Resourcefulness and the Hypercompetitive Shift'. *Organization Science* 7(3), pp. 221–42 among others.

[7] See, e.g. influential books like R. A. D'Aveni (1994). *Hypercompetition.* Free Press: New York; and C. M. Christensen (1997). *The Innovator's Dilemma: When New Technologies Cause Great Firms to Fail.* Harvard Business School Press: Boston, Massachusetts.

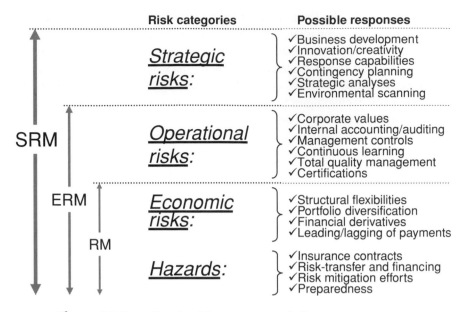

Figure 4.2 *Extending the risk management challenge*

The emergence of an operational risk perspective has fostered a combined focus on exogenous economic risks as well as endogenous processing risks, often organized in a central enterprise-wide risk management function headed by a Chief Risk Officer.[8] The operational risk concerns are also highly related to the adoption of total quality management techniques and lean management practices aimed at process rationalizations and ongoing improvements through continuous learning. These developments have fostered a commonly expressed view that risk management is not just about avoiding the likelihood of downside losses, but is as much related to the aims of improving processing efficiencies and operating effectiveness to enhance corporate performance. The newer focus on enterprise risk management (ERM) adopts an internal-process-oriented risk management focus. The ERM practices seek to integrate various aspects of management practice to extend the focus from insurable and financial risks to incorporate also operational effectiveness and structural features of the organization.

The integrative risk management perspective has been partially captured by value-at-risk perspectives initially developed to address the aggregate risk assessments of large market-related risk portfolios. Hence, a common argument has been that since risk factors are interrelated, their effects can partially outweigh each other, so there is a need to consider the overall risk exposure in a manner

---

[8] See, e.g. A. P. Liebenberg and R. E. Hoyt (2003). 'The Determinants of Enterprise Risk Management: Evidence from the Appointment of Chief Risk Officers'. *Risk Management and Insurance Review* 6(1), pp. 37–52; and A. E. Kleffner, R. B. Lee and B. McGannon (2003). 'The Effects of Corporate Governance on the Use of Enterprise Risk Management: Evidence from Canada'. *Risk Management and Insurance Review* 6(1), pp. 53–73.

that takes potential risk diversification effects into account. However, this principle is obviously more difficult to apply to economic and operational risk factors that are harder to quantify in meaningful ways. Another argument for a centralized integrative risk management function has arisen as a natural response to the increasing demands for regulatory compliance that has urged a focus on proper accounting and control processes while documenting that major risk factors have been addressed. This has frequently meant that major economic and operational risk factors have been identified, their potential economic impacts assessed and various responsive actions considered. Such analyses have typically been conducted in conjunction with the implementation of tailored management accounting systems and internal control processes to ensure that costly deviations and errors rarely occur.

However, other risks that are harder to identify and measure may be underrepresented in our current approaches to the corporate risk management challenge. Here, we argue that it is useful to add a distinct strategic risk management (SRM) focus that can extend conventional risk concerns and give specific consideration to strategic risks, many of which constitute the most important corporate exposures. Yet, when promoting this, we also realize that there is no developed risk management approach to deal effectively with these types of risk that are hard to quantify and often extremely difficult to foresee. The reality of increasingly turbulent and competitive business environments is that many of the future risk factors are difficult to identify or extrapolate in meaningful ways. Nonetheless, the corporation must be able to respond effectively when these types of unforeseeable events occur. That is, we must consider ways in which to deal with many new, diverse and complex challenges associated with increasingly dynamic industrial contexts that evolve over time (see Box 4.1 *Identifying significant environmental changes*). It is not clear at the outset what exactly makes up these responsive practices, but they must somehow be related to the organization's ability to engage in creative thinking that allows them to take actions with the potential to circumvent environmental challenges as they arise. Hence, the ability to take responsive actions arguably bound in a corporate capacity to take innovative initiatives, develop new commercial opportunities and execute these alternative commercial ventures when changing business conditions show a need for it.

One way to deal with the requirement for strategic responsiveness may be facilitated by the adoption of a real options perspective when analyzing available business opportunities. Real options in effect comprise commercial projects that can be implemented by engaging in an initial investment. That is, a real option can be conceived as a business opportunity that can be executed under favourable market circumstances and left alone under unfavourable conditions. This embedded flexibility to act on, defer or leave the business opportunity constitutes an option that can be exploited in corporate decision-making under rapidly changing market conditions. This perspective can encourage executives to think about possible options that the corporation already may possess. Once the business

Box 4.1 Identifying significant environmental changes

Industry structure

A rather conventional approach to analyze the competitive situation in a given industry is to conduct a review in accordance with the so-called 'five-forces' model introduced by Michael Porter.[9] One critique of this model is its static nature, i.e. it presupposes a rather well-defined industry without consideration for major disruptive influences. However, despite these shortcomings, the model arguably constitutes a reasonable analytical foundation to understand better a given industry context. Andy Grove, the former CEO of Intel, suggests the use of a slightly extended version of the model that also takes into account the influence of firms that operate in complementary industrial areas and looks at substitution as a particular phenomenon describing new ways of conducting business that may have the potential to revolutionize the current industry structure.[10]

Grove's six forces diagram

The *six forces diagram* is very much inspired by Andy Grove's experiences as the CEO of Intel Corporation during the mid-1980s. Intel was initially started as a producer of memory chips and for years dominated this market as a technology leader. However, in the early 1980s the company was being out-competed by Japanese firms with superior competencies in global mass production. As this threat became increasingly apparent, it so happened that an engineer within the firm had developed the first microchip and actually sold this product to interested customers supported by the intervention of various line managers based on rational decision criteria.[11] This initiative became the new business focus of Intel as it adapted to the changing business conditions.

While memory chips became increasingly commoditized in ways that made Intel's technological competencies less effective as a competitive market response, the computer industry also experienced some fundamental changes. Where computers previously had been dominated by fully integrated main-frame producers, the new expansive growth of the personal computer fragmented the market into specialized complementers,

---

[9] M. E. Porter (1980). *Competitive Strategy: Techniques for Analyzing Industries and Competitors*. Free Press: New York – the model considers the relative influence of new market entries, product substitutes, the bargaining powers of suppliers and buyers, and the degree of rivalry among industry peers.

[10] A. S. Grove (1997). *Only the Paranoid Survive: How to Exploit the Crisis Points that Challenge Every Company and Career*, HarperCollins Business: London.

[11] For a more detailed account of the complex internal processes that drove these developments, see, e.g. R. A. Burgelman (2002). *Strategy is Destiny: How Strategy-Making Shapes a Company's Future*. Free Press: New York.

including producers of software and microchips as well as computer manufacturers. Hence, the adaptive initiative developed deep within Intel became its solution to reposition itself in view of the paradigm change that had taken place in the industry.

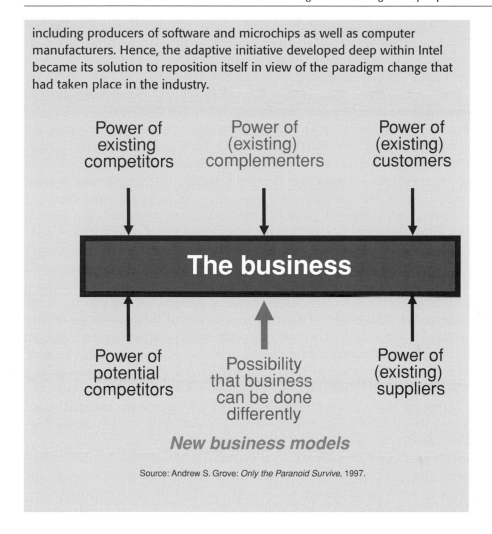

Source: Andrew S. Grove: *Only the Paranoid Survive*, 1997.

opportunities available to the corporation have been identified, they arguably extend the range of alternative choices management can engage in when competitive conditions change and require some form of adaptive response. In this way, we can see real options as business opportunities that constitute responsive commercial ventures with characteristics that resemble the options instruments adopted for financial hedging purposes. Obviously, the development and execution of real options derive from more complicated environmental conditions than conventional financial options contracts and somehow evolve as a result of more complex corporate strategy processes. The changing conditions for financial options are simply reflected in the price volatility of the underlying assets, whereas the value of the business opportunity that underpins a real option is influenced by many factors in the evolving business environment (we return to these issues in later chapters).

We have so far discussed the use of a range of sophisticated hedging and risk-transfer instruments adapted for use in conjunction with particular risk management techniques geared to handle different types of exposures. Financial derivatives of many shapes and colours have been introduced to deal with a variety of market-related risks. Insurance and reinsurance contracts combined with alternative risk-transfer solutions have emerged to deal with various casualty and natural catastrophe risks. Internal control processes and management accounting systems have been introduced to deal with different kinds of operational risks. In this context, we may see a potential for adopting identified real options as potential vehicles for addressing important strategic exposures related to competitive moves, technological innovations, changes in industry and economic structures, etc. Hence, the range of different hedging instruments can be seen as a complementary 'toolbox' for the handling of different types of corporate exposures.

Financial derivatives are typically used to hedge the price risks associated with the various cash flows that pass through the corporation over time as a consequence of both commercial and financial transactions. The price risks can be related to the volatility of financial rates as well as variations in the relative prices of commodities and finished goods. The financial exposures can arise from mismatched foreign exchange payments over future time periods that emanate from the receivables and payables of commercial and financial commitments. They may also arise from excessive mismatches in the interest rate sensitivities of corporate assets and liabilities. Derivatives and risk-transfer instruments are traded in specialized segments of the international financial and capital markets and can be used to modify and manage the financial exposures. Due to the finite maturity of many financial derivatives, longer-term economic exposures may, however, be dealt with through diversified investment in production capacity across economic regions as a way to diversify underlying exposures. It may also be possible to create manufacturing flexibilities across foreign entities that can allow the corporation to take advantage of more persistent price differentials in foreign currency rates, input prices, etc.,[12] and thereby provide a basis for exploiting arbitrage opportunities and factor cost advantages (Figure 4.3).

When it comes to competitive, technological and economic risk factors, the corporate effects are usually unique to the individual firms and, therefore, it is not possible to develop financial hedging tools where natural counterparts would be willing to trade and take positions in these instruments. Instead, real options – or business opportunities developed through combinations of firm-specific assets, resources and competencies in new business opportunities – can arguably provide the means to react to changed strategic situations that will impose new exposures on the corporation.

---

[12] See, e.g. B. Kogut and N. Kulatilaka (1994). 'Operating Flexibility, Global Manufacturing and the Option Value of a Multinational Network'. *Management Science* 40(1), pp. 123–41.

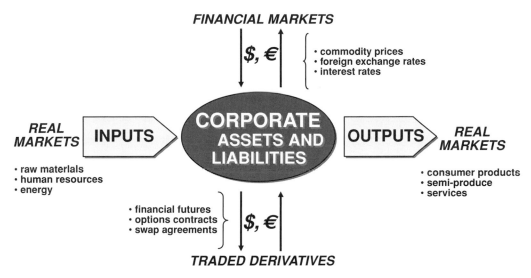

Figure 4.3 *Distinguishing between financial and real market exposures*

4.3   Real options and strategic exposures

The real options can be identified around different types of option structures that shape incremental flexibilities in corporate investment decisions. Expansion options provide the opportunity to extend the scale and scope of business activities. Deferral options provide the ability to defer a strategic investment decision to a later point in time. Abandonment options give the possibility to abandon further commitments to a strategic investment. Contracting options provide the ability to terminate, dispose of or subcontract business activities. Switching options provide the ability to change the use of corporate assets for other business purposes. In short, it may be possible to identify many different types of real options that provide the corporation with inherent flexibilities in its business activities and strategic investments.

The most common real option structures are *expansion* and *deferral* options that depict the flexible choice of investing in new business opportunities or postpone them to later more opportune points in time. These option structures can be construed as simple call options that provide the holder with the possibility but not the obligation to start new business activities at some point in time within a certain time frame. The expansion option perspective can be applied to the development of various strategic growth options. The deferral option perspective can be applied to the timing of major irreversible business investments where postponement may be beneficial until a time where market conditions are better known and uncertainties have decreased to more acceptable levels. The value of a financial call option is derived from the potential for future exercise at a

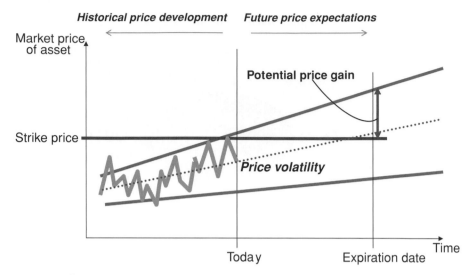

Figure 4.4 *Option value and volatility of market prices*

significant economic gain because market developments are volatile (Figure 4.4). The theoretical option premium ascribed to this value potential can be estimated by the use of analytic solutions (see Appendix 2 for a brief discussion of how the premium on a call option can be determined).

Pursuing a real options perspective to analyze potential strategic responses requires that different potential option structures embedded in corporate assets, resources and competencies can be identified. To the extent that a process of real options recognition can be devised to uncover all of the relevant business opportunities throughout the organization, there is a need for a central analytical process to compare and evaluate the alternative responses represented by the options under a given risk scenario. As the real options perspective builds on valuations of firm-specific business opportunities as opposed to potential gains from financial market developments, real options can extend the analytical toolbox from derivative instruments to consider also the response potential embedded in the flexible structure of corporate assets and resources. This introduces a new set of risk management instruments to deal with corporate exposures that also include strategic concerns and thereby increases the scope of exogenous risk factors considered in the risk management process (Figure 4.5).

The consideration of structural flexibilities and real options in the form of business opportunities that are available to the organization can be used to extend the scope of approaches to be applied in the corporate risk management process. The conventional risk-transfer markets, comprising financial derivatives, insurance contracts and various capital market solutions, can be used to modify the corporate exposures to different market risks, casualty events and disaster scenarios where operational exposures typically are handled by imposing internal control systems (Figure 4.6).

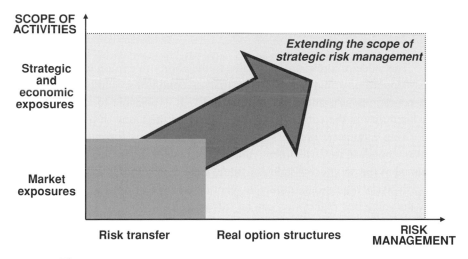

Figure 4.5 *Real options as extension of the risk management scope*

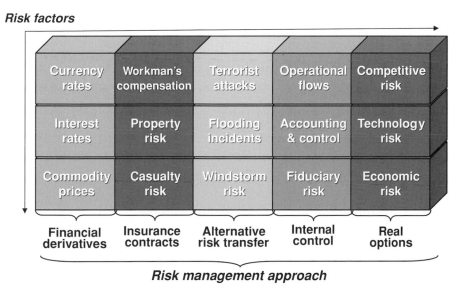

Figure 4.6 *Different instruments and approaches to deal with corporate risks*

In contrast, the market does not offer any traded instruments to deal with strategic risks like competitive moves, technology innovation and changes in global demand conditions because the derived exposures typically are firm specific. In this situation, the identification of different real option structures that form the corporate action space can provide the means to modify and manage the implied exposures by devising appropriate responses.

4.4   Real options frameworks

The value of a real option relates to the ability to exploit the underlying business opportunity under favourable market conditions, while leaving it if market conditions turn out to be unsatisfactory. It is possible to assign a value to this flexibility in the same way as we determine the value of a financial call option, using a numeric option valuation solution. In this formula, the market price corresponds to the investment value of the underlying business opportunity determined as the net present value of future cash flows, with a strike price equal to the cash layout required to initiate the venture (see Appendix 3 for a description of how the value of a real option can be calculated).

It is not option valuation per se that may be the most important consideration because real options as firm-specific constructs are not acquired in a public market place per se and, therefore, reaching an exact option value is not necessarily that critical. What seems important though is a corporate ability to recognize, create and develop the underlying business opportunities as efficiently as possible. Hence, it is probably more economical to create them in-house as opposed to through acquisitions. Conversely, it is not sufficient to have a large portfolio of real options if the holder is unable to exploit them effectively.[13] Therefore, it is equally important for the corporation to impose decision processes that ensure effective exercise of the underlying business opportunities in view of ongoing market developments. That is, the corporate ability both to create and exercise real options in a portfolio of business opportunities under challenging environmental conditions is a prerequisite to achieve optimal performance outcomes from responsive actions (Figure 4.7).

From a risk management perspective, real options are interesting because they can provide a basis for adapting and modifying the business volume to changing

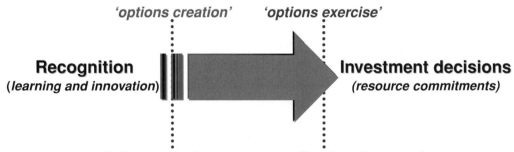

Figure 4.7 *The real options chronology in risk management*

---

[13] See T. J. Andersen (2006). 'Options Reasoning and Strategic Responsiveness: Discussion and Empirical Assessment' in T. J. Andersen (ed.), *Perspectives on Strategic Risk Management*. Copenhagen Business School Press: Copenhagen.

economic prospects and reorganizing activities in accordance with new market conditions that may open up for alternative commercial activities. The creation of real options as alternative strategic business projects may be furnished through internal venturing activities initiated by functional specialists and operational managers within the organization and championed by middle managers to the attention of corporate management.[14] Conversely, the evaluations of alternative real options are made at the executive level and require that the relevant option structures have been identified for further assessment. Hence, a more complete understanding of the real options approach to manage strategic risks probably should combine decentralized creation processes with more centralized evaluation practices to support the corporate exercise and investment decisions (see Box 4.2 *A real options approach*).

Box 4.2 A real options approach

The creation of real options is obviously necessary for the firm's subsequent exploitation of different strategic opportunities. However, options creation is not a sufficient condition for superior performance. First of all, the costs associated with the options creation process matter. It is not a question of establishing as much organizational flexibility as possible because the cost of creating this flexibility in some cases can be prohibitive. Also, some flexibility is more meaningful and important to the firm than others, i.e. optimal options creation processes are cost efficient and effective in developing relevant option structures. Furthermore, to create excess returns, the business opportunities contained in the firm's portfolio of real options must be adopted (exercised) in an optimal manner throughout their lifetime. Therefore, a major challenge is to devise processes that allow the firm to better optimize real options exercise that will result in superior returns.

An important step towards effective strategic options management practices is to recognize that firms must be able to create and identify new relevant real options in a relatively costless manner and then effectively exploit them under turbulent market conditions. The development of relevant options depends on capabilities that can assess the potential value of business opportunities under turbulence even though they represent new innovations with vague commercial contours. Options exercise, in turn, depends on abilities to scan effectively the environment and assess business conditions based on financial, organizational and strategic risks. These organizational capabilities are supported by informal knowledge networks and effective communication between functional specialists and decision-makers located in different parts of the organization.

---

[14] See, e.g. R. Burgelman (1988). 'Strategy Making as a Social Learning Process: The Case of Internal Corporate Venturing'. *Interfaces* 18(3), pp. 74–85.

One may argue that strategic flexibility is essential for the ability to react to changing market conditions and adapt in ways that can circumvent the adverse effects of increasing turmoil and exploit the upside potential of emerging opportunities. This may bound in a versatile corporate resource base where essential competencies can be recombined and redirected towards new activities relatively easily without incurring prohibitive restructuring costs. It may also depend on an effective internal venturing capacity to maintain a channel for real options creation and turn it into a portfolio of business opportunities at different stages of development. Creating an overview of the resulting real options portfolio may constitute a very practical way to assess the potential for alternative responsive actions in view of specific environmental changes.

In this assessment, it is not the absolute value of the real option that matters per se, but it can be useful when deciding between immediate exercise and deferral of business projects that require large irreversible investments. In this situation, the decision heuristic suggests that the net present value of the investment must exceed the premium ascribed to the deferral option that is foregone if the real option is exercised. This is a precautionary rule adopted to ensure that business ventures behind the real options are not introduced prematurely. As far as options creation is concerned, a layman's logic would suggest that internal development projects should make small initial commitments to test out the viability of new technologies and subsequently the commercial potential of the business opportunity. This is quite consistent with an internal venturing process where lower level resource commitments are usually of limited size. However, once the venture is developed into a full-scale real option ready for market implementation, the deferral option logic applies to make sure that large investments are not made prematurely. The eventual timing of a large irreversible business investment should balance a trade-off between the risk of premature market entry against the risk of increasing competitive pressures. The same logic may obviously be applied to external venturing activities.

We can use an options-theoretical logic to assess the potential associated with a portfolio of real options represented by new ventures or business opportunities at different development stages that have been identified by corporate management. The underlying logic hinges upon qualified judgments regarding the value potential of the real options and the potential time value remaining in the real options. The value potential corresponds to the option's intrinsic value, i.e. the gain that can be obtained from immediate exercise.[15] The time value of an option reflects the incremental value potential to be gained from the volatility of underlying market conditions until the option expires. Indicators of these factors can be extracted from the option valuation formula as presented in Appendix 3. The natural logarithm of the investment value over the cash outlay ($\ln(P/S)$)

[15] See T. Leuhrman (1998). 'Strategy as a Portfolio of Real Options'. *Harvard Business Review* 76(5), pp. 89–99.

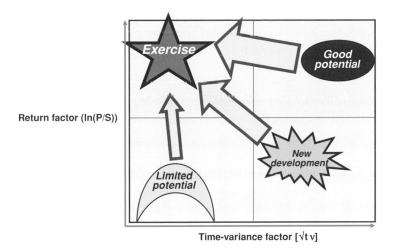

Figure 4.8 *A real options framework*

indicates the return from options exercise. The square root of the time remaining to exercise multiplied by the volatility of the investment value ($\sqrt{t}\, v$) indicates the remaining value potential of the option. Based on assessments of these two factors across all of the real options in the portfolio, it is possible to decide how to position the options in terms of immediate exercise and further development (Figure 4.8).

Strategic options with high return and low time-variance factors should be exercised soon because economic returns are high and there is little uncertainty associated with an exercise. Real options with high returns and high time values are promising for future exercise because return is high and there is significant time value left. These should be held back until uncertainty has settled somewhat. Ventures showing low to medium returns and high time values represent promising but uncertain future earnings potential and, therefore, should be nurtured, whereas those with low returns and low time values are deadbeats to be discarded. This may provide a somewhat crude assessment of the potential associated with the real options portfolio, but it does nonetheless provide an overview of alternative strategic actions that can be taken immediately and those with longer time horizons.

If environmental conditions are changing at a given moment, the viable strategic options to consider are the ones with high intrinsic values and limited time values left, whereas options with high time value may be too risky to consider for immediate implementation. While this type of analysis in principle requires that the viable strategic options are identified in advance, there may also be a basis for using such an analytical framework to help identify areas where real options seem to be lacking and thereby possibly encourage considerations about internal ventures that already may exist in latent forms embedded in the corporate resource endowment.[16] As such, the very framework might be useful as a way to underpin creative strategic thinking processes in the quest to identify relevant strategic options.

4.5   Application of the real options logic: managing innovation in the pharmaceutical industry (*external venturing*)[17]

Product innovation is vital to the survival and success of pharmaceutical companies. At the same time, huge costs are involved in developing drugs and the outcome of these efforts is highly uncertain. Consequently, the development of drugs is probably the most important strategic risk faced by pharmaceutical companies.

Furthermore, it is claimed that the traditional research and development (R&D) model within the pharmaceutical industry no longer works:

> It is fair to say that large pharmaceutical companies have not been as innovative as they need to be. The standard paradigm centred around a few conventional drug targets has proven a much harder approach than first believed. In stark contrast, smaller firms that have pursued biologics have had a pretty spectacular turn in the past decade – opportunities large pharma have failed to grasp . . . Engaging with the small company sector and academia has proven to be fertile ground for innovation.[18]

Novo Nordisk is a company that has opened the boundaries and looked beyond its own in-house research activities to gain access to early-stage research projects and thereby potential new technologies. It is a worldwide healthcare company operating within diabetes care and biopharmaceuticals segments, marketed in 179 countries and maintains a market share in the world insulin market of 52 per cent.

Novo Nordisk allocates approximately 20 per cent of its research budget to external R&D partnering with small biotechnology companies, etc. within diabetes, biopharmaceuticals and delivery technologies. The company states that: 'Partnerships, both project-related and longer-term commitments, are one way of bridging gaps in areas where Novo Nordisk sees room to pursue business opportunities.'[19] This implies that in-licensing agreements, contract research and

---

[16] See, e.g. E. H. Bowman and D. Hurry (1993). 'Strategy Through the Options Lens: An Integrated View of Resource Investments and the Incremental Choice Process'. *Academy of Management Review* 18(4), pp. 760–82.

[17] This example is inspired by D. V. Richea (2007). 'Novo Nordisk – A Case Study on the Creation and Exercise of Real Options in the Pharmaceutical Industry Through Pharma-Biotech Collaborations'. Strategic Risk Management Report, Copenhagen Business School.

[18] Quoted from John Bell, Regius Professor of Medicine, University of Oxford, printed in Novo Nordisk Annual Report (2005), p. 26.

[19] Novo Nordisk Annual Report (2006), p. 32.

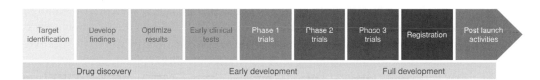

Source: Adapted from the Novartis drug development process (http://nibr.novartis.com).

Figure 4.9 *The drug development process*

co-funded studies are used to stimulate cross-fertilization of ideas and develop organizational learning that will eventually benefit the patients. The company is pursuing development efforts that appear medically viable and commercially sound. At the same time, the company is scouting for suitable drug candidates discovered elsewhere and seeking to form partnerships that can help bring them to market. Novo Nordisk encourages an open learning environment with other firms in the business. As argued in the annual report: 'It takes a global outlook to excel in biotechnology. And it takes patience to reap the rewards.'

In this new model of innovation, Novo Nordisk enters into an R&D collaboration agreement about technology transfer, licensing, co-development, etc. for a specified technology or drug lead with a range of smaller biotechnology companies. Normally, Novo Nordisk will be contractually obliged to make an up-front payment (or equity investment) in the biotechnology company with a possibility to extend the cooperation depending upon partnership performance or business conditions by making a series of payments over a given time frame. The contracts give Novo Nordisk the right to acquire an exclusive licence to manufacture and commercialize the technology or drug if it proves successful. Furthermore, Novo Nordisk can withdraw from the collaboration at any time if it finds it suitable to do so, ending the commitment of further funding if the research does not proceed as expected or if business conditions suddenly change for the worse.

The step-by-step approach is closely connected to the drug development process, which is split into phases, where the decision to proceed with the next phase depends on the outcome of the previous phase (Figure 4.9).

This approach constitutes a type of abandonment option structure whereby the company is testing whether the initial investments lead to expected results and can subsequently abandon future investments if results are disappointing or alternatively extend the investment if the interim outcomes are favourable. In that way, the typical cooperation with a biotechnology company has the characteristics of a real option, where Novo Nordisk buys into the unknown upside potential, has the opportunity to abandon the project and, therefore, limits the potential downside losses to the amount invested in the project. This constitutes a chained abandonment structure.

For example, Novo Nordisk entered into a development and licence agreement for the development and commercialization of a system for pulmonary delivery of insulin (with an option to develop the technology for delivery of other compounds in two undisclosed therapeutic areas outside diabetes) with Aradigm Corp. in June 1998 to ensure that Novo Nordisk would be the first company to provide an innovative technology for diabetes treatment, if the system proved successful.[20] Aradigm could receive up to US$50 million in milestone and equity investments, of which US$9 million, including purchase of Aradigm stocks, are made up front. However, further investments from Novo Nordisk would be conditioned on achieving specific clinical and product development milestones aiming to limit Novo Nordisk's downside risk. When part of the uncertainty surrounding the success of the technology was resolved, in October 2001, the companies entered into a manufacturing and supply agreement, where Novo Nordisk committed itself to provide manufacturing capacity for the project, while Aradigm granted Novo Nordisk an exclusive worldwide licence to register, use, market, distribute, sell and produce products from the development activities. When most of the uncertainty surrounding the technology had been dissolved in September 2004, Novo Nordisk committed completely to the project and received full manufacturing rights to the technology, and a right to purchase all of Aradigm's facilities and manufacturing equipment related to the project, while Aradigm retained ownership of intellectual property rights and would thereby receive royalties on future sales.

Furthermore, Novo Nordisk formed a five-year strategic research collaboration with TransTech Pharma Inc. (TTP) in September 2001 utilizing TransTech's proprietary small-molecule discovery engine, TTP Translational Technology®, to create novel clinical candidates for the treatment of human diseases.[21] Even though TTP received a milestone payment from Novo Nordisk in October 2004 as well as in September 2005, as a result of progress made with a drug candidate resulting from this collaboration, Novo Nordisk announced in February 2007 an agreement whereby it renounced the joint R&D project and TTP obtained an exclusive licence from Novo Nordisk to its clinical glucokinase activator (GKA) programme. Under the terms of the agreement, TTP obtained all rights worldwide to Novo Nordisk's GKA programme, including pre-clinical and clinical compounds. TTP made an up-front payment to Novo Nordisk for the licensed rights, and was also committed to additional payments as development milestones were reached, as well as royalties on commercial product sales. The main driver behind the decision was to focus its research efforts, as stated: 'Novo Nordisk today announced a decision to focus all its research and development (R&D) resources on the company's growing pipeline of protein-based pharmaceuticals. As a result of this decision the company's R&D activities within small molecules for oral treatment of diabetes will be discontinued and existing projects divested';[22] and 'this allows us to focus our R&D on therapeutic proteins which is where we have our core competences, while keeping a financial stake in the

[20] See various press releases from the two companies and articles in the business and medical press.
[21] See various press releases from the two companies and articles in the business press.
[22] Stock Exchange Announcements, 15 January 2007.

GKA programme'.[23] That is, Novo Nordisk decided that they will be able to use resources more favourably by focusing their activities.

All in all, the Novo Nordisk innovation model has enabled the company to manage uncertainty linked to the drug development process through risk sharing and conditional agreements with various partners. Novo Nordisk has broadened its research base and assumed a portfolio of technological opportunities, many of which would not be possible to develop solely through internal venturing due to the specialized competencies required. Consequently, Novo Nordisk has extended its access to future growth opportunities through strategic partnerships, in-licensing agreements, contract research and co-funded studies. Secondly, the fact that one-fifth of the company's R&D investments are carried out through external partnerships provides enhanced flexibility, as they can abandon these projects if desired, and can choose only to invest further in those projects that exhibit the greatest potential as uncertainty decreases.

4.6   Extending the real options perspective

Adopting a real options approach to consider potential responsive actions in view of changing environmental conditions presupposes that the corporate analysts have been able to identify all of the underlying business opportunities that are available to the organization. The identification of relevant business opportunities as foundation for alternative real options requires a deep understanding of the corporate resource base and how various competencies may be recombined to support corporate business activities. It also requires a fundamental understanding as to where the business environment seems to be moving as informed by insights into regulatory conditions, customer demands, competitor moves, etc. However, the reality is that it can be extremely difficult to foresee these events because we tend to think within a prevailing competitive dynamic. Yet, we know that mega-changes in these types of exogenous market conditions most likely will lead to strategic 'inflection points' where the organization is forced to rethink the entire way in which it conducts its business activities.[24]

One way to accommodate analyses of environmental changes and open the scope for what might happen is the concept of *scenario planning*, where a basic idea is to think through possible ways in which the future competitive landscape might shape up.[25] By allowing the formation of alternative scenarios, there is less risk of contracting the same mould of competitive thinking. By considering the possibility for extreme alternative realities, there is also a basis for assessing the corporate preparedness to handle abrupt risk events in the future. This planning

---

[23] Press release, 21 February 2007.
[24] R. A. Burgelman and A. S. Grove (1996). 'Strategic Dissonance'. *California Management Review* 38(2), pp. 8–28.
[25] Scenario planning will be discussed further in Ch. 7.

framework for thinking more openly about possible competitive scenarios can be combined with a real options approach.[26] That is, for each of the environmental scenarios developed in the planning process, corporate management can think through what the appropriate strategic responses could be, which implicitly means that the usefulness of an existing real options portfolio of business opportunities is being assessed. Incidentally, these considerations may furnish more creative thinking to uncover latent options that already may exist within the confines of the corporation. It also provides a basis for rethinking the viability and timing of alternative business opportunities and gaining a better understanding of the dynamic relationships between alternative actions available to the corporation.

Hence, we have argued that the use of financial derivatives and alternative risk-transfer instruments can be extended by adopting a real options lens to interpret alternative business opportunities available to the corporation as possible responses if and when conditions change. This uncovers a need for specialized expertise to handle particular types of exposures through engagement in special instruments, together with a need for a central corporate management process to deal with the overarching strategic risk issues. This suggests an organizational structure that combines specialized risk management units with a corporate office function that is more closely liked to the formal strategy process.

This chapter has promoted a real option perspective as a potentially useful way to deal with hard-to-quantify strategic exposures, but we should also be aware of the limitations of a real options approach. It is argued that real options thinking may lead to over-commitment to new initiatives while the monitoring efforts associated with the handling of a real options portfolio will impose additional administrative costs. Awareness of these concerns is a first step towards avoiding the potential downsides, and if they can be subdued real options can be a useful way to assess corporate responsiveness to important strategic risks.

4.7   Conclusion

We have discussed derivative instruments and financial hedging techniques, as well as insurance contracts and alternative risk-transfer instruments as the means to obtain cover for conventional market-based risks and environmental hazards. In this chapter we extended the scope of corporate risks to consider also commercial and strategic risks that often represent higher levels of uncertainty and hard-to-quantify exposures. The insights about financial derivatives were extended with real options reasoning as a possible way to deal with the uncertainty surrounding strategic risks. Real options were conceived as structured flexibilities or portfolios of commercial projects representing new business opportunities that expand the scope of corporate choices that eventually can increase strategic

---

[26] K. Miller and H. G. Waller (2003). 'Scenarios, Real Options and Integrated Risk Management'. *Long Range Planning* 36(1), pp. 93–107.

responsiveness in the face of environmental uncertainty. Whereas these considerations build on financial and strategic rationales, the concerns about operational
disruptions, fraudulent behaviours, reputational risks and so forth have urged
the development of more control-based risk management approaches. These risk
management frameworks have also been introduced with an aim of integrating
the analysis of all of the risk factors to which the corporation is exposed. Here,
we suggest that a real options perspective can be a useful way to incorporate
longer-term commercial and strategic risks in these considerations.

References

Andersen, T. J., 2006. 'Options Reasoning and Strategic Responsiveness: Discussion and
    Empirical Assessment', Chapter 10 in Andersen, T. J. (ed.), *Perspectives on
    Strategic Risk Management*. Copenhagen Business School Press: Copenhagen.

Bank for International Settlements, 2006. *Basel II: International Convergence of Capital
    Measurement and Capital Standards: A Revised Framework – Comprehensive
    Version*. Available online from www.bis.org.

Bowman, E. H. and Hurry, D., 1993. 'Strategy Through the Options Lens: An Integrated
    View of Resource Investments and the Incremental Choice Process'. *Academy
    of Management Review* 18(4), pp. 760–82.

Burgelman, R. A., 1988. 'Strategy Making as a Social Learning Process: The Case of
    Internal Corporate Venturing'. *Interfaces* 18(3), pp. 74–85.

    2002. *Strategy is Destiny: How Strategy-Making Shapes a Company's Future*. Free
    Press: New York.

Burgelman, R. A. and Grove, A. S., 1996. 'Strategic Dissonance'. *California Management
    Review* 38(2), pp. 8–28.

Christensen, C. M., 1997. *The Innovator's Dilemma: When New Technologies Cause
    Great Firms to Fail*. Harvard Business School Press: Boston, Massachusetts.

D'Aveni, R. A., 1994. *Hypercompetition*. Free Press: New York.

Eisenhardt, K., 1989. 'Making Fast Strategic Decisions in High-Velocity Environments'.
    Academy of Management Journal 32(3), pp. 543–76.

George, M., Rowlands, D. and Kastle, B., 2004. *What is Lean Six Sigma?* McGraw-Hill:
    New York.

Grove, A. S., 1997. *Only the Paranoid Survive: How to Exploit the Crisis Points that
    Challenge Every Company and Career*. HarperCollins Business: London.

Kleffner, A. E., Lee, R. B. and McGannon, B., 2003. 'The Effects of Corporate Gover-
    nance on the Use of Enterprise Risk Management: Evidence from Canada'. *Risk
    Management and Insurance Review* 6(1), pp. 53–73.

Kogut, B. and Kulatilaka, N., 1994. 'Operating Flexibility, Global Manufacturing and
    the Option Value of a Multinational Network'. *Management Science* 40(1),
    pp. 123–41.

Leuhrman, T., 1998. 'Strategy as a Portfolio of Real Options'. *Harvard Business Review*
    76(5), pp. 89–99.

Liebenberg, A. P. and Hoyt, R. E., 2003. 'The Determinants of Enterprise Risk Manage-
    ment: Evidence from the Appointment of Chief Risk Officers'. *Risk Management
    and Insurance Review* 6(1), pp. 37–52.

Miller, K. and Waller, H. G., 2003. 'Scenarios, Real Options and Integrated Risk Management'. *Long Range Planning* 36(1), pp. 93–107.

Porter, M. E., 1980. *Competitive Strategy: Techniques for Analyzing Industries and Competitors*. Free Press: New York.

Richea, D. V., 2007. 'Novo Nordisk – A Case Study on the Creation and Exercise of Real Options in the Pharmaceutical Industry Through Pharma-Biotech Collaborations'. Strategic Risk Management Report, Copenhagen Business School.

Saunders, A. and Cornett, M. M., 2003. *Financial Institutions Management: A Risk Management Approach*. McGraw-Hill Irwin: Boston, Massachusetts.

Slywozky, A. J., 2007. *The Upside: How to Turn Your Greatest Threat into Your Biggest Growth Opportunity*. Capstone Publishing: Chichester, West Sussex.

Thomas III, L. G., 1996. 'Dynamic Resourcefulness and the Hypercompetitive Shift'. *Organization Science* 7(3), pp. 221–42.

Womack, J. P. and Jones, D. T., 2005. *Lean Solutions: How Companies and Customers can Create Value and Wealth Together*. Simon & Schuster: London.

5 Integrative risk management perspectives

In this chapter we look at some of the traditional risk management practices adopted by many companies to deal with their most essential exposures. The applicability of financial hedging is discussed and the limitations of this approach are pointed out while arguing that organizations should take a more integrative look across different types of risk effects and consider exposures over different time spans. As a natural outgrowth of this discussion it appears that companies should complement their risk management activities with a more strategy-oriented perspective in their hedging considerations.[1] Finally, the practical challenges associated with managing the myriad of risks faced by modern corporations are addressed.

5.1 The need to look across risks

It is common practice in many, if not most, companies to hedge their anticipated future foreign-currency-denominated cash flows over a certain period of time, cf. the example from the Danish pharmaceutical company Lundbeck (see Box 5.1 *Lundbeck – foreign exchange exposure*).[2]

The main reason for engaging in these hedging exercises is to limit negative short- to medium-term impacts from foreign-currency-denominated cash flows when they are converted to the home currency of accounting and thereby reduce adverse earnings effects from exchange rate fluctuations in the major invoicing currencies. These exposures typically relate to transactions recorded in the books as corporate receivables or payables, the local value of which will vary with changes in the foreign exchange conversion. The bulk of booked international commercial transactions do not extend beyond the current and next accounting year and can be hedged, for example, by engaging in forward foreign exchange or financial futures contracts that, for the same reason, only rarely exceed a maturity of twelve to eighteen months. In addition to this, corporate net assets may

---

[1] See, e.g. T. J. Andersen (2006). 'An Integrative Framework for Multinational Risk Management' in T. J. Andersen (ed.), *Perspectives on Strategic Risk Management*. CBS Press: Copenhagen; and J. McGee, H. Thomas and D. Wilson (2005). 'Risk, Uncertainty and Strategy', Ch. 14 in *Strategy Analysis and Practice*, McGraw-Hill: London.

[2] The information in this insert is extracted from the Lundbeck Annual Report (2005).

> ## Box 5.1 Lundbeck – foreign exchange exposure
>
> The bulk of the Group's commercial transactions are settled in foreign currencies.
>
> The associated foreign exchange exposure is reduced by hedging open positions in the most important foreign currencies by engaging in forward foreign exchange and currency option contracts and, to a minor extent, by matching expected foreign exchange inflows by foreign currency liabilities.
>
> Foreign currency management is handled by a specialized central function in the finance department located at parent company headquarters.
>
> The Group has a general aim of hedging anticipated foreign currency cash flows for a period of up to twelve months and up to eighteen months in the case of US dollars.

vary considerably with the exchange rate and these positions are also hedged in some instances.[3] Consequently, the risk exposure is mainly seen from transaction and translation perspectives to avoid erratic earnings outcomes from changes in foreign exchange rates as they influence commercial cash flows and the profit and loss statement.

A corporate risk management objective such as reducing the volatility of periodic earnings can be beneficial, as it reduces the probability of financial distress.[4] Different company stakeholders may be adversely affected by extreme performance volatility, and especially by downside results, as a distressed financial situation enhances the possibility that the company might cease to exist in the future. The stakeholders may include suppliers that tailor production schedules and capacity investments to company-specific needs, customers that may depend on specific services or guarantees provided by the company and employees who risk losing their jobs and livelihood in case of bankruptcy. Hence, to protect these important and valuable stakeholder relationships, it makes economic sense to reduce the risk of bankruptcy to an acceptable level.[5]

Similarly, if the potential bankruptcy risk increases, companies may face external financing costs of such a high level that they have to cut back on investment spending because they have insufficient internally generated cash to finance the

---

[3] Rational financial arguments would consider this type of hedging superfluous unless the hedging exercises have eventual effects on the future corporate cash flows, such as potential asset sales, tax payments or the like. If the sole hedging effect is to manipulate the formally recorded earnings, financial analysts are supposedly able to see that it corresponds to a costly practice with no real benefits.

[4] In practice this will correspond to efforts to reduce the variability in corporate cash flows. Whereas accounting practices may affect the formal registration of earnings and expenses on the official accounts, they will tend to follow developments in the underlying cash flows over longer periods of time.

[5] For an extended discussion of these rationales, see, e.g. K. D. Miller (1998). 'Economic Exposure and Integrated Risk Management'. *Strategic Management Journal* 19, pp. 497–514.

scheduled investment projects.[6] As a consequence, efforts to reduce the variability in corporate cash flows and earnings can add value by making more and more favourably priced financial means available to ensure that the company has sufficient funding for sound investment projects. A comparable and even simpler argument is that lower cash flow volatility reduces the need to maintain cash reserves at low returns and thereby allows corporate management to release excess cash for investment in alternative, more value-enhancing business activities.[7]

Conventional financial theory argues that investors can diversify firm-specific investment risk and that accordingly risk management within a publicly traded company is of no value to the equity holders. However, the firm-specific investment rationale points to the fact that other important stakeholders such as customers, managers, employees, suppliers, etc., cannot diversify the risks associated with their firm-specific investments. Therefore, if and when exposures increase in the firm it will have to incur higher transaction costs as it tries to induce important stakeholders to maintain their business interactions with the firm.[8] Consequently, risk management can add value by lowering the risk faced by non-diversified investors and by stimulating essential stakeholders to engage in firm-specific investments that constitute sources of competitive advantage (see Box 5.2 *The firm-specific investment rationale*).

Box 5.2 The firm-specific investment rationale

If the corporate bankruptcy risk is high, essential stakeholders may be reluctant to make longer-term commitments to the firm in their unique relationships that are important for the firm's ability to create value. Firm-specific investments commit resources towards activities carried out between particular counterparts that are valuable in these specific interactions and thereby constitute a potential loss or risk exposure if the resources must be used for other business purposes. Such a situation may arise, for example, if the firm is unable to honour a prior commitment or fails to engage in an agreed or pre-planned interaction with another organization. In this case, the counterpart must divert the resources it has committed to the firm-specific relationship for other uses.

Active risk management in the firm reduces the risk that these situations of relational un-fulfilment arise that may impose losses on counterparts among the firm's essential stakeholder groups. Hence, risk management may also

---

[6] This is advanced as a major argument for corporate risk management effects. See K. A. Froot, D. S. Scharfstein and J. C. Stein (1994). 'A Framework for Risk Management'. *Harvard Business Review* 76(6), pp. 91–102.

[7] This argument is, for example, advanced by R. C. Merton (2005). 'You Have More Capital than You Think'. *Harvard Business Review* 83(11), pp. 84–94.

[8] For a discussion of the firm-specific investment rationale, see H. Wang, J. B. Barney and J. J. Reuer (2003). 'Stimulating Firm-Specific Investment Through Risk Management'. *Long Range Planning* 36(1), pp. 49–59.

constitute an encouragement to the firm's important stakeholders to commit resources in firm-specific investments. The firm-specific investments can, for example, comprise development of customized production or specialized technologies applied to products and services offered in knowledge-intensive businesses. These kinds of firm-specific investments made by employees, suppliers, customers and partners constitute a class of resources that are often valuable, rare and hard to imitate and substitute and, therefore, may provide the basis for creating superior economic value that constitutes a sustainable competitive advantage for the firm.[9]

Hence, effective risk management capabilities can lead to lower bankruptcy risk and thereby reduce the exposures embedded in the firm's relational engagements with customers, suppliers, partners, managers, employees, etc. A lower level of risk makes it more likely that various counterparts among essential stakeholders will invest in the firm-specific resources needed to furnish valuable longer-term business relationships.

The underlying rationale for currency hedging practices, then, is to reduce excessive fluctuations in corporate cash flows that stabilize the earnings development and thereby reduce bankruptcy risk and induce performance-enhancing investments. However, since commercial transactions typically reach no more than twelve to eighteen months into the future, there is a limit to how far it is possible to smooth the future effects of fluctuations in foreign exchange rates through conventional hedging approaches. Furthermore, the effects of changes in foreign exchange rates are not limited to direct effects on the profit and loss account from conversion of already booked transactions, but they are also related to changes in the commercial conditions under which the firm operates in the international markets. Hence, changes in major currency parities might affect supply and demand conditions among competitors in the industry due to changes in the relative terms of trade. For example, a depreciation of the currency in an important foreign market may increase the cost base that is accounted for in local currency, thereby shifting the supply curve upward and thus causing an increase in foreign-currency-denominated prices that reduce the competitiveness of goods sold in overseas markets[10] (Figure 5.1).

Conversely, if prices are held unchanged in the foreign markets, the firm will receive decreasing amounts measured in the local currency as the overseas sales are converted at the current foreign exchange rate, which will squeeze the

---

[9] These exemplify the so-called VRIO-conditions for gaining sustainable competitive advantage as promoted by the resource-based view of the firm. For a recent update of this theoretical rationale, see J. B. Barney (2002). *Gaining and Sustaining Competitive Advantage* (2nd edn). Prentice Hall: Upper Saddle River, New Jersey.

[10] Obviously this argument assumes a direct cost-related pricing scheme imposed on goods and services offered in the market. While this may represent an over-simplification of the foreign currency scenario, we are likely to see gradual price adaptations that eventually will resemble this description.

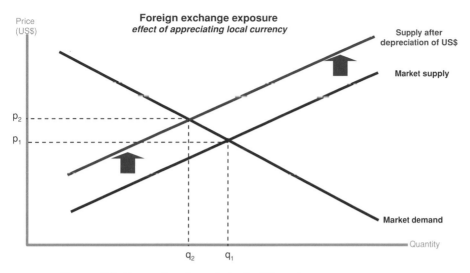

Figure 5.1 *Demand and supply in the US market*

profitability of the international commercial transactions. That is, the company's ability to sell its products in overseas markets, and thereby its global competitive position, is influenced by movements in the foreign exchange rates and thus constitutes an important strategic concern. The discussion about UK membership of the euro-zone and the appreciation of the pound sterling during the year 2000 illustrates the potential importance of changes in foreign exchange rates for assessments of the competitive environment in a domestic manufacturing industry (see Box 5.3, *UK automotive manufacturing competitiveness under pressure*).[11]

Box 5.3 UK automotive manufacturing competitiveness under pressure

The Rover crisis in March 2000 highlighted the ongoing debate about if and when the UK might join the euro-zone. According to BMW, the appreciating value of the pound sterling against the Deutschmark removed DEM 1 billion from its balance sheet in 1999. However, BMW was not the only firm to highlight the adverse effects of currency movements on the competitive position of UK-based business activities during 1999 to 2000. The Japanese car producers located in the United Kingdom that export most of their production to continental Europe were also concerned.

New investment in Nissan's renowned plant in Sunderland was under threat. During spring 2000, Nissan announced that their Sunderland facility, which was judged to be one of the most productive car plants in Europe at the time, was aiming to cut costs by 30 per cent by the end of 2002 in order

---

[11] Adapted from *EIROnline* (December 2000). 'Problems Mount for UK Automotive Manufacturers in Face of Increased Competitive Pressures'.

to offset the adverse effects of the foreign exchange rate development. Soon after the Rover crisis, Nissan also warned that the appreciation of the pound could jeopardize a proposed £150 million expansion of the site to build the new Micra model.

In March 2000, Honda announced that it was cutting vehicle production at its UK plant by more than 50 per cent. Honda blamed slowing demand in Europe for UK-built models, the strength of the pound sterling and weak domestic sales caused by uncertainty over new car prices. In June of the same year, Honda announced that it would reduce the UK content in its cars from an average of 70 to 50 per cent and even lower over the following two years. By November, Yoshide Munekuni, the chairman of Honda's board of directors, was quoted as saying that the company would 'definitely not' be advancing to build a car plant in the United Kingdom if it had been looking around today for a European manufacturing location. Honda later confirmed that it had suspended plans to build a new small car at its Swindon plant, which was due for introduction in 2002.

Toyota also voiced strong concerns over the competitive situation in the United Kingdom. Tadaaki Jagawa, executive vice-president of procurement, issued a stern warning that the continued strength of the pound sterling against the euro could prompt Toyota to reconsider its investments in the United Kingdom. He expressed their sentiments in the following manner: 'The UK government has said it may join the euro in five years, but we won't be around five years from now.' In the meantime, Toyota would require some suppliers to switch pound-sterling-denominated contracts to invoicing in euros to help reduce the currency exposure.

In February 2000, just before US-based Ford would announce its future plans for the Dagenham facilities, Nick Scheele, the company's European chairman, noted that their UK activities were the prime target for European economic restructuring as the pound sterling was rising in value against the euro. He called for governmental clarifications about British entry to the single currency area, but at the same time stated that: 'No manufacturer would be helped if Britain went in at a rate of DEM 3.20 to the pound. The right level is DEM 2.55–2.60.' Following statements like these, Peugeot, the French car maker, announced that its €150 million investment in a new paint facility at its Coventry plant could be under reconsideration. Without this investment, scheduled to take place in 2003, the very future of the plant was uncertain. Accordingly, Jean-Martin Folz, Chief Executive Officer of PSA Peugeot Citroën, said that: 'Before taking this decision we will have to review the advantages of doing this investment in the UK.'

Changes in foreign exchange rates can affect the corporate cash flows directly due to the company's transaction exposures as well as global competitiveness in the industry through future changes in relative output (and input) prices related to

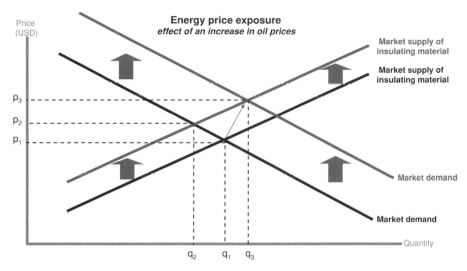

Figure 5.2 *Demand and supply of commodity*

the so-called operating exposures. An operating exposure constitutes the longer-term element of a company's economic exposures as future international trans-actions that are expected, but have not yet been booked, matter to the overall valuation of the corporation.[12] Both transaction and operating exposures should be accounted for in a currency hedging strategy, as it is the sensitivity of the firm's net present value of future cash flows to foreign exchange rate movements that matters from a corporate value perspective.

Similarly, changes in interest rates and commodity prices may affect demand and supply conditions in the underlying product markets. For example, it is well known that the demand for many durable consumer goods and housing varies with changes in the interest rate level, as the cost of borrowing is an important factor in the buying decision. Likewise, oil may be an important energy source in manufacturing processes and accordingly a rising oil price could increase production costs, which everything else equal should reduce demand to the extent that cost increases are transposed into higher product prices. However, for other companies, such as manufacturers of insulation materials, things could be more complicated. Here, rising oil prices might actually increase overall demand for insulation because higher energy prices make it more economical to invest in better insulation and thereby obtain savings on oil bills (Figure 5.2).

One point is to recognize the importance of the interdependency among the various macroeconomic and financial variables; another is to measure the actual corporate exposure to these variables. However, a straightforward method to mea-sure the corporate exposure to macroeconomic sources of risk is to estimate the

---

[12] By economic exposures we refer to factors that can influence the future cash flows of the company.

relationship between the company's real commercial cash flow and the relevant macroeconomic risk factors using multiple regression analysis, although the estimation of these relationships is associated with some uncertainty. The uncertainty is caused by interdependencies between the dependent variables and structural changes in the external environment, such as changes in the competitive situation, new market entrants, political regime shifts, etc. Nonetheless, measurement of macroeconomic exposures can support management in its risk assessments and thereby enhance the effectiveness of hedging strategies. The importance of basic economic risk factors and their effect on corporate cash flows becomes clearer and can be taken into consideration in the development of economic risk strategies (see Box 5.4 *Assessing economic exposures*).[13]

Box 5.4 Assessing economic exposures

Oxelheim and Wihlborg suggest that an appropriate way to measure corporate exposures to macroeconomic sources of risk is to estimate the relationship between the company's real commercial cash flows and a range of macroeconomic-, industry- and company-specific variables that may affect the corporate cash flows over time using multiple regression analysis. In other words, the company's real commercial cash flows become the dependent variable and various macroeconomic and company-specific variables the independent variables, which can be described as follows:

$$CF_t = \beta_0 + \beta_s\,FX_{s,t} + \beta_m\,MV_{m,t} + \beta_z\,FV_{z,t} + \varepsilon_t$$

CF_t = commercial cash flows over period t

β_s = regression coefficients for each of the s currencies

β_z = regression coefficients for each of the z firm-specific factors

$MV_{m,t}$ = prices for m macroeconomic variables over period t

ε_t = residual error term

β_0 = constant regression coefficient

β_m = regression coefficients for each of the m market factors

$FX_{s,t}$ = foreign exchange rates for s currencies over period t

$FV_{z,t}$ = indicators for z firm-specific variables over period t

t = time indicator over the period of study

The exact specification of the equation depends on econometric considerations, for example, whether the equation should be measured in terms of levels or changes and whether it should be specified in linear or non-linear form, as well as which relevant independent variables should be included, such as currency rates, interest rates, industry and company

---

[13] Adapted from L. Oxelheim and C. Wihlborg (2005). 'A Comprehensive Approach to the Measurement of Macroeconomic Exposure' in M. Frenkel, U. Hommel and M. Rudolf (eds.), *Risk Management: Challenge and Opportunity* (2nd edn). Springer: Berlin.

specific factors, etc. Furthermore, the chosen time period should be determined in light of the company's ability to adapt its commercial operations as changes in the environmental contingencies occur.

Each of the regression coefficients reflects the effect of a change in the dependent variable on the company's commercial cash flows given that all other independent variables remain unchanged. In other words, each coefficient will express the sensitivity of the company's commercial cash flows caused by changes in each of the independent variables.

As an example, Oxelheim and Wihlborg estimate Volvo Car's macroeconomic exposure and find the following best fit equation (based on step-wise regression in order to handle the high correlation issue among various exchange rates and other variables), where the dependent as well as the independent variables are measured as a percentage rate of change from the preceding quarter:

$$CF = 5.5 \times \text{Real SEK/DEM currency rate}$$
$$+ 30.1 \times \text{Producer prices in Germany (Adj. } R^2 = 0.03)$$

In other words, a real appreciation of the SEK of 1 per cent will have a negative effect of 5.5 per cent on commercial cash flows, while an increase of 1 per cent in the German producer prices at a constant foreign exchange rate will lead to a 30 per cent increase in Volvo's commercial cash flows based on historical relationships. These results can be compared to Volvo's financial position to evaluate the extent to which these positions actually constitute a hedge against Volvo's true commercial exposure.

Changes in interest rates and commodity prices can affect company cash flow directly through increased borrowing costs and expenditures as well as indirectly by changing the relative demand for products and services. Therefore, hedging interest rate and commodity price exposures per se might not be effective, as the associated effects on demand for corporate outputs can impose additional effects that must be considered in the exposure calculations. Hence, when assessing the longer-term effects of interest rate and commodity price exposures, the company should counterweigh the potential effects on relative demand conditions for various inputs and outputs they trade in. Further, it may be argued that the hedging strategies pursued by major competitors could affect the longer-term competitive environment as well and, therefore, should be monitored and taken into consideration. For example, the hedging practices pursued by various players in the US airline industry could affect the domestic competitive position (see Box 5.5 *Oil prices and the airline industry*).[14]

---

[14] Extracted from *Commodities Now* (June 2005), 'Airlines Hedging Strategies: The Shareholder Value Perspective', by Blanco, Lehman and Shimoda. See www.commodities-now.com.

Box 5.5 Oil prices and the airline industry

Hedging practices at leading US airlines during 2005:

American Airlines – 15 per cent hedged in 2005, Q1
United Airlines – 11 per cent hedged for 2005
Delta Airlines – not hedged
Northwest Airlines – about 25 per cent hedged for 2005 Q1 and 6 per cent
   for 2006
Continental Airlines – not hedged
Southwest Airlines – 85 per cent hedged
US Airways – no fuel hedges as of 31 December 2004
America West – 45 per cent hedged for 2005 and 2 per cent for 2006
Alaska Air – 50 per cent hedged for 2005
JetBlue Airways – 22 per cent hedged for 2005
(the airlines are listed by order of size measured in terms of passenger
   volume)

The interrelatedness observed between different financial and commodity price risks may also exist across other types of risk, such as natural hazards, man-made disasters and terrorist events, as these incidents can affect macroeconomic conditions and various financial market variables. For example, a number of companies suffered serious disruptions in production due to incidents of the severe acute respiratory syndrome (SARS) in the Far East during 2003. Even though only 8,000 people were infected, with one in ten dying, it still cost an estimated US$60 billion in lost output throughout South and East Asia.[15] Similarly, the Asian Tsunami in 2004 had an adverse effect on economic activity across the entire region, and many airlines, hotels and tour operators were seriously affected.

A number of economies have experienced the negative economic consequences of foot-and-mouth disease outbreaks in the past, including the United Kingdom and Denmark, in the form of reduced consumption, production and business confidence (see Box 5.6 *The impact of a foot-and-mouth disease outbreak*).[16] Consequently, some hazards may influence supply and demand conditions across particular industries and thereby affect general consumer behaviours. Such events can have strategic implications for a company that far exceed the direct economic losses imposed by the events themselves. The direct loss effects are evaluated in most companies and used to inform decisions on the extent to which the exposures should be transferred through traditional insurance coverage. However, the longer-term economic and strategic exposures of the various hazards ought to be assessed as well.

---

[15] Information from *The Economist* (15 June 2006), 'When the Chain Breaks'.
[16] Adapted from the Reserve Bank of New Zealand and the Treasury (14 February 2003), 'The Macroeconomic Impacts of a Foot-and-Mouth Disease Outbreak', Information Paper, Department of the Prime Minister and Cabinet.

Box 5.6 The impact of a foot-and-mouth disease outbreak

An analysis of the potential macroeconomic impacts of a limited foot-and-mouth disease outbreak in New Zealand is outlined below.

The stipulated reduction (loss) in the foreign exchange rate of the New Zealand dollar would mainly be caused by an expected fall in export prices and overseas sales volumes that will reduce demand for the NZ$ and require additional foreign borrowings of around NZ$8 billion as a result (see figure below).

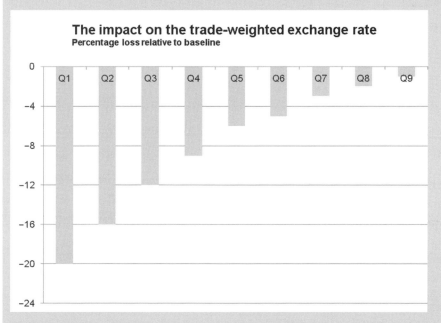

The impact on the trade-weighted exchange rate
Percentage loss relative to baseline

The waning overseas demand is likely to cause a temporary downturn in economic activity:

Delays in and cancellations of investment projects may result in a short-term drop in investments of around 20 per cent, with long-term investments running 6 per cent below the baseline.

The level of both permanent production output and capital stock additions will be below baseline.

The resulting economic loss is estimated to be around 2.5 per cent of annual GNP.

5.2   Shortcomings of traditional hedging practices

In many situations, it will not be possible to reduce identified economic exposures through the use of traditional risk-transfer mechanisms (including derivative securities and insurance covers) if the time frame for the economic exposure exceeds the common maturity of the financial instruments. The most

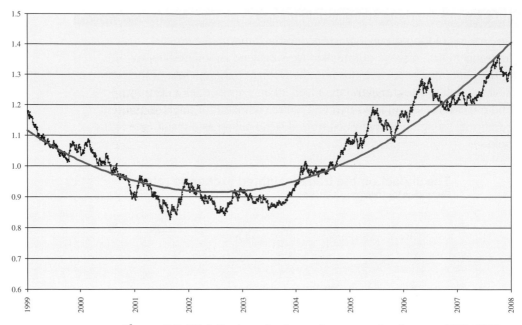

Figure 5.3 *US dollar/euro foreign exchange rate development 1999–2008*

frequently traded derivatives rarely exceed eighteen months of maturity and reinsurance contracts are commonly renewed on an annual basis. That is, use of
financial instruments for hedging purposes is generally suitable to cover short- to
medium-term risk periods only. For example, the US dollar strengthened somewhat after the euro was introduced as an accounting currency in the beginning of
1999 until 2002. In contrast, the dollar continued to weaken against the euro after
the introduction of common coins and notes in 2002 and has continued this trend
on and off until well into 2008, when it started to rebound again (Figure 5.3).

Since these periods of continuous directional trends exceed the maturity of
most currency derivatives, it is virtually impossible to hedge against these long-
term waves in the foreign exchange rate development through the use of conventional financial instruments. One consequence of this is that financial hedging based on instruments like forward foreign exchange and currency options
contracts primarily serves to smooth the earnings development, whereas use of
these derivatives fails to influence the effects of longer-term currency trends (see
Box 5.7 *The impact of financial hedging – an example*).

Hence, companies may need to incorporate other hedging strategies to cope
with longer-term economic risks, for example, as illustrated by the considerations
in the UK automotive manufacturing industry with respect to a potential entry
into the euro-zone. Thus, managing longer-term economic risks becomes a general management issue and not a specialized tactical issue solved by specialists
in the treasury department. That is, effects of short- to medium-term transaction exposures and the longer-term operational exposures are in many instances

Box 5.7 The impact of financial hedging – an example

Many companies will try to hedge their foreign currency receivables by adopting a 'balanced' approach. Accordingly, they may typically leave part of the net position open and take a chance on favourable market developments, while hedging the remainder of the net position through an equal emphasis on locked-in hedges using forward foreign exchange contracts (or currency futures) and flexible currency options contracts. In this case, the company may have an equal split between open, locked-in and flexible hedging positions (see figure below).

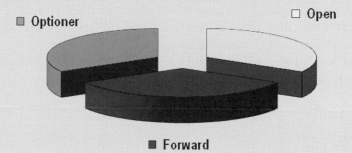

Such a combined hedging strategy will allow the company to reduce the effects of short term foreign exchange rate movements and lessen the development of corporate earnings over the period. Since the hedging techniques are applied to transaction exposures on an ongoing basis, the hedging outcomes will continue to reflect the underlying longer-term currency trends, but with vastly reduced period-by-period earnings fluctuations (see graph below for a corporate example).

Currency indices

As appears, the realized foreign currency earnings after engaging in financial hedging follow a smoother path (grey line) compared to the development in a comparable market index (black line) of foreign exchange rates.

intertwined. Therefore, exposed companies should seek to incorporate longer-term strategy-oriented perspectives when they consider their economic exposures. That is, the financial hedging of transaction exposures should be pursued with a view to the complementary effects of financial instruments and underlying business choices associated with longer-term economic risks. This also provides a basis for incorporating financial, economic and strategic risk considerations into the company's strategic planning process and thereby addresses the broader question of how fluctuations in market rates and economic variables affect the company's future competitive position.

5.3   An integrative approach to other types of risk

It is not just financial variables that may affect demand and supply conditions in the different commercial markets where the company operates. Changes in political, macroeconomic, social and technological conditions may equally affect the competitive developments in various industries and the rivalry among the companies operating in them. A given change in one of these exogenous factors may often have repercussions for other external environmental variables. Besides, the various companies within the same industry will often be affected differently by such changes due to firm-specific peculiarities as well as their responses to such exogenous changes are likely to differ. Hence, there is not necessarily a one-to-one correspondence between changes in the external environment and how the competitive position of a particular company will be affected. Furthermore, the globalization of corporate business activities has made international offshoring, outsourcing, input sourcing and manufacturing integral parts of the business model pursued by multinational enterprises. The tighter coupling of these cross-border activities in the corporate structure has made the companies more vulnerable to exogenous environmental changes in the external environment, while the wider global reach of the organization has added new risks that are beyond corporate control (see Box 5.8 *Political risks in the global network economy – import quotas*, Box 5.9 *Global resource access as a risk factor – HR shortages* and Box 5.10 *Effects of exogenous hazards – Nokia and L. M. Ericsson*).[17] These developments obviously underscore the very need for corporate management to monitor changes in the global environment and assess

---

[17]   The content of the third insert is adapted from M. Christopher and H. Peck (2004). 'The Five Principles of Supply Chain Resilience'. *Logistics Europe* 12(1), pp. 16–21 and data extracted from Yahoo! Finance and AOL Money & Finance.

the potential effects of central external variables and thereby provide an informed basis that may enable the companies to respond in a timely manner.

Box 5.8 Political risks in the global network economy – import quotas

Global outsourcing of production and sourcing of semi-produce increases the time of international transportation and thereby introduces other risks related to the enhanced flow time caused by transit handling, which may reduce guarantee of supply and eliminate the flexibility associated with just-in-time processing. Due to significant time-lags between pre-ordering and final delivery, there is also a substantial time-window during which the company is exposed to political risks. For example, many companies in the European textile industry experienced this in 2005 – although of a shorter duration only – when the European trade commissioner gained sudden approval to impose restrictions on textile imports from China. As a result, much of the pre-ordered clothing foundered at the EU borders and many apparel manufacturers and retailers were left scrambling to find alternative suppliers.

Box 5.9 Global resource access as a risk factor – HR shortages

An increasing number of companies create value through an enhanced base of intangible assets. Employee knowledge and capabilities are often critical for the corporate competitiveness, while retaining and recruiting staff is a key risk in many companies. Some Danish firms experienced this risk in light of the favourable economic conditions during 2006 to 2007, where lack of labour became pronounced in many industries. For example, GN Great Nordic was seriously left behind in their R&D operations due to a shortage of engineers. As a result, the company had to consider overseas recruiting efforts while the introductions of new products were delayed, with a decrease in economic turnover as an inevitable consequence.

Box 5.10 Effects of exogenous hazards – Nokia and L. M. Ericsson

In March 2000, the worldwide demand for mobile telephones was booming. Two of the international market leaders in mobile phones were the Finnish electronics company Nokia and its Swedish rival L. M. Ericsson. Far away from Finland and Sweden, a lightning bolt hit a power line in Albuquerque, in central New Mexico, United States and caused a fluctuation in the power supply, which resulted in a fire in a furnace in a nearby semiconductor plant owned by Dutch firm Philips Electronics NV. As it happened, this factory supplied ASIC chips for the manufacturing of the most recent product lines at both Nokia and L. M. Ericsson.

The fire was brought under control in minutes. The plant was likely to disrupt production for around a week – at least that is what the plant told

Nokia and Ericsson. However, the damage to the factory from smoke, soot and water was much more extensive than the fire itself, because it contaminated the sensitive production environment as well as its entire stock of millions of finished chips. It became clear soon afterwards that the problem was so serious that supplies would be disrupted for months. Nokia was about to roll out a new generation of mobile phones that depended on the ASIC chips, potentially disrupting more than 5 per cent of the company's annual production.

L. M. Ericsson lost an estimated €400 million in new product sales as a result of the fire. An insurance claim later offset some of the direct economic losses. Nevertheless, Ericsson was forced to halt completely the manufacturing of mobile phones. In contrast, Nokia was able to maintain production levels throughout because it had alternative sourcing possibilities, which eventually cemented its position as global market leader.

The economic effects of the different approaches to the described risk event can be assessed by comparing the stock price development of the two public companies over the years after the event (see graph below).

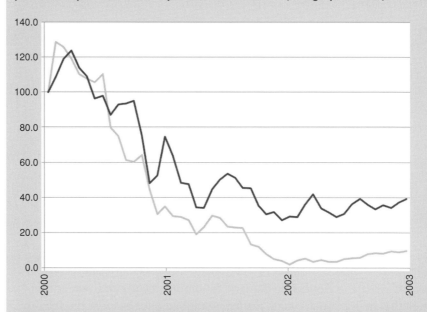

Development in monthly stock prices 2000–2003 (January 2000 = index 100)

It appears that the stock prices of both companies were affected negatively by the adjustments to the 'dot.com bubble' during 2000. However, it is also quite apparent that the market valuation of one company, Nokia (black line), fared considerably better than the other close competitor (grey line) in the industry.

The streamlining of the corporate value chains via the adoption of 'lean' practices through inventory and capacity reduction, outsourcing, single sourcing, etc. aimed at reducing operating costs has become widespread among multinational enterprises. However, the cost savings may at times be achieved at the expense of increased risk exposures, as the tightly coupled global company structures become more vulnerable to unexpected events.[18] For example, a reduction in the company's inventory or in the number of suppliers will increase the vulnerability to situations of supply disruption. Similarly, the adoption of lean practices might result in lost production due to minor delays or malfunctions that arise occasionally at different points along the corporate value chain. Furthermore, outsourcing means that some of the control slips away from the company, which might affect the quality as well as assurances of delivery. Thus, the result of increasingly efficient processes could be that the company is left with less control over important elements of the value chain with fewer buffers to counter unexpected events, which with other things being equal might reduce the company's ability to react to unexpected events (see Box 5.11 *Potential consequences of global outsourcing and lean practices*).[19] Therefore, this underpins the need for the companies to investigate how their value chains are affected by various exogenous events and not least assess how these events may be interrelated, and thereby allow corporate management to consider relevant precautionary measures.

Even minor delays or malfunctions at different points on a globally dispersed corporate value chain may have severe economic repercussions as the disruptive effects accumulate and may lead to severe loss of production and sales.

5.4   Managing the different images of risk

The previous sections underpin the need to manage risks in a more integrated manner as the corporation is exposed to a variety of risks that in many instances may be related to each other directly or indirectly. However, different risks may often interact in highly complex and unpredictable ways and in other cases not at all. Therefore, even while it may be challenging to predict the medium-term development in, for example, the £/US$ foreign exchange rate, it is exceedingly more difficult to establish and quantify the impact of changing foreign exchange rates on the global demand for the company's products, let alone the impact on close competitors. Consequently, there is considerable uncertainty surrounding predictions of the company's future cash flow effects and, as a consequence, it is difficult to determine what exactly should be hedged.

---

[18] For a discussion of the effects of 'tight coupling', see, e.g. C. Perrow (1999). *Normal Accidents: Living with High-Risk Technologies*. Princeton University Press: Princeton, New Jersey, pp. 3–14.

[19] The insert incorporates the familiar long-linked value-chain configuration introduced by M. E. Porter (1985). *Competitive Advantage*. Free Press: New York.

Box 5.11 Potential consequences of global outsourcing and lean practices

We currently observe a major trend towards outsourcing of corporate activities in the multinational enterprise to overseas locations in search of temporary factor cost advantages and global operational efficiencies. The relentless move to gain economic efficiency is often complemented by an urge to obtain lean practices that often leads to reduced inventory and capacity levels. However, the associated efficiency gains may be achieved at the expense of increasing operational exposures as the tightly coupled systems become more vulnerable to potential exogenous shocks (see figure below).

Environmental developments and operational risks

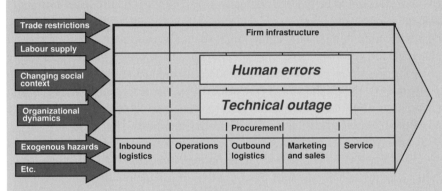

Lower inventory and capacity buffers in a tightly coupled multinational company structure can make the organization more vulnerable to unexpected environmental developments, including:

- supply disruptions caused by sudden trade disputes, civil unrest, terrorist events, etc.;
- broken connections to outsourced entities due to civil unrest, political crises, natural catastrophes, etc.; and
- disruptions in IT-connectedness due to major infrastructure breakdowns, hacking, etc.

Moreover, some risks represent true uncertainties that are impossible to quantify with any precision and may even be completely unknowable in advance. World demographic trends, foreign exchange rates, interest rates, commodity prices, casualty losses, etc. are recorded regularly in public databases and constitute measurable risks that consequently can be predicted within the boundaries of normal variations. Conversely, many strategic risks represent true uncertainty that cannot be recorded and hence not measured and predicted, such as new product innovations, disruptive technologies, changes in consumer taste, etc. These risks seem to grow in number as the business environments become increasingly

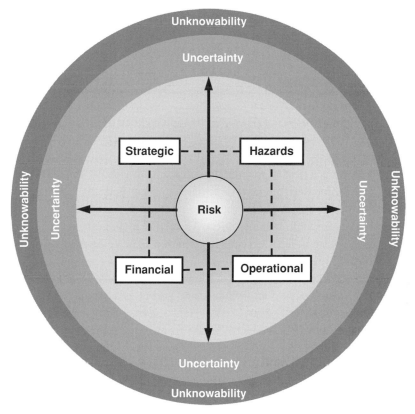

Figure 5.4 *Different images of risk*

dynamic. Furthermore, the risk contours of contemporary companies operating in the global economy are increasingly exposed to turbulence and risk dynamics that are unknown and hence constitute a sphere of 'unknowability', where future events are virtually impossible to foresee (Figure 5.4).

Hence, modern corporations are faced with a variety of predictable and unforeseeable risks and sometimes with unknowable economic consequences that may interact in complex ways that add to the embedded environmental uncertainties. Nevertheless, the corporation must relate to these risks, and particularly the most important ones, by trying to identify, assess and monitor the implied exposures and reacting to risk events in a timely manner. This is obviously difficult when dealing with unknowable risks that add completely new requirements to effective risk management processes regarding the ability to enhance strategic responsiveness in dealing with unforeseeable and hard-to-quantify exposures. At first glance, this seems to be an immense and rather impossible task. However, companies that have the capability to sense environmental changes, including changes in the competitive landscape, and mobilize internal resources in an appropriate and timely way can achieve a cutting edge, as these response capabilities enable the company to take advantage of new opportunities and avoid the disastrous effects of emerging threats.

5.5   Conclusion

Different types of risks are often interrelated and, accordingly, formulating corporate responses cannot be handled adequately by dispersing all of the risk management responsibilities to specialized functional units. While the hedging of short-term transaction exposures, by engaging in various financial instruments, must be handled by functional specialists, these hedging activities should be contained within a wider corporate umbrella that also takes the longer-term operational exposures into consideration. Thus, risk management decisions must be made in ways that utilize the specialized market expertise in functional units while assuming a longer-term company-wide risk perspective aimed at addressing net exposures rather than covering each individual company risk at the time. Since many risk factors can be interrelated, any particular risk may affect the value of the entire company in complex ways. Hence, it may be beneficial to consider the potential diversification gains to be had from these interactions before deciding on how to cover excess exposures.

Additionally, some of the very firm-specific exposures that derive from operational and strategic risk factors cannot be covered through use of financial instruments such as derivative securities and insurance contracts. Consequently, conventional risk-transfer solutions and strategic choices regarding global organization, etc. often have complementary roles when hedging the company's long-term exposures. For this reason, hedging decisions and the risk management process in general should become an integral part of the corporation's strategic planning process. Furthermore, companies face innumerable risks that are hard to foresee and with unknowable characteristics. At first glance, the complexity of these risk relationships might be overwhelming to get a hold on. However, adopting a structured and systematic approach to identify risks and assess their multi-dimensional effects on the company can help the company by outlining the contours of its most important exposures. Adopting an enterprise-wide risk management perspective allows the company to approach risk management in a structured and systematic manner to identify, assess and integrate the most significant exposures in a way that links the risk handling to the company's strategic planning process. This framework will be described and discussed further in the next chapter.

References

Andersen, T. J., 2006. 'An Integrative Framework for Multinational Risk Management' in Andersen, T. J. (ed.), *Perspectives on Strategic Risk Management*. CBS Press: Copenhagen.

Barney, J. B., 2002. *Gaining and Sustaining Competitive Advantage* (2nd edn). Prentice Hall: Upper Saddle River, New Jersey.

Christopher, M. and Peck, H., 2004. 'The Five Principles of Supply Chain Resilience'. *Logistics Europe* 12(1), pp. 16–21.

Froot, K. A., Scharfstein, D. S. and Stein, J. C., 1994. 'A Framework for Risk Management'. *Harvard Business Review* 76(6), pp. 91–102.

McGee, J., Thomas, H. and Wilson, D., 2005. *Strategy Analysis and Practice*. McGraw-Hill: London.

Merton, R. C., 2005. 'You Have More Capital than You Think'. *Harvard Business Review* 83(11), pp. 84–94.

Miller, K. D., 1998. 'Economic Exposure and Integrated Risk Management'. *Strategic Management Journal* 19, pp. 497–514.

Oxelheim, L. and Wihlborg, C., 2005. 'A Comprehensive Approach to the Measurement of Macroeconomic Exposure' in Frenkel, M., Hommel, U. and Rudolf, M. (eds.), *Risk Management: Challenge and Opportunity* (2nd edn). Springer: Berlin.

Perrow, C., 1999. *Normal Accidents: Living with High-Risk Technologies*. Princeton University Press: Princeton, New Jersey, pp. 3–14.

Porter, M. E., 1985. *Competitive Advantage*. Free Press: New York.

Wang, H., Barney, J. B. and Reuer, J. J., 2003. 'Stimulating Firm-Specific Investment Through Risk Management'. *Long Range Planning* 36(1), pp. 49–59.

6 Current risk management practice and the rise of ERM

This chapter takes a closer look at some of the main drivers behind the demand for a new risk paradigm and outlines the risk management practices evolving from this development. The key components of enterprise risk management (ERM), as a proponent for the new risk paradigm, are described and compared with more traditional approaches to risk management. In this light we discuss the extent to which the new integrative risk paradigm enables corporations to manage their exposures in increasingly dynamic business environments, where organizations are faced with high levels of uncertainty and a decreasing ability to foresee events. The discussion identifies potentially crucial shortcomings associated with the current enterprise-wide risk management approaches, which suggest that some amendments to the generic ERM framework are required to ensure that risk events are identified in time and handled in ways that allow the company to gain foresight and become more responsive.

6.1 Drivers of the new risk paradigm

Risk management has long been considered a standard management activity, although the risk focus generally has been limited to those exposures that can be observed, measured and financed through insurance and other financial hedging products, including derivative instruments, or that can be contained through implementation of internal control systems. The main aim in conventional risk management has been to protect the company against the adverse economic effects of various risk events. Critical stakeholders responded to Barings's collapse in the 1990s, the failure of Long-Term Capital Management and other recent corporate scandals by demanding enhanced self-discipline, more ethical behaviours and public risk disclosure. These efforts have enforced a focus on downside loss potentials resulting in growing public pressures for more systematic and comprehensive approaches to risk management.

The Dey Report sponsored by the Toronto Stock Exchange in 1994, the German Control and Transparency in Business Act (KonTraG) imposed during 1998, the Turnbull Report in the United Kingdom from 1999 and the corporate governance recommendations for the Copenhagen Stock Exchange by the Nørby Committee in 2001 all exemplify various risk management initiatives taken by industry,

Public policy initiatives

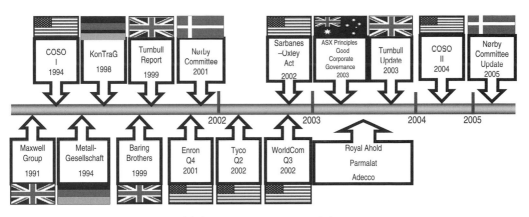

Figure 6.1 *Corporate events and the trend towards new risk regulation*

professional, semi-public and governmental institutions. Despite these efforts, a number of spectacular corporate scandals still occurred in their wake, involving companies like Enron, Tyco, WorldCom, Royal Ahold, Parmalat and others, which drove public opinion and politicians towards firmer legislative action. The most notable of these legislative initiatives was the Sarbanes–Oxley Act in the United States in 2002, holding boards, CEOs and other senior executives accountable for potential risks – thus in effect forcing them to conduct complete corporate risk reviews rather than being confined to reviewing smaller pieces of the risk puzzle. As a consequence, the Committee of Sponsoring Organizations of the Treadway Commission (COSO) in the United States developed the COSO ERM framework[1] and we saw updated risk management guidelines developed by the Turnbull Review Group and others (see Figure 6.1).

The primary aim of these initiatives has been to ensure that the companies have appropriate controls in place to counter identified risks.[2] However, today companies are also faced with the potential disruption associated with shorter product life cycles stemming from continuous and faster innovation processes that further dynamize the competitive environment. The higher intensity of knowledge and intellectual capital embedded in human resources makes protection of important strategic assets inherently more difficult as job characteristics change and links with suppliers and customers are becoming increasingly important. Similarly, it is generally becoming less effective to protect patents in new technology areas

---

[1] The Treadway Commission was initially formed to analyze how to impose adequate control systems to circumvent fraudulent corporate behaviour dating back to the late 1980s and has developed a formalized framework for integrated risk management practices over an extended period between 2002 and 2004.

[2] See, e.g. M. Power (2007). *Organized Uncertainty: Designing a World of Risk Management*. Oxford University Press: New York, which gives an account and interpretation of these initiatives.

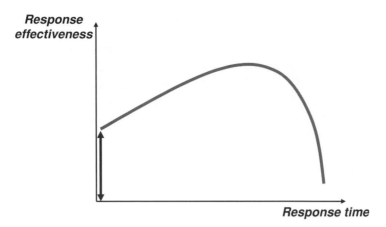

Figure 6.2 *Strategic response capabilities*

where firms are tied together in larger intertwined industry networks. With the increasing internationalization of corporate business activities and related global sourcing structures as key components of the business model, new exposures may emerge, with many of the underlying risk factors being out of the company's control.

A more dynamic nature of business environments means that companies are facing new kinds of exposures with higher elements of uncertainty, which consequently reduce the ability to forecast environmental conditions and potential risk events. This means that the formal strategic and investment planning frameworks based on forecasts become inadequate. On the other hand, foresight is more important as the company's ability to sense emerging environmental changes becomes crucial. Thus, companies must try to organize in ways that allow them to increase their sensitivity to external market changes and develop an ability to respond faster and effectively when unexpected surprises and abrupt changes occur. The company's ability to respond to changes and surprises is often referred to as its strategic response capabilities.[3]

The effects of strategic response capabilities are illustrated in Figure 6.2. The positive intercept on the secondary axis of response effectiveness indicates that an effective response may occur instantaneously, for example, when a competitor introduces a new product and the company has already prepared a response to cope with this event. This could be the case if the company is ready to introduce a new competing product immediately in response to a sudden competitive move. The positive slope of the graph illustrates that additional redeployment of resources may be possible along the way to enhance effective responses, for example, to modify features around the distribution of the newly introduced product and

---

[3] The concept of 'strategic response capabilities' is adopted from R. A. Bettis and M. A. Hitt (1995). 'The New Competitive Landscape'. *Strategic Management Journal* 16, pp. 7–19.

the like. A company with a higher and steeper response curve displays faster and more effective responses over a given time span, where incremental effects will eventually fade out and show diminishing return characteristics. Hence, risk management is not just a matter of having the right control systems in place to monitor predefined exposures, but is also a question of maintaining sufficient flexibility in the organization to allow effective reactions to new and unexpected risk events. This also includes an ability to identify and develop potential business opportunities that can increase responsiveness to changing competitive realities and drive future growth.

In view of increasing environmental demands and the political push for more formal risk management systems, there has been much emphasis on the introduction of new risk management frameworks. These enterprise-wide risk management approaches have become commonly known under a general heading of ERM. Ideally, ERM seeks to support managers in limiting downside losses from major exposures while simultaneously supporting them to think more systematically about opportunities that represent upside potential. It is the stated aim of these risk management frameworks to provide managers with a more complete understanding of the magnitude, interrelatedness and importance of different exposures through a holistic, systematic and structured analysis of various risk factors. This approach should provide an analytical foundation that enables corporate managers to make informed decisions and take actions to exploit risk situations and growth opportunities profitably.

6.2   Risk management practices

Many surveys on risk management have been carried out in the past and they all show a similar pattern, namely that risks are generally managed in silos focusing on financial risks and environmental hazards, while operational and strategy-related risks receive less attention.[4] At the same time, the companies pursue a more structured and formal approach when they are dealing with insurable hazards and financial market risks compared to operational disruption and especially strategic exposures. As a consequence of the rooting in conventional insurance and financial hedging approaches, risk management has often been organized in units focused on the handling of corporate insurance programmes frequently under the auspices of the finance department.[5] In other words, many

---

[4] In reality very few companies integrate the risk management activities across the organization. Some European companies seem slightly ahead with regard to risk management integration where their North American counterparts may be hampered by the prevalence of stringent corporate governance rules and guidelines.

[5] See, e.g. K. Andersen and A. Terp (2006). 'Risk Management' in T. J. Andersen (ed.), *Perspectives on Strategic Risk Management*. CBS Press: Copenhagen.

contemporary risk management practices are rather narrowly focused on insurable risks and financial hedging. This emphasis may appear rather contradictory in view of recent surveys of Danish corporate executives who indicate that cover for insurable hazards and financial risks typically has higher emphasis, even though they are not considered the most important risks.[6] In contrast, strategic exposures are considered highly important, but nonetheless still receive limited attention and are usually not formally considered in the planning for corporate risk covers.

Similar investigations suggest that a predominant driver for risk management continues to be protection and cost-savings. That is, risk management practices are often rather defensive by nature and in many instances compliance-driven.[7] Accordingly, risk management is typically not seen as an integrated part of the corporate ability to create new business opportunities. Thus, it is hardly surprising that the companies generally pursue a somewhat traditional risk management approach focused on financial exposures, insurable risks, process controls and internal auditing. One reason why financial market risks and environmental hazards are scrutinized in a more structured way than operational and strategic risks relates to the fact that these risks are better documented and, therefore, easier to handle. Another complementary and straightforward explanation is that insurance companies and other financial institutions simply demand a mapping of the underlying exposures to commit to insurance arrangements against them. All the while, there is a need for a structured approach to identify and characterize specific risks if they are to be priced and exchanged between financial intermediaries. Yet, there is less focus on some of the more unruly and emergent risk factors. For example, fundamental dependence on information and communication technologies (ICT) has increased the vulnerability of corporate ICT installations. Events like global virus attacks and international hacking into central institutional databases especially point to the significance of IT security. Even though operational risks are receiving more focus from financial regulators[8] and enforcement of the Sarbanes–Oxley Act increases conventional risk awareness, similar formalized requirements have not yet spilled over into similar demands for extended corporate risk management practices.

As appears from the analysis of risk assessment by corporate executives, strategic risks are considered more important than financial and hazard risks that yet seem to constitute most of the risk management coverage (Figure 6.3).

[6] P. W. Schrøder (2006). 'Impediments to Effective Risk Management' in T. J. Andersen (ed.), *Perspectives on Strategic Risk Management*. CBS Press: Copenhagen.

[7] S. Gates (2006). 'Incorporating Strategic Risk into Enterprise Risk Management: A Survey of Current Corporate Practice'. *Journal of Applied Corporate Finance* 18(4), pp. 81–90.

[8] The most recent revision of the capital adequacy proposals from the Bank for International Settlements (BIS) in Basel, referred to as Basel II, incorporates operational risks, which can be important in the data-intensive banking industry, and actually proposes development of risk simulation techniques, etc. to assess these exposures.

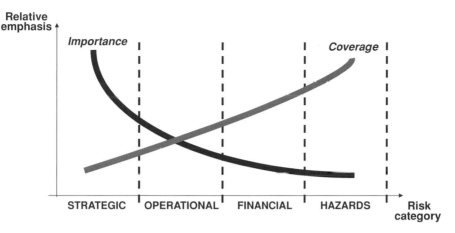

Figure 6.3 *Current risk assessments*

Hence, it is rather surprising that the management of strategic risks receives a relatively modest emphasis and is often considered on a more informal basis. Even though it may be possible to manage these exposures through ad hoc approaches US-based analyses[9] indicate that nearly 90 per cent of the 100 largest one-month drops in shareholder value could be attributable to strategic or operational risk events (Figure 6.4). A number of other studies have reported similar findings (see Box 6.1 *Further risk management studies*).[10]

Box 6.1 Further risk management studies

Deloitte & Touche examined instances of major shareholder value losses among the top 1,000 global companies from 1994 to 2003. They found that almost half of these global companies lost more than 20 per cent of their market value in a one-month period relative to the Morgan Stanley Capital International (MSCI) world stock index. Further, they examined the 100 events that accounted for the largest observed value losses among these firms. The various events were grouped into the four categories of strategic, operational, financial and external risks. The analysis revealed that strategic risks counted as the key driver in sixty-six of the instances, operational risk in sixty-one of the instances, while financial and external risks were key drivers in thirty-seven and sixty-two of the instances respectively. (This does not add up to 100, because more than eighty of these 100 companies experienced

---

[9] The MMC Research (2002). 'Causes for Stock Drops – Fortune 1000 Group', Mercer Management Consulting Research.

[10] The insert builds on a study by Deloitte Development LLC (2005). 'Disarming the Value Killers: A Risk Management Study', available online at www.deloitte.com; and T. Bussa and R. Knight (2003). 'Ernst & Young, Oxford Metrica, Risks That Matter: Sudden Increases and Decreases in Shareholder Value and the Implications', available online at www.oxfordmetrica.com.

risk triggers of more than one type, which underpins the importance of assessing possible risk interdependencies).

Ernst & Young jointly with Oxford Metrica examined shifts in shareholder value across the largest 1,000 global companies over the five-year period from August 1996 to July 2001. They found that 40 per cent of the top 1,000 global companies lost value of over 30 per cent in their worst month relative to the MSCI world stock index. Furthermore, the largest 100 losses were analyzed to determine the types of risk events that caused the loss in market value. Classifying the various events as relating to strategic, operational or financial risks, they found that the key trigger in 72 per cent of the instances could be ascribed to a strategic event, while the underlying risk in the remainder of the instances was evenly distributed between operational and financial risk factors.

Furthermore, they even found that two-thirds of these risks could have been anticipated and handled by known risk management practices, tools and techniques. In other words, their results seem to indicate that a proactive management approach to deal with strategic risks and operational disruption can add value and, therefore, should receive more attention from senior executives (see Box 6.2 – *Evaluating all of the corporate risk exposures*). As a consequence, the findings indicate that more structured approaches to the management of operational and strategic risks have the potential to create market value.

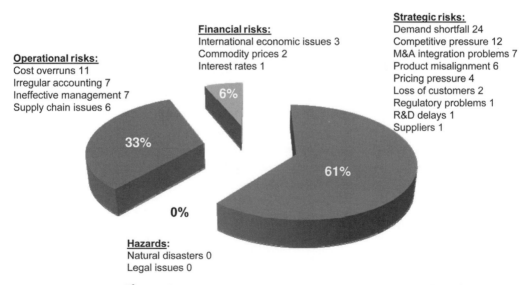

Operational risks:
Cost overruns 11
Irregular accounting 7
Ineffective management 7
Supply chain issues 6

Financial risks:
International economic issues 3
Commodity prices 2
Interest rates 1

Strategic risks:
Demand shortfall 24
Competitive pressure 12
M&A integration problems 7
Product misalignment 6
Pricing pressure 4
Loss of customers 2
Regulatory problems 1
R&D delays 1
Suppliers 1

Hazards:
Natural disasters 0
Legal issues 0

Figure 6.4 *The primary causes for drop in stock price (number of companies)*

Box 6.2 Evaluating all of the corporate risk exposures

There is some recognition that strategic risk factors constitute some of the most important corporate exposures and, therefore, represent a major area of concern for effective risk management practices.

The management of environmental *hazards and financial risks* is mainly focused on protection against downside loss effects caused by damages to productive economic assets.

Managing *operational risks* is primarily aimed at avoiding downside effects caused by disruptions to business activities, but also tries to achieve upside gains from increased process efficiencies and improvements through learning.

The handling of *strategic risks* imposes new requirements for improved responsiveness to events that are difficult to foresee and hard to quantify. These entail an ability to deflect downside effects of environmental threats as well as an ability to realize upside gains from business opportunities (see figure below).

The risk management pyramid

Risk management practices:

Strategic risks – increase responsiveness through creation of new business opportunities in decentralized entrepreneurial processes; be observant to changing environmental conditions through dispersed alertness combined with central risk monitoring; stage initial development investments and time large irreversible business commitments; establish general priorities, common goals and values, and general risk awareness through corporate planning process.

Operational risks – impose process control systems; establish auditing function to monitor internal and external compliance; engage in continuous improvement processes (these are related to the organizational learning concept and existing lean, TQM and six-sigma practices).

Hazards and financial risks – assess environmental risk factors; quantify corporate exposures and monitor them; engage in risk mitigation efforts to reduce vulnerability; engage in risk-transfer arrangements to hedge and manage the economic exposures of the corporation.

6.3   ERM – the new risk paradigm

The ERM approach has been introduced with the purpose of assessing the many potentially important corporate exposures more systematically, including operational and commercial risks, within an integrative enterprise-wide framework, considering both the potential for downside losses and upside gains offered in an uncertain environment. The holistic, systematic and analytical approach of ERM represents a shift in the way of thinking about the risk management challenge. Enterprise risk management thrives on a different mindset compared to traditional risk management. Some of the distinctive characteristics of the ERM frameworks include the following points.

- The aim is to create competitive advantage and exploit natural hedges rather than primarily focusing on losses and costs and gaining protection from traditional risk-transfer solutions.
- Different risks are integrated across the organization and managed centrally instead of being managed separately in specialized units.
- The risk management process is linked to strategic objectives incorporated in business plans where traditional risk management practices are loosely linked to objectives.
- The risk management perspective is extended from a primary focus on financial market risks and insurable hazards to consider also operational and commercial exposures.
- The risk management activities are incorporated into the core business processes as opposed to being practised as an ad hoc checklist exercise.

A central aim of the enterprise risk management approach is to provide the companies with a formalized framework and structured processes that should make the corporation more anticipatory and effective in embracing, evaluating and managing exposures in an uncertain environment. The risk management practices proposed by the Committee of Sponsoring Organizations of the Treadway Commission (COSO),[11] the joint Australian/New Zealand risk management standard (AS/NZS 4360)[12] and the Federation of European Risk Management Associations (FERMA) common standard[13] are all representative examples of current enterprise risk management frameworks (see Box 6.3 *An ERM framework*). Whereas the ERM framework more or less contains the same key components as the other frameworks, the specific elements of the framework should be tailored to the particular needs of individual companies. In other words, the ERM framework is not supposed to constitute a one-size-fits-all proposition, but rather to outline an idealized framework for risk management guidance.

The enterprise risk management frameworks retain the conventional risk management cycle comprised by risk identification, risk analyses, risk evaluation and risk responses as a central process element (Figure 6.5). That is, ERM explicates how the risk management process should identify, analyze and respond to important corporate exposures and explains how risk management responses should comply with the overall corporate objectives. Hence, the ERM framework recognizes that structured risk assessment practices must be adopted in recognition of overarching corporate objectives and use of management controls to monitor exposure developments and risk management outcomes. ERM should be anchored within the organization and the framework describes how the management of risk should be organized, which systems to use in support of risk management activities and the capabilities, features of corporate culture and leadership styles that are required.

The risk management process

Within an ERM context, the risk management strategy is developed in view of the company's overall strategic objectives and the adjacent risk management activities are supposedly integrated with corporate business processes. The link to the overall corporate objectives should ensure alignment between risk strategies, major business objectives and the overarching corporate mission. In the absence of such a strategic embeddedness, there is no business policy context, and the risk management exercise could end up becoming a formal checklist drill. Since risks are inherent in all strategic decisions and business activities executed by a company, the risk management practices should be an integral part of the corporate business processes. This is also important because risk situations are

---

[11] See COSO (2004). 'Enterprise Risk Management – Integrated Framework'. This document can be downloaded from www.coso.org/ERM-IntegratedFramework.htm.
[12] See the Standards New Zealand website: www.standards.co.nz.
[13] See FERMA (2003). 'A Risk Management Standard', which can be downloaded online from www.ferma.eu.

Box 6.3 An ERM framework

The central aim of the enterprise risk management framework is to provide the company with a structured approach that enables it to be more anticipatory and effective in embracing, evaluating and managing corporate exposures under uncertain environmental conditions.

It is the aim of ERM to assume a holistic, enterprise-wide and integrated approach to manage all key risks and opportunities of the corporation in a systematic manner, with the intent of maximizing corporate value (see a representative illustration below).

ERM framework

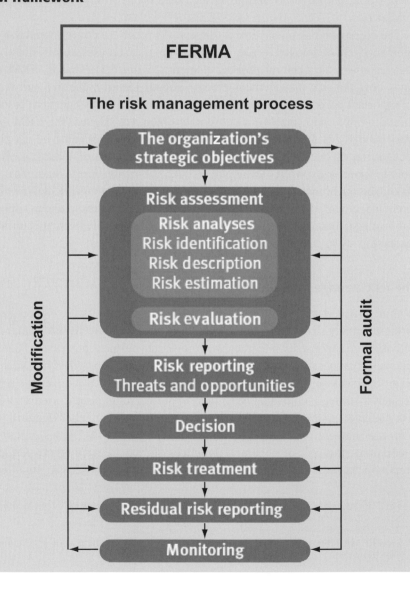

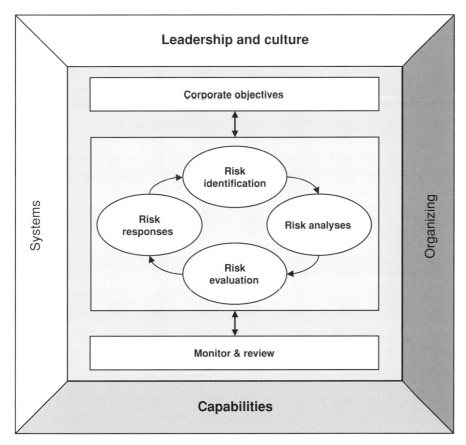

Figure 6.5 *Key components in an ERM framework*

managed and controlled better by actors that are close to the possible sources of the new exposures.

Risk identification

The first step of risk identification should be to track corporate risk areas in terms of potential losses and opportunities. A focus on important risk factors combined with insight about the corporate business activities provides a better understanding of how different events may affect the ability to achieve longer-term objectives in view of identified threats and opportunities. However, individual organizational actors may differ in their interpretation of possible risk factors. Therefore, it is important to develop a shared understanding of major corporate exposures and their interrelatedness in a way that is adapted to the specific environmental conditions. Establishing a common risk management vocabulary or 'risk language' among corporate decision-makers will ease internal communication. This can ensure a consistent view on corporate exposures across the organization when dealing with potential exposures and may make it easier to coordinate responsive actions that need collaboration between functional entities.

Adopting a common risk management framework can underpin a consistent examination of corporate exposures and allow cross-functional comparisons when assessing the aggregate corporate exposures. Business disruptions can typically arise along the corporate value chain and particularly so in the interfaces between different functional units within a larger operational system. These internal processing conditions can affect the generation of cash flows both in terms of operating expenses and sales revenues and may provide a good basis for understanding vulnerable business activities and identifying opportunities for process and product improvements. The identification of corporate risks may be supported by a common process classification scheme that makes it easier to compare and communicate information and insights about major exposures.

Risk analyses – quantification and aggregation

The adoption of structured measurement methodologies can support managers in their formal decisions about the severity of identified risks by establishing common risk parameters, enabling aggregation of exposures and setting targeted risk limits. However, it is difficult to estimate many of the risks, for example, in areas of operational disruption and commercial exposures, due to the lack of data availability. Even if it is possible to estimate these risks with the aid of quantitative models, the resulting risk measures can be challenged because the models may build on relatively restrictive assumptions.[14] Although the development and assessment of risk factors should be measured and the related exposures quantified, the play with numbers should never override the use of judgment. The input from experienced staff with special expertise is valuable when the assumptions that go into the models are developed, as are their insights when the model outputs are interpreted. Simple analytical approaches, including scenario analyses and computer simulations, can be useful, as these techniques raise the awareness of different risk factors and their interactions based on objective measures of uncertainty in the analyses.

Risk evaluation and responses

Once the various risk factors have been identified, the corporate exposures derived from them should be mapped and aggregated for oversight and general assessment. A widely used and simple tool for assessment and risk prioritization is to plot the exposures on a two-by-two grid in terms of their potential economic impact on the one side and the likelihood of the events occurring on the other.

[14] See, e.g. R. S. Dembo and A. Freeman (1998). *Seeing Tomorrow: Rewriting the Rules of Risk.* John Wiley & Sons: New York.

The approach must be supported by objective assessment criteria and can help overcome the estimation barrier that otherwise may apply to operational and commercial exposures. In this risk analysis, the company should compare the potential outcomes with performance indicators expressed in the corporate objectives. This will enable the company to determine whether or not the risks are mission critical and whether excess exposures should be modified. One clear advantage of this approach is that it prevents information overload. The risk prioritization identifies a multitude of unimportant potential risk factors, while ensuring a focus on the key risks to be managed, monitored and reported. The ERM framework formalizes the company's overall exposures in relation to a general risk appetite. It makes performance variability and aggregate loss exposures explicit within acceptable corporate limits and anchors the exposure to individual business units and profit- and cost-centres at different organizational levels. Appropriate use of the ERM framework requires that risk management strategies must be decided in view of the enterprise as a whole rather than on the basis of narrow divisional or functional assessments. As a consequence, decisions to avoid, retain, reduce, transfer or exploit risks should in principle be evaluated at the corporate level and not on a stand-alone basis.

The internal environment

An effective enterprise-wide risk management approach requires an appropriate organizational structure comprising elements of leadership, culture, organizing, capabilities and systems (Figure 6.5). When considering the intricate conditions around an appropriate risk management organization, it may be useful to adopt different organizational frameworks to analyze the relationship between essential organizational characteristics (see Box 6.4 *Analyzing the internal environment*).[15]

Leadership and culture

Imposing an ERM framework on the corporate risk management process may require a change in managerial attitude supported by the full backing of senior executives and the board of directors. It may require a change in the corporate risk management culture to facilitate operational and cross-functional involvement in the risk management process from managers in all parts of the organization. The ERM framework starts at the top, with the board assuming an oversight role in line with its corporate governance responsibilities. The board of directors must provide general direction by emphasizing risk management and outlining the risk appetite of the enterprise, while stipulating general risk management policies. The corporate executives are ultimately responsible for the execution of the risk

---

[15] See, e.g. J. R. Galbraith (1977). *Organization Design*. Addison-Wesley Publishing Company: Reading, Massachusetts.

Box 6.4 Analyzing the internal environment

When analyzing the appropriateness of the organization's internal environment, it may be useful to use one or more of the conventional analytical frameworks developed by organization scholars and corporate consultants.

Two common analytical frameworks

Galbraith's organizing model

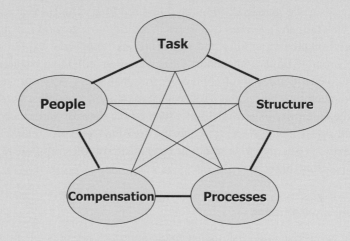

McKinsey's 7S framework

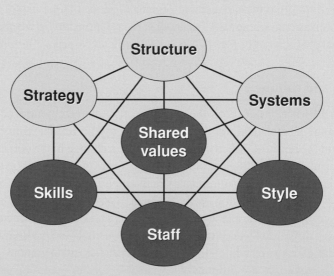

The underlying idea behind these frameworks is that the different elements that typically make up a comprehensive organizational structure should constitute an appropriate fit that together make up a cohesive whole as the basis for effective corporate culture and efficient execution of internal processes.

management process and must give the process corporate priority to ensure buy-in throughout the organization and setting the tone for a positive risk culture.

The board's ability to support the corporate risk management efforts is crucial to the success of ERM and some studies indicate that managerial skill enhancement is necessary to achieve successful risk management practices.[16] The directors must enhance their knowledge about risk management if enterprise-wide risk management is to become a core competence at the board level. Furthermore, successful implementation seems to depend on the presence of visible, top-level champions who believe in the effort and actively demonstrate support for it. Therefore, a strong belief in the active management of corporate risks with clear communication that this is a central focus is important to develop a robust risk management culture.

The permeation of risk awareness throughout the entire organization seems to be a critical factor for successful implementation of an ERM framework. One study suggests that the adoption of ERM is unlikely to be successful if the risk management concept fails to become an ingrained part of the corporate culture.[17] A corporate culture of openness and trust seems important because it creates an environment where employees can discuss sensitive risk concerns and learn from past mistakes, while sharing ideas about new opportunities.

Organizing

The ERM frameworks propose that a formal reporting structure delineating specific roles and responsibilities to designated staff members within the organization is important to successful implementation of enterprise risk management. Yet, there are a variety of alternative options available when considering how to establish an effective risk management organization (a possible solution is shown in Figure 6.6).

The main argument for a formalized risk management structure is that the organizational model must have 'teeth' so the risk management process constitutes a central corporate function with direct reporting lines to an executive officer and the top management team. A number of risk-conscious companies have advanced considerably in their efforts to establish effective enterprise risk management systems in accordance with these principles by establishing specialized risk offices to handle the enterprise-wide risk management process (see Box 6.5 *Risk management set-up at Novo Nordisk A/S*).[18]

[16] See B. Weinstein, K. Blacker and R. W. Mills (2003). 'Risk Management for Non-Executive Directors: Creating a Culture of Cautious Innovation'. Henley Discussion Paper No. 2. Henley Management College.

[17] A. E. Kleffner, R. B. Lee and B. McGannon (2003). 'The Effect of Corporate Governance on the Use of Enterprise Risk Management: Evidence From Canada'. *Risk Management and Insurance Review* 6(1), pp. 53–73.

[18] The information is extracted from the Novo Nordisk Annual Report (2006).

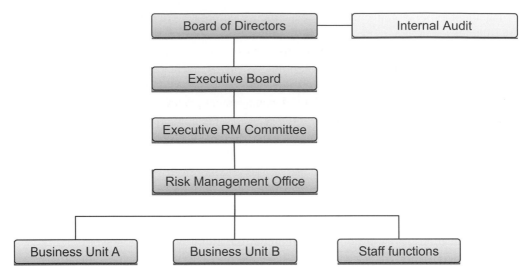

Figure 6.6 *The organizational oversight structure*

Box 6.5 Risk management set-up at Novo Nordisk A/S

Executive management has established a dedicated Risk Management Board of senior executives representing all key business activities and selected support functions. Chaired by the Chief Financial Officer, it reports to Executive Management and the Board of Directors. The Risk Management Board meets at least four times a year.

It sets the strategic direction and challenges for risk management, and analyzes the risk and control information generated by the individual business areas. This process helps to reduce blind spots and consider potential cross-functional impacts. Risks are assessed and quantified in terms of potential financial impact and reputational damage in quarterly reports to Executive Management and the Board of Directors. The potential impact is specified for each risk, as are associated mitigation efforts.

The Risk Office is the secretariat of the Risk Management Board. It drives and consolidates risk reporting from discovery and development, through manufacturing and logistics, to marketing and sales. In addition, risks related to support functions such as regulatory, business development, finance, legal and IT and people and organization are included. This is done in consultation with relevant Novo Nordisk committees, management groups and boards.

Within the formalized ERM framework, each of the corporate business entities and the senior managers that head them assume responsibility for the risk management process and are held accountable for managing the key risks identified within their respective business areas. Hence, the responsibility for specific business risks is delegated to the unit managers and enforced through their formal reporting to an executive risk management committee seconded by a central risk office function. However, identifying, controlling and managing many intertwined risks across an entire enterprise can be complex and may require focused managerial attention and specialized expertise. To this end we have seen a new management role emerging, the Chief Risk Officer (CRO), who oversees the corporate risk management function. The appointment of a CRO will further underpin the importance of corporate risk management.[19]

The central risk management function can be responsible for integrating the management of all or only certain risk areas. However, an effective corporate risk management function should somehow be able to develop an integrative management approach to handle aggregate corporate exposures and take responsibility for the appropriate identification, assessment and handling of enterprise-wide risks under the supervision of an executive risk committee. This may require different combinations of educational, facilitating, advisory, supervisory, monitoring and controlling tasks across the organization that leave sufficient room for functional units to assume a proactive role in the risk management process, while maintaining sufficient overview of enterprise-wide risks. It requires a balance between engaging organizational members in the management to reducing downside losses and enhancing upside gains, while also orchestrating and coordinating the enterprise-wide risk management process. The formal responsibilities include establishing the processing framework with risk management policies and requirements for risk reports, while introducing relevant risk indicators, developing risk management capabilities and communicating the corporate risk profile to key stakeholders.

The CRO and the risk management function can assume a role as co-coordinator as well as risk owner. However, risk-ownership might only take place within the financial industry where market-based risks are easier to quantify and control. In keeping with this, COSO points out that companies have found the CRO's role most successful when it is set up as a staff function providing support, facilitation and coordination to line management. The risk function must be tied closely to the major lines of business and viewed as important by members of the management team in those businesses to be successful, as this provides them with a better understanding of the business areas they support.

Internal audit is one of the few bodies within many organizations that look systematically at all risks across the company. Consequently, it has knowledge of business activities and administrative processes company wide, which often makes it a natural choice for providing key assistance in the implementation of the ERM framework. Hence, the internal audit function could assist the executive management team in introducing ERM, but should not have responsibility for the

---

[19] See A. P. Liebenberg and R. E. Hoyt (2003). 'The Determinants of Enterprise Risk Management: Evidence from the Appointment of Chief Risk Officers'. *Risk Management and Insurance Review* 6(1), pp. 37–52.

risk management process because they act in an advisory capacity rather than a decision-making position in order to retain impartiality and objectivity.

Capabilities

For ERM to work, the risk management concepts, process applications and needed capabilities must be an integral part of the corporate training curriculum. Yet, the requirement for specific capabilities may vary considerably between different business and functional entities in the corporation as the handling of different types of risk can require quite diverse sets of skills and competencies. Hence, it is important to define the appropriate level of risk management capabilities and the relative sophistication of specialized expertise needed for each of the prioritized risk areas. Establishing general risk awareness and communicating prevailing risk policies through training and learning is key in the development of a risk management culture. Therefore, organizational and individual learning practices must be engaged in the implementation of an ERM framework. Finally, it may be necessary to consider an appropriate incentive structure to encourage desired risk management behaviours through corporate compensation schemes.

Systems

Computerized communication systems, internal information networks, Web-based technology solutions, etc. may provide useful support for the ERM efforts, as they enable managers across the company to share risk knowledge and enhance risk management capabilities, as well as identifying and controlling exposures in different parts of the organization. However, technology is an enabler only, whereas the engagement of people within the organization is essential when responding to corporate risks.

6.4   Limitations of the ERM framework

A common critique of ERM is that it is construed as a control framework and establishes a formalized extension of the corporate audit with a view to regulatory requirements. That is, it may extend the Sarbanes–Oxley (section 404) compliance efforts into an enterprise risk management process.[20] Although the different ERM frameworks emphasize that risk management should be developed in the context of the company's overall strategy and be part of the core business processes, the fact is that the main aim of the various frameworks is to ensure that

[20] See, e.g. J. Roth (2007). 'Myth vs Reality: Sarbanes–Oxley and ERM'. *Internal Auditor* 64, pp. 55–60, who states that SOX deals with financial reporting risks, whereas ERM deals with all risks.

intended strategies are executed and the related objectives accomplished, which means that these frameworks give priority to controls.

As a matter of fact, the various frameworks provide suggestions on neither how new business opportunities can be identified and assessed, nor how alternative strategies should be evaluated.[21] Consequently, the risk management practices within these frameworks are not an integrated part of the company's strategy formulation and objective-setting processes. This may be a critical deficiency, as general risk evaluations are essential complements in strategic decision-making. However, these potential shortcomings are not surprising as the various ERM frameworks have emerged as responses to widely reported corporate scandals that have happened over the past decades, with an aim of protecting against the adverse economic effects of the implied corporate risks. Accordingly, the ERM frameworks have without a doubt strengthened the control environment in the corporate sector and thereby reduced the losses accruing from many negative events.

However, the danger in imposing comprehensive and rather *control-oriented* frameworks is that the risk management process becomes a formal checklist drill serving to satisfy restrictive regulations and create comfort that executives and board members have done their duty if things should go wrong. Even worse, implementing a very restrictive ERM framework may constrain creative thinking and hold back the development of responsive solutions to changing conditions. To the extent that this happens, the formal risk management process can become a straightjacket as opposed to an effective enhancer of good risk practices as intended. As a consequence, the introduction of ERM frameworks may turn into a heavy-duty bureaucratic exercise, where the upside benefits are reduced and the downside risk effects are superseded by excessive administrative costs. A complete and fully documented control of all of the company's potential exposures may require substantial staff resources, resources that often are not provided specifically for the purpose. In some cases, experienced managers and functional staff must handle the risk management exercise simultaneously with their daily business duties and they often breathe a sigh of relief when the bureaucratic exercise has been completed. As a result, a proper risk awareness culture may not be fostered and, worse, potential changes in the risk landscape might not be identified in a timely manner because they are forgotten in formal reporting practices.

Incidentally, a recent study indicates that the Sarbanes–Oxley Act of 2002 may have enforced a precautionary mindset among US corporations that has resulted in a reduction in risk-taking behaviours. The study shows that Sarbanes–Oxley seems to have reduced the R&D efforts of US corporations, suggesting that this legislative initiative has curbed the inclination to embark on innovation

---

[21] P. Henriksen and T. Uhlenfeldt (2006). 'Contemporary Enterprise-Wide Risk Management Frameworks: A Comparative Analysis in a Strategic Perspective' in T. J. Andersen (ed.), *Perspectives on Strategic Risk Management*. CBS Press: Copenhagen, pp. 107–30.

and thereby killed the goose that lays the golden egg.[22] The study and its key findings are summarized in Box 6.6 *Sarbanes–Oxley's chilling effect on corporate risk-taking*.[23]

Box 6.6 Sarbanes–Oxley's chilling effect on corporate risk-taking

Bargeron, Lehn and Zutter from the University of Pittsburg have investigated the possible effect of the introduction of the Sarbanes–Oxley Act (SOX) on the risk-taking behaviour of US corporations. Their study compares risk-taking in US corporations with counterparts in the United Kingdom over time periods before and after SOX.

They investigate the investment behaviour of US firms in comparison to their UK counterparts over the periods 1995 to 1997, 1998 to 2000 and 2003 to 2005 based on a sample of 4,239 US corporations and 989 UK corporations, representing more than 80 per cent of companies in the S&P 500 Index and nearly 70 per cent of companies in the FTSE 100 Index.

They find that R&D intensity (measured as the ratio of R&D expenditures to total assets) as well as the capital intensity (measured as the ratio of capital expenditures to total assets) are significantly higher for the US corporations during all three above-mentioned periods. However, the difference in the ratio has declined over time. As R&D expenditures and to some degree capital expenditures involve investment in risky business projects, the relative decline in the ratios corresponds to a reduction in risk willingness among US corporations. The negative effect of SOX on the US corporate risk-taking is supported further by the finding that the difference between the ratio of cash holdings to total assets between US and UK corporations has widened considerably in the period after SOX. That is, the propensity to invest in non-operating low risk assets has increased among US corporations compared to their UK counterparts in the period after SOX. All in all, their findings are consistent with the view that SOX has had a chilling effect on corporate risk-taking in the United States.

They further investigate initial public offerings (IPOs) in the United States compared to the United Kingdom based on a sample comprising all completed common stock IPOs over the period 1990 to 2006. It should be emphasized that the US and UK stock markets to a large extent showed comparable developments in market returns over the period, which makes it

---

[22] Tom Siebel, former CEO of software company Siebel Systems, stated that 'we might have killed the goose that lays the golden egg ... You're mitigating every possible risk that can be conceived. Risk didn't used to be a bad thing' in T. Kontzer (2004). 'Siebel Sees Sarbanes–Oxley Taking Toll on Economy'. *Information Week*, 13 October 2004.

[23] L. Bargeron, K. Lehn and C. Zutter (2007). 'Sarbanes–Oxley and Corporate Risk-Taking'. Presented at the American Enterprise Institute on 18 June 2007. Available online at www.aei.org.

appropriate to use the United Kingdom as a benchmark. Their findings are shown in the table below.

	Pre-SOX (1990–2002)	Post-SOX (2003–2006)
Number of IPOs, US	6,417	963
– hereof within high R&D industries	2,472	283
Number of IPOs, UK	1,284	598
– hereof within high R&D industries	314	154
Sum of proceeds, US, US$ million	680,840	230,286
– hereof within high R&D industries	229,088	39,259
Sum of proceeds, UK, US$ million	147,639	38,687
– hereof within high R&D industries	14,690	4,484

Note: Proceeds are end-of-year 2005 CPI-adjusted.

It is evident from the table that the relative share of IPOs among US corporations has dropped from 83 per cent in the pre-SOX period to 62 per cent in the post-SOX period. Furthermore, the annual number of IPOs in the United States has decreased substantially post-SOX, whereas the number of IPOs in the United Kingdom has increased. Thus, the findings support the view that the introduction of SOX has reduced US-based private companies' inclination to go public.

Furthermore, the share of IPOs among US high R&D industries decreased from 39 per cent in the pre-SOX period to 29 per cent in the post-SOX period, compared with 24 and 22 per cent respectively for the similar counterparts in the United Kingdom. This pattern is even more pronounced if the high R&D industries' share of the proceeds is taken into consideration. While the UK high R&D industries account for a slightly increased share of the UK proceeds post-SOX compared with pre-SOX, the US high R&D industries' share of the US proceeds drops from 34 per cent pre-SOX to 17 per cent post-SOX. This result provides further support for the view that SOX has reduced corporate risk-taking in the United States.

Finally, they evaluate the stock markets' assessment of equity risk among US and UK companies through conventional measures of total equity risk, market risk and firm-specific risk based on daily as well as monthly stock returns over the period 1994 to 2006. They find that the total equity risk and its two components, market risk and firm-specific risk, have decreased significantly for US companies relative to their UK counterparts since the adoption of SOX, a finding that is strongest within R&D-intensive industries.

> Consequently, the findings reveal that the equity of US companies has become less risky compared with UK companies subsequent to SOX.
> All in all, the various measures of risk applied in the study tell a similar story: that SOX seemingly has chilled risk-taking by US corporations.

The various ERM frameworks implicitly suggest that a hierarchical organizational structure with direct reporting lines to the upper management echelons is required. However, this can lead to centralization of power with a high degree of central coordination of activities that in turn may reduce the involvement of business managers and functional specialists. As a consequence, important organizational actors could be kept out of the loop and disengaged in the important roles as environmental observers and creators of solutions. One outcome of this might be lower organizational flexibility, slower decision-making and reduced responsiveness. As a result, the ERM frameworks may not support the demand for enhanced strategic response capabilities in light of the increasingly uncertain environmental conditions that circumscribe contemporary organizations. Imposing a hierarchical organizational control structure may in some instances be inconsistent with existing corporate business practices and decision processes. This potential obstacle is frequently noted as one of the main barriers for the implementation of enterprise-wide risk management frameworks due to the resistance it can create among managers in the corporate business units.[24]

Finally, we may question whether the establishment of a formalized risk management structure across all organizational entities is a suitable way to handle the often diverse types of risk that apply to different businesses and functional entities. As discussed previously, the many risks faced by the company are multifaceted. Some risks can be identified, measured and quantified and thus constitute relatively predictable risks that are easier to control. Other risk factors are known with uncertainty, i.e. we do not possess recorded event losses that could inform about potential outcomes, which makes it difficult to quantify the exposures. Yet, other risks are even hard to foresee at all and they may actually constitute the most significant corporate exposures. This segment of unknowable risks seems to be a major characteristic of contemporary business environments, including factors like changing customer needs, leaps in technology use, etc. (Figure 6.7). All the while, the prediction of aggregate corporate exposures is complicated by the complex interactions that may exist between risk events that are outside the scope of conventional control approaches to risk management.

---

[24] See, e.g. B. Weinstein (2003). 'Risk Management versus the Loose Organisation'. Working Paper. Henley Management College, available online at www.henleymc.ac.uk; W. Smiechewicz (2001). 'Case Study: Implementing Enterprise Risk Management'. *Bank Accounting and Finance* 14(4), pp. 21–7; G. Dickinson (2001). 'Enterprise Risk Management: Its Origins and Conceptual Foundation'. *Geneva Papers on Risk and Insurance* 26(3), pp. 360–6; and M. Haubenstock (1999). 'Organizing a Financial Institution to Deliver Enterprise-Wide Risk Management'. *Journal of Lending and Credit Risk Management* 81(6), pp. 46–52.

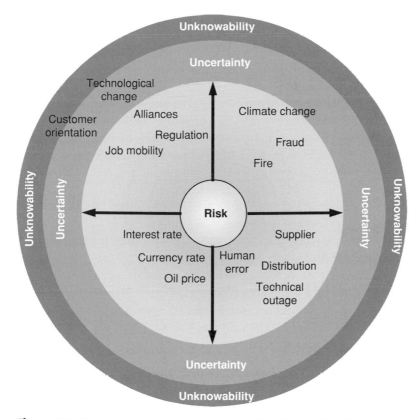

Figure 6.7 *Environments become uncertain with unknowable risks*

While predictable risks can be controlled centrally as well as decentrally, unpredictable risks characterized by unknowability or sheer complexity are impossible to control centrally and, therefore, should be managed through decentralized actions that enable timely reactions. Therefore, the organization of risk management activities within the company calls for an appropriate balance between central management controls and decentralized responsiveness, which is an issue scarcely touched upon by the ERM frameworks.

6.5   Conclusion

Corporate misconduct in the past has created growing public pressures for changes in corporate governance and risk management regulations. Current risk management practices are frequently focused on financial risks and insurable hazards managed in rather isolated silos within the organization, while operational and commercial risks take a back seat. In this context, public policies demand more integrated, systematic and comprehensive risk management approaches to ensure that companies have the right control systems in place. However, the business environment is dynamic, which means that companies are faced with risk factors characterized by uncertainty, immeasurability and low ability to forecast. Therefore, risk management is not just a matter of having the right controls in place, but should also ensure flexibility within the organization in support of effective responses to new risks.

Enterprise risk management is offered as an example on a new risk paradigm. The aim of ERM is to provide the companies with frames and structures that enable them to be more anticipatory and effective at evaluating, embracing and managing risks. However, the ERM frameworks may display a number of deficiencies.

- They are inherently control frameworks with limited emphasis on the need to create risk awareness and enhance responsiveness.
- They represent hierarchical organizational structures that may reduce flexibility and speed of decision-making.
- They impose formal risk management practices without relationship to the company's strategy-making process.
- They propose a joint structure to handle all types of risk across the organization, which is insufficient to deal with multifaceted corporate risks characterized by complexity and unknowability.

The next chapter outlines the most common analytical approaches associated with the ERM frameworks. The current critique of the ERM frameworks suggests a move towards a risk management approach that is integrated with the company's strategic management processes in a way that provides a better balance between internal controls and the ability to develop flexible responses. This discussion is extended in the ensuing chapter, including proposals for possible remedies to circumvent the identified shortcomings.

References

Andersen, T. J. (ed.), 2006. *Perspectives on Strategic Risk Management*. CBS Press: Copenhagen.

Andersen, K. and Terp, A., 2006. 'Risk Management' in Andersen, T. J. (ed.), *Perspectives on Strategic Risk Management*. CBS Press: Copenhagen.

Bargeron, L., Lehn, K. and Zutter, C., 2007. 'Sarbanes–Oxley and Corporate Risk-Taking'. Presented at the American Enterprise Institute on 18 June 2007. Available online at www.aei.org.

Bettis, R. A. and Hitt, M. A., 1995. 'The New Competitive Landscape'. *Strategic Management Journal* 16, pp. 7–19.

COSO (Committee of Sponsoring Organizations of the Treadway Commission), 2004. 'Enterprise Risk Management Framework'. Available online at www.erm.coso.org.

Dembo, R. S. and Freeman, A., 1998. *Seeing Tomorrow: Rewriting the Rules of Risk*. John Wiley & Sons: New York.

Dickinson, G., 2001. 'Enterprise Risk Management: Its Origins and Conceptual Foundation'. *Geneva Papers on Risk and Insurance* 26(3), pp. 360–6.

FERMA (Federation of European Risk Management Associations), 2003. 'A Risk Management Standard'. Available online at www.ferma.eu.

Galbraith, J. R., 1977. *Organization Design*. Addison-Wesley Publishing Company: Reading, Massachusetts.

Gates, S., 2006. 'Incorporating Strategic Risk into Enterprise Risk Management: A Survey of Current Corporate Practice'. *Journal of Applied Corporate Finance* 18(4), pp. 81–90.

Haubenstock, M., 1999. 'Organizing a Financial Institution to Deliver Enterprise-Wide Risk Management'. *Journal of Lending and Credit Risk Management* 81(6), pp. 46–52.

Henriksen, P. and Uhlenfeldt, T., 2006. 'Contemporary Enterprise-Wide Risk Management Frameworks: A Comparative Analysis in a Strategic Perspective' in Andersen, T. J. (ed.), *Perspectives on Strategic Risk Management*. CBS Press: Copenhagen, pp. 107–30.

Kleffner, A. E., Lee, R. B. and McGannon, B., 2003. 'The Effect of Corporate Governance on the Use of Enterprise Risk Management: Evidence from Canada'. *Risk Management and Insurance Review* 6(1), pp. 53–73.

Kontzer, T., 2004. 'Siebel Sees Sarbanes–Oxley Taking Toll on Economy'. *Information Week*, 13 October.

Liebenberg, A. P. and Hoyt, R. E., 2003. 'The Determinants of Enterprise Risk Management: Evidence from the Appointment of Chief Risk Officers'. *Risk Management and Insurance Review* 6(1), pp. 37–52.

Power, M., 2007. *Organized Uncertainty – Designing a World of Risk Management*. Oxford University Press: New York.

Roth, J., 2007. 'Myth vs Reality: Sarbanes–Oxley and ERM'. *Internal Auditor* 64, pp. 55–60.

Schrøder, P. W., 2006. 'Impediments to Effective Risk Management' in Andersen, T. J. (ed.), *Perspectives on Strategic Risk Management*. CBS Press: Copenhagen, pp. 65–87.

Smiechewicz, W., 2001. 'Case Study: Implementing Enterprise Risk Management'. *Bank Accounting and Finance* 14(4), pp. 21–7.

Weinstein, B., 2003. 'Risk Management versus the Loose Organisation'. Working Paper. Henley Management College, available online at www.henleymc.ac.uk.

Weinstein, B., Blacker, K. and Mills, R. W., 2003. 'Risk Management for Non-Executive Directors: Creating a Culture of Cautious Innovation'. Henley Discussion Paper No. 2. Henley Management College.

7   Strategic risk analyses

This chapter will discuss a variety of analytical tools that may be adopted for risk management purposes. Initially, common tools applicable to analyze trends and emerging issues within predictable and known business environments are put forward, and a resemblance to strategic management is revealed through examples. Uncertainty is added to the spectrum, and the use of templates such as scenario planning and real options is outlined. It is shown how these approaches may enable the corporation to evaluate the effect of a changing risk landscape and to take necessary precautionary measures. Environmental uncertainty affects the corporation and introduces unexpected events that can cause major deviations to plans. The relevance of contingency planning is discussed and it is argued that it may work in simple and predictable environments to handle more severe deviations. However, it is subsequently argued that it must be complemented by a culture of mindfulness known from high reliability organizations in more complex and unpredictable environments. The chapter is rounded off with a discussion of risk management under unknowable environmental conditions as it must deal with 'unk unks'.[1] The role of values, behaviour and corporate culture in dealing with uncertainty and unforeseeable events is considered.

7.1   Environmental scanning in a predictable world

Corporations often face environmental changes that seem to come out of thin air. The previous chapter suggested that nearly 90 per cent of the drops in shareholder value can be attributed to strategic and operational risk events. This accentuates the question of how the corporation can better identify and foresee events that often appear initially as weak signals at the corporate periphery where the actual transactions take place.[2] Hence, the ability to involve the relevant

[1] Unk unks refer to unknown unknowns, i.e. unforeseeable events the consequences of which cannot be known beforehand. Nasem Nicolas Taleb (2007) objects to people who think they can map the future, arguing that they ignore the large deviations and thus fail to take the 'Black Swans', i.e. the abrupt and unexpected events with extreme effects, into account. See N. N. Taleb (2007), *The Black Swan – The Impact of the Highly Improbable*. Penguin Books: New York.

[2] G. S. Day and P. J. H. Schoemaker (2006). *Peripheral Vision: Detecting the Weak Signals That Will Make or Break Your Company*. Harvard Business School Press: Boston, Massachusetts.

people in the organization to be observant and sensitive to changes in the risk environment may enable the recognition of important environmental changes sooner and allow the firm to react to them in a more timely manner.

Admittedly, it is difficult if not impossible to tell the future, and these weak signals are often difficult to see and not least to interpret. For example, Taleb (2007) points out the general failure of forecasters to predict the abrupt and often drastic changes that occur from time to time. For example, the emergence of major technologies, including the computer, the PC, the Internet and the laser, were unplanned, unpredicted and unappreciated upon their discovery and well after their initial use. Similarly, few people, if any, expected the US sub prime mortgage market melt down over the course of 2007 and the subsequent consequences for the international financial system, despite the early emergence of weak economic signals. The macroeconomic context in the preceding period was characterized by excess global liquidity, historically low interest rates, increasing current account deficits in leading economies and not least abnormal increases in real estate prices.[3] These trends could have been monitored and evaluated to foresee the build-up of a housing bubble and raise relevant 'what if' questions about the potential economic consequences if the bottom should drop out of the housing markets. Hence, we claim that preparing for responses on emerging risk events can increase the efficiency in dealing with uncertainty. Thus, the corporation should have a structure in place to identify and evaluate key trends, emerging issues and events.

Environmental scanning can be conceived as incorporating four modes of viewing the environment and searching for important environmental developments.[4]

Formal search, where the corporation in a structured way obtains information of relevance to specific issues as input to the planning process and decision-making.

Conditional viewing, where the corporation tracks pre-selected information from particular sources aimed at identifying the contours of specific evolving issues.

Informal search, where the corporation actively looks for information through unfocused and unstructured efforts to increase understanding of specific developments to assess potential impacts and the need for responsive action.

Undirected viewing, where the corporation scans many diverse sources of information without specific informational needs in mind to sense new trends and enable the corporation to think about environmental developments in unconventional ways.

---

[3] The microeconomic factors related to financial regulation and industry practices also appear to have played a crucial role in the build-up of the price bubble in the housing markets. See L. Laeven and F. Valencia (2008). 'Systemic Banking Crises: A New Database'. IMF Working Paper, 08/224.

[4] In this context, 'viewing' means looking *at* information, while 'searching' means looking *for* information. For a discussion of the four modes, see, e.g. C. W. Choo (1999). 'The Art of Scanning the Environment'. *Bulletin of the American Society for Information Science*. February/March, pp. 21–4.

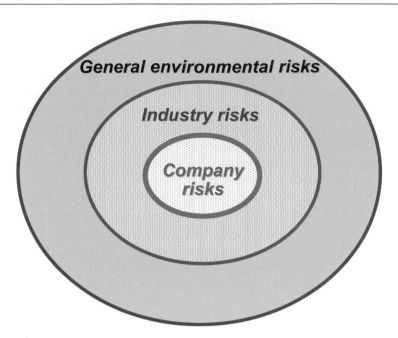

Figure 7.1 *An organizing framework for risk analyses*

The corporation must choose the right balance between those four modes of scanning. Too much focus on undirected viewing might result in huge costs, information overload and not least a lack of focus. On the other hand, unilateral use of conditional viewing and formal search, although cost-efficient, might result in a too-narrow scanning of the environment and might cause the corporation to miss out on fundamental changes. Generally, the more complex and volatile the business environment is, the greater the need for undirected viewing. Formal search and conditional viewing applies more to central planning activities with the aim of integrating and coordinating existing corporate activities for economic efficiencies. Informal search and undirected viewing refers mostly to the observance of people at decentralized functional entities in the organizational periphery closer to where the operational, supplier and customer transactions are carried out. Hence, the ability to process information to optimize current activities as well as scanning the periphery for new emerging market trends suggests a dual emphasis on central planning and decentralized observance.

There is no standardized way to scan the environment and analyze the broad amalgam of possible risk factors. However, one way to approach systematically the analysis of a wider risk spectrum is first to consider the general environmental conditions that circumscribe the entire community, then to consider business conditions specific to the industrial environment in which the corporation operates and then finally to focus on the factors that are internal to the company's own operations (Figure 7.1).

General environmental risks

General environmental risks comprise a number of exogenous factors completely outside the control of corporate management that circumscribe the general business environment affecting all actors across industries and sectors, albeit in different ways. These types of risks are often categorized to consider particular factors, such as political events, economic developments, social trends, technological innovations and the like, which may be analyzed within the so-called PEST or PESTEL frameworks[5] (see Box 7.1 – *Drivers of change in non-life insurance* – for an example of how this type of analysis may be used).[6]

Box 7.1 Drivers of change in non-life insurance

Political issues: The personal non-life insurance industry is faced with increased political pressures to introduce more transparent products and pricing schemes that allow the consumer to compare different market offers. Furthermore, the adoption of new regulations on capital requirements (the Solvency II rules) will affect the insurance industry by imposing higher capital requirements.

Economic issues: An increasing trend in the demand and supply of welfare benefits will generally impose a higher proportion of consumption being spent on services.

Social issues: The insurance industry is faced with a trend towards higher demands from younger employees for personal growth and job satisfaction. It is common that both spouses are working, which imposes higher pressures for a balance between the time spent with family, on the job and in the general spare time.

Technology issues: The increased use of the Internet to compare prices between competing insurance companies on similar products either through brokers or directly on price and product sites will affect the competitive dynamic. The improvements in streaming video and availability of low-cost bandwidth will make it easier to speak directly to customers through their computers. The Internet has also changed the way in which companies in other industries communicate and trade with the customers.

---

[5] The acronym PESTEL refers to political, economic, socio-economic, technological, environmental and legal conditions. See, e.g. a standard strategy textbook like G. Johnson, K. Scholes and R. Whittington (2005). *Exploring Corporate Strategy*. Pearson Education: Harlow, United Kingdom ('The Environment', Ch. 2, pp. 63–105) for a discussion of this framework.

[6] The example builds on a strategy analysis conducted by one of the authors for Alm. Brand Insurance during 2004. The Alm. Brand non-life insurance company is the fourth largest insurance company in Denmark and offers all types of insurance to private customers and small businesses. The distribution of products is handled by twenty-five offices across the country, the company's own insurance agents and different partnerships, which include the largest real estate agency in Denmark and a major car importer.

Environmental issues: Terror is becoming an important environmental concern, particularly after 11 September, and has put severe strains on the prices for property reinsurance. Furthermore, climatic changes can affect weather conditions and impose higher disaster losses and subsequently higher reinsurance rates.

Legal issues: The potential removal of the access to door-to-door selling can have a major effect on the current sales practices. The existing legislation makes it possible for insurance agents to contact customers directly, for example, by phone, without prior consent. Hence, an important distribution channel will disappear if this is made unlawful.

Industry risks

Industry risks refer to factors identified at the industry level where competitive conditions may influence corporate exposures, while corporate actions may affect industry developments. Some typical frameworks adopted at this analytical level include, for example, Porter's five-forces model,[7] Porter's national diamond model,[8] industry network structures (the value migration between different industry segments),[9] competitive analyses,[10] mapping of strategic groups, market segmentation, etc. Conventional industry analysis considers conditions that are specific to the particular business environment, including new product developments, process innovations, changing customer needs, industry regulations, etc. Competitor analysis is often adopted to determine the strategies of existing and potential competitors, possible strategic moves and their expected consequences (see Box 7.2 – *Industry threats and opportunities in non-life insurance*).[11]

Box 7.2 Industry threats and opportunities in non-life insurance

An analysis of the profit dynamics in the industry can use Porter's five forces model. The model makes assessments about the industry's attractiveness based on the effect of five key forces, namely: (1) the threat of new entrants; (2) the bargaining power of buyers; (3) the bargaining power of suppliers; (4) the threat of substitute products or services; and (5) the intensity of competition in the industry. Each of these points is examined below.

---

[7] M. E. Porter (1980). *Competitive Structure*. Free Press: New York.
[8] M. E. Porter (1990). *The Competitive Advantage of Nations*. Free Press: New York.
[9] A. Slywotzky (1996). *Value Migration: How to Think Several Moves Ahead of the Competition*. Harvard Business School Press: Boston, Massachusetts.
[10] R. D'Aveni (1994). *Hypercompetition*. Free Press: New York.
[11] This insert illustrates how Porter's five-forces model (Porter, 1980) may be used for this type of analysis. Obviously this approach can be extended in various ways, e.g. using Grove's six-forces model (see Box 4.1 in Chapter 4) or D'Aveni's hypercompetitive framework (D'Aveni, 1994), etc.

(1) Insurance is a complex business and requires specific skills and experience. Customers are often conservative and retain all of their policies with one of the major insurance companies, so it is difficult for niche players to enter the market. Furthermore, it takes substantial marketing costs to establish a market presence as the industry sells standardized products to a mass market. Consequently, the threat of new entrants is low.

(2) The non-life-insurance products are in demand because they provide the customers with safety and peace of mind. The cost of switching from one insurer to another is relatively high and is a rather time-consuming process. However, a market survey shows that customers see no significant differences between the major market players, so new customers could possibly be attracted by better price quotes. The survey further indicates that nearly one-third of the customers are 'disloyal' to their current insurance provider. That is, the bargaining position of the buyer is generally low, but a certain portion of the customers may be accessible through differentiated product offers and competition on price quotes.

(3) The higher reinsurance premiums affect the costs in the industry and less consolidated insurance companies will have to retain a larger proportion of their risks because they cannot afford the higher costs of obtaining reinsurance coverage. Consequently, these companies become more vulnerable and large industry incumbents are in a better position.

(4) There are few direct alternatives to non-life insurance policies besides self-insurance through personal savings. However, this will not provide full coverage until the full amount of the potential loss has been saved.

(5) The nature of the business is relatively stable, with changes in products, production technologies and customer behaviour changing infrequently. The market is dominated by the major players, which account for around 65 per cent of the market, and they do not differ significantly from each other in terms of market offerings. This leads to intense price competition to maintain or gain market share. That is, the rivalry among the major market players is very high.

The character of the market is changing somewhat due to increased distribution partnerships with major banks whereby some market activities co-evolve possibly to develop new market opportunities. Hence, an increasing share of the non-life insurance sale is taking place through the banks that have closer relationships to their customers through widespread branch networks. An extended analysis shows significant differences in the distribution channels available to the insurance companies as some use the banks as a major distribution channel, while others use insurance agents, where the latter may be vulnerable to prohibition of door-to-door selling.

Company risks

Company risks relate to risk factors that are endogenous to the corporation as they are caused by organizational processes, technological systems and actions taken by members of the organization. The type of company risks to consider may typically include things like operational disruption, technological breakdown, misreporting, legal mistakes, fraudulent behaviours, inability to observe and react to market changes, etc. Some of the common frameworks and tools that can be used in the analysis of the company's internal environment include the McKinsey 7S model, value-chain analysis,[12] the VRIO framework[13] (to assess the sustainability of essential corporate resources), analysis of core competencies,[14] etc. (see Box 7.3 – *Assessing company risks* – for an example as to how the frameworks can be selectively applied to analyze the company's internal risk environment).

Box 7.3 Assessing company risks

Many of the operational activities in the value chain are dispersed to the local market entities, whereas centralization of certain common activities, for example, claims handling, could be located at a central function more efficiently without adversely affecting the service provided by the sales staff in the field. This is so due to a strong core operational processing system that ensures an efficient underwriting and claims handling. Furthermore, the potential to launch effective e-insurance systems is strong.

The firm has strong competencies in risk management, underwriting, claims assessments and compensation handling. This is reflected in a favourable claims ratio and customer portfolio compared to competitors. However, a lack of competencies in customer relationship building and servicing is a weakness in view of the opportunities described in Box 7.2 *Industry threats and opportunities in non-life insurance*.

The company has a strong set of shared values to guide the employee behaviours towards customers and colleagues. These values are supported by more than 90 per cent of the staff according to a recent staff survey.

The strong architecture between risk management price calculations, inbound logistics underwriting, claims assessment and compensation handling is a definite strength. However, the company's unified distribution is possibly a weakness due to the potential removal of door-to-door selling.

The company's financial position is relatively weak due to recent loss of equity capital and a corresponding decrease in the solvency ratio. This will

[12] M. E. Porter (1985). *Competitive Advantage*. Free Press: New York.
[13] J. B. Barney (2002). *Gaining and Sustaining Competitive Advantage* (2nd edn). Prentice Hall: Upper Saddle River, New Jersey.
[14] C. K. Prahalad and G. Hamel (1990). 'The Core Competence of the Corporation'. *Harvard Business Review* 68(3), pp. 79–91.

limit the scope for business expansion. Furthermore, the expense ratio is relatively high compared to main competitors, which is a risk in an industry characterized by intensive price competition. Conversely, recent technology investments in a more effective core insurance system and e-insurance platform are expected to improve the cost ratio and future profitability.

The above-mentioned analytical tools and approaches are typically used to assess the strategic position of the corporation in terms of developments in external market conditions and internal organizational capabilities. That is, these tools often focus on existing perceptions of the macro environment and industry conditions. However, there are alternative analytical approaches that can be adopted to stretch prevailing beliefs about the environmental context.[15] The formal strategic management and planning frameworks that incorporate these analytical tools adopt their own terminologies contained within a common strategy language. This corresponds to the recommendation proposed by ERM proponents of developing a common risk vocabulary within the corporation to stress an emphasis on risk management and facilitate internal communication in the risk-handling activities. Table 7.1 provides an example of a common risk management language based on four broad categories of strategic, hazards, financial and operational risks.

The common language can be constructed in many ways. For example, COSO has two broad risk categories and ten sub-categories,[16] while the risk-consulting firm Protiviti introduces three broad categories and eighteen sub-categories.[17] Thus, it should be recognized that such a common language can be tailored to the company's specific circumstances and needs. Typically, a tailored common language is developed through interviews and workshops at various levels of the organization. These procedures are in many ways analogous to the strategic management activities aimed at developing a common understanding of the strategic situation and communicate an overarching future direction for the company. The main advantage of establishing a common language is that it ensures a more consistent way of looking upon and analyzing risks across the organization.

---

[15] See, e.g. W. C. Kim and R. Mauborgne (2004). 'Blue Ocean Strategy'. *Harvard Business Review* 82(10), pp. 76–84. In this article the authors criticize current planning analysis for a singular focus on beating competition in the existing market space ('red ocean') rather than creating an uncontested market space ('blue ocean') and thereby capturing new demand. Hence, their analytical framework may be applied to scan the potential risk environment for both contested and uncontested market shares within a coherent analytical approach. Assuming a corporate social responsibility (CSR) perspective may be another way to extend the risk horizon to include risk factors that otherwise might slip from the horizon. See, e.g., B. Kytle and J. G. Ruggie (2005). *Corporate Social Responsibility as Risk Management: A Model for Multinationals.* Harvard University, John F. Kennedy School of Government.

[16] See COSO (2004). 'Enterprise Risk Management – Integrated Framework', available online at www.coso.org.

[17] See the Protiviti Risk Model[SM]. Available online from www.protiviti.com. Other consulting firms, such as Deloitte Touche Tohmatsu and Ernst & Young, have developed their own common risk management languages.

Table 7.1 *Common risk management language (aviation example)*

Strategic	Hazards	Financial	Operational
Aero political changes	Terrorism	Oil prices	Disaster recovery
Environmental	Malicious acts	Interest rates	Business continuity
regulations	Social and political	Currency rates	plans
Emission and	unrest	Access to capital	Aircraft disaster
pollution	Epidemics	Access to liquidity	Damage to assets
Security regulations	Natural disasters		Strikes
Aviation regulations	Fire		Security practices
World economic	Workplace safety		Utility outages
growth	Internal fraud and		Telecommunication
Competitors	theft		failure
Power of fuel	Theft and fraud		Failure of other
suppliers			third-party services
Power of aircraft			System reliability
suppliers			Ineffective external
Power of airports			Outsourcing
Power of unions			Employee turnover
Power of customers			communication
Partnering			
Qualified personnel			
Shareholder structure			
Image and brand			

The strategic analysis is typically summarized in a SWOT analytical frame-work, where strengths and weaknesses identified in the internal corporate environment and opportunities and threats identified in the external market environment are compared against each other and prioritized.[18] Table 7.2 exemplifies a SWOT analytical summary based on the evaluations performed in the previous boxes.

As it appears, the summary of the strategic analysis within the SWOT framework can actually help to identify important strategic risk factors. However, the SWOT analysis does not explicitly state the relative importance of the various risk factors. This shortcoming can be circumvented by completing a risk map, which can be considered the SWOT equivalent within the risk management field and is elaborated through a more formal approach to rank the various risk issues.

The results from the SWOT analysis can essentially feed into the initial assessment phase of the risk management process. However, as the SWOT framework normally focuses on strategic and economic risk factors, the SWOT analysis might

---

[18] SWOT analysis has been used for many years and its roots certainly date back to K. Andrews (1971). *The Concept of Corporate Strategy*. Homewood: Chicago, Illinois. This framework can be a useful approach to assess the potential impact of exogenous economic and strategic risk factors and evaluate possible strategic responses.

Table 7.2 *SWOT analysis (insurance example)*

Strengths	Weaknesses
Core insurance system	Customer leaving rate too high
E-insurance platform	Customer relationship building
Quality of the customer portfolio	Unified distribution
Risk management skills and knowledge	Strategic positioning
Culture	Solvency low
	Expense ratio too high
Opportunities	**Threats**
E-insurance	Consolidation within the industry increasing
Distinct positioning in the market	Bank insurance
Insurance customers' loyalty low	Increasing transparency in prices
Partnerships	Strong price competition
	Access to door-to-door selling might be prohibited

Table 7.3 *Rating criteria – likelihood (example)*

Score	Rating	Description
6	Frequent occurrence	Occurs more often than three times a year
5	Almost certain	Occurs one to three times per year
4	Likely	Occurs once every one to three years
3	Moderate	Occurs once every three to ten years
2	Unlikely	Occurs once every ten to twenty-five years
1	Rare	Occurs more seldom than once every twenty-five years

Note: This rating framework is used in Saxo Bank A/S.

be complemented with assessments of operational risk factors and hazards.[19] When the various risk factors have been identified, the associated exposures should be evaluated with the aim of determining those risks that represent the most material economic effects. The various risk factors are assessed from two perspectives, namely the likelihood that the underlying risk event will occur and the economic impact the specific risk event is expected to impose on the company.[20] The criteria for rating the likelihood are generally based on qualitative assessments and managerial judgments expressed in a ranking of the different events. The ranking efforts may, for example, be illustrated and expressed in a 'scoring system' (Table 7.3).[21]

[19] See, e.g. S. M. Walker (2001). *Operational Risk Management – Controlling Opportunities and Threats*. Connley Walker Pty Ltd: Melbourne for examples of operational and hazards risk modelling techniques.

[20] No one is actually able to predict the probability, cf. e.g. Taleb (2007). Thus, emphasis should be on the relative likelihood and expected impacts of the events (and what to do if they materialize).

[21] For an illustration of an ERM rating standard, see, e.g. FERMA (www.ferma.eu/tabid/195/Default.aspx).

Table 7.4 *Rating criteria – impact (example)*

Score	Rating	Description
6	Catastrophic	Could threaten the firm's existence
5	Severe	Loss estimates exceed two months of profit before tax, but do not threaten the existence of the firm
4	Major	Estimated losses between ten days and two months of profit before tax
3	Significant	Estimated losses of one to ten days' average profit before tax
2	Moderate	Estimated losses of 10 to 100 per cent of the average daily profit before tax
1	Minor	Loss estimates below 10 per cent of the average daily profit before tax

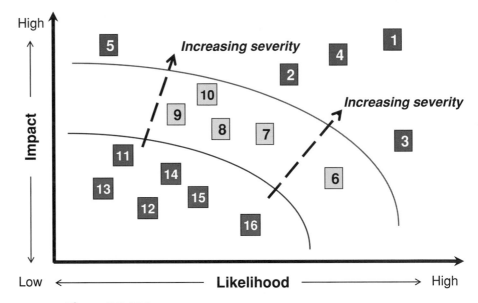

Figure 7.2 *Risk map*
Note: Ranking number 5 in the graph represents a low likelihood, high impact catastrophe event. Even though the total score may be relatively low due to a low likelihood of occurrence, they should be considered, e.g. in the form of business continuity plans.

The criteria for assessing the economic impact of the identified risk factors also often have to be based on qualitative judgments. These risks typically represent exposures that are hard to quantify, so the rating may express a rough indication of the potential direct economic losses caused by the event as well as the expected effects on the company's future earnings potential (Table 7.4).

Once the two rating scales (likelihood of event, expected economic impact of event) have been adopted in a qualitative assessment of all the identified risk factors, they can be plotted into a two-by-two framework. The final assessment of the corporate risk profile is then done on the basis of the resulting risk map (Figure 7.2). The most important risks that require the urgent attention of corporate

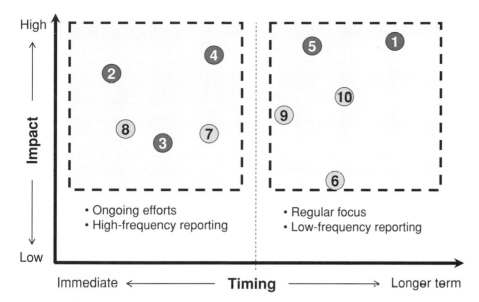

Figure 7.3 *Risk timing*

management are made up by the (grey colour) events positioned in the north-eastern corner of the map representing high likelihood – high impact events. In contrast, the low likelihood – low impact events (black colour) in the south-western corner do not warrant the same managerial attention.

Furthermore, some risks may have short-term effects, while others may have longer-term potential effects. Thus, the timing aspect should be considered when prioritizing and allocating responsibility to the various exposures. Some important risk factors need immediate and ongoing treatment (mitigation initiatives, process controls, high-frequency monitoring) and are normally dealt with at the tactical and operational levels in the organization. Other important risk factors may have longer-term and less immediate potential effects (emergent risks or 'phantom' risks, regular low-frequency monitoring) and are generally treated at the tactical and strategic levels in the organization (Figure 7.3).

However, the risk (timing) map shows the assessment of the various risk factors in isolation where potential interdependencies are not taken into account. Yet, the risk analysis can be extended with an impact-influence analysis aimed at determining the interdependencies between the various risk factors and thereby pinpointing those risks that might have the greatest potential impact. This result can subsequently form the basis for discussions about how risks might be mitigated or exploited effectively. The so-called influence matrix is an appropriate tool for such an analysis.[22] The idea behind the influence matrix is to evaluate the

---

[22] The influence matrix resembles the design structure matrix used in project management. It was first proposed in engineering by D. V. Steward (1981). *Systems Analysis and Management:*

	1	2	3	4	5	6	7	8	9	10	11	12	13	14	15	16	17	18	19	20	Total
1 E-insurance		(2)	1	1	1	1	(2)	2	(0)	0	2	1	0	0	1	2	2	2	0	1	21
2 Distinct positioning in the market	0		1	1	1	1	0	1	0	0	0	0	0	1	1	0	0	1	0	0	8
3 Insurance customers' loyalty	0	0		1	1	1	0	1	0	0	0	0	0	0	2	0	0	0	0	1	7
4 Partnerships	0	0	0		1	1	0	2	0	0	1	2	0	1	1	1	2	0	0	0	12
5 Consolidation in the industry	0	0	0	1		1	0	2	0	0	0	0	0	0	0	0	0	1	0	0	5
6 Bank insurance	0	1	1	1	0		0	0	0	0	0	2	0	0	2	0	0	1	0	0	8
7 Transparent prices	0	0	1	0	2	0		2	0	0	0	0	0	0	2	0	0	0	0	1	8
8 Price competition	1	0	1	1	2	0	0		0	0	0	0	0	0	2	0	0	0	2	0	9
9 Access to door-to-door selling	2	0	0	2	2	2	0	1		0	2	0	0	0	1	0	2	0	0	2	16
10 Core insurance system	0	0	1	1	0	0	0	0	0		0	0	0	0	0	0	0	0	0	2	4
11 E-insurance platform	2	2	1	1	0	1	0	0	0	0		0	0	0	1	0	2	2	0	1	13
12 Quality of the customer portfolio	0	0	0	0	0	0	0	2	0	0	0		0	0	0	0	0	1	0	2	5
13 Risk management skills and knowledge	0	0	0	0	0	0	0	2	0	0	0	2		1	0	0	0	0	0	1	6
14 Culture	0	2	2	0	0	0	0	0	0	0	0	2	0		1	0	0	0	0	0	7
15 Customer leaving rate	0	0	2	0	1	0	0	1	0	0	0	0	1	1		0	0	0	0	2	8
16 Customer relationship building	2	2	2	1	0	0	0	1	0	0	0	0	0	1	2		0	2	0	1	14
17 Unified distribution	0	0	0	0	2	0	0	0	0	0	0	0	0	1	0		0	0	1		4
18 Strategic positioning	2	2	1	1	0	1	0	0	0	0	0	0	0	1	1	0	0		0	0	9
19 Solvency	0	0	0	2	2	1	0	1	0	0	0	0	0	1	0	1	0		0		8
20 Expense ratio	0	1	1	0	2	0	0	2	0	0	0	0	0	1	0	0	0	0			7
Total	9	12	15	14	17	10	2	20	0	0	5	10	0	6	20	3	9	10	0	17	179

Figure 7.4 *Influence matrix (example)*

interaction between the various risk factors on a qualitative basis in the absence of exact relationships.[23] Thus, the influence matrix is the qualitative counterpart to the quantitative approach applied in value-at-risk assessments, where it is possible to calculate exact relationships between risk factors based on historical accounts of price developments.[24] The ranking of the various risk factors can be illustrated in the form of an example (Figure 7.4).

First, it evaluates the extent to which each individual risk factor has an impact on each of the other risks using a graduation scale: 0 for no or insignificant impact; 1 for some impact; and 2 for high impact. For example, e-insurance is a key element in establishing a distinct position in the market, and accordingly, row 1 – column 2 is assigned the weight of 2. Similarly, e-insurance will enhance the transparency of prices considerably and, consequently, row 1 – column 7 is assigned the weight of 2. Conversely, e-insurance will have no effect on the access to door-to-door selling and, accordingly, row 1 – column 9 is assigned the weight of 0. In this way, the assessment is carried on for each risk factor.

The across columns 'total' of measures (*sideways*) along each row indicates how the risk factors affect all of the other risk factors and, accordingly, captures

Structure, Strategy and Design. Petrocelli Books: New York. Eppinger et al. developed it further as a management tool. Refer to S. D. Eppinger, D. E. Whitney, R. P. Smith and D. A. Gebala (1994). 'A Model-Based Method for Organizing Tasks in Product Development'. *Research in Engineering Design* 6, pp. 1–13. See C. H. Loach, A. DeMeyer and M. T. Pich (2006). *Managing the Unknown: A New Approach to Managing High Uncertainty and Risk in Projects*. John Wiley & Sons: New York, p. 101.

[23] The interrelatedness between different market risks can be expressed as correlations between market returns (often formalized in a variance-covariance matrix). However, this type of precision does not exist for operational and strategic risk factors.

[24] These calculations typically assume that historical price data series are normally distributed with stable correlation coefficients between different prices.

the importance of the specific risk factor and its relative ranking. For example, the risk e-insurance receives a total score of 21, which is the highest score, and consequently this risk is evaluated as the one with the greatest risk impact. Concluding from this analysis, the handling of e-insurance should therefore receive top priority, as an appropriate strategy for handling this risk will affect other issues as well.

The across row 'total' of measures (*top-down*) along each column indicates how much each risk factor is being influenced by all of the other risk factors – the so-called passive score. For example, the risk factor 'customer leaving rate' together with 'price competition' receive the highest total score of 20, and accordingly constitute the risks that are most affected by all of the other risks. In contrast, those risks that receive very low passive scores cannot be addressed (indirectly) by handling other risks due to the absence of interdependency. For example, the risks 'access to door-to-door selling', 'core insurance system', 'risk management skills and knowledge' and 'solvency' receive a passive score of 0, which means that these risks can only be addressed by initiatives directed specifically towards them.

7.2   Scenario planning – a simple technique in an unpredictable world

The above-mentioned tools are rather static in nature as the analyses lead to one implicit belief about the future. Many companies normally develop their strategic plan based on this official picture of the future, focusing on how key issues can be solved most effectively, and thereby failing to take other alternatives into account. In a world of mounting uncertainty, this approach is increasingly hazardous, as too narrow a focus might result in blind spots, with the risk of surprises arising as a result[25] (see Box 7.4 *Brent Spar – a public nightmare* and Box 7.5 *Nokia – the risk of relocation*).[26]

Box 7.4 Brent Spar – a public nightmare

In 1995, the oil company Royal Dutch Shell gained approval from the British authorities to dispose of the Brent Spar offshore oil container by sinking it into the ocean as the best option compared to onshore dismantling.

---

[25] G. S. Day and P. J. H. Schoemaker (2004). 'Peripheral Vision: Sensing and Acting on Weak Signals'. *Long Range Planning* 37, pp. 117–21.

[26] These inserts are based on information extracted from M. H. Bazerman and M. D. Watkins (2004). 'Organizational Roots: The Role of Institutional Failures' in *Predictable Surprises – The Disasters You Should Have Seen Coming and How to Prevent Them*. Harvard Business School Press: Boston, Massachusetts; and from C. Brückner and C. G. Ciocan (2008). 'The Risks of Relocation: Nokia Moving Production from Germany to Romania'. Strategic Risk Management Report, Copenhagen Business School.

However, they experienced a public nightmare in April 1995 when activists from Greenpeace boarded and occupied the oil platform, just a few weeks before it was planned to sink the platform into the sea. Greenpeace claimed that the toxic residues in Spar's storage tanks would damage the environment. The event received considerable media coverage, and Royal Dutch Shell experienced mounting dissatisfaction across Europe with its plans. As a result, Shell stations were boycotted and vandalized. Further, in June of the same year, the public pressure forced Shell to abandon its plan to sink the platform and instead opt for a more expensive and dangerous – but probably more environmentally friendly – onshore solution. While the associated cost increases were less important, the real concern to Shell management was the tarnished image resulting from this incident and the potential adverse impact this might have on company sales.

According to the Head of Shell UK, Shell had covered all of the scientific, technical and legalistic angles, but failed to include hearts and emotions, admitting that Shell probably was too inward thinking.

Box 7.5 Nokia – the risk of relocation

In 2007/2008, Nokia decided to close down its mobile-phone production facility in Bochum, Germany, and move it to Jucu in Romania.

Nokia set up its production facilities in Bochum in the late 1980s, and received nearly €90 million in subsidies from the German Government during the 1990s to ensure long-term employment in the area. However, in early 2007, Nokia entered into negotiations with the Romanian Government about opening a mobile-phone production facility in Romania. The Romanian Government committed to invest heavily in infrastructure such as highways, rail and air connections and to offer Nokia and its most important suppliers property free of charge to be set up around a Nokia Village. This also implied tax exemptions to companies located in the area on buildings and land. In return, Nokia committed to employ 3,500 people by 2009.

In February 2008, Nokia opened its plant in Jucu. In January 2008, Nokia announced, without any preliminary announcements, that the Bochum plant would be closed and the workforce laid off by the end of June 2008.

The initial response was overwhelmingly negative. Demands for compensation for the workforce and government officials publicly changing their mobile phones from Nokia to other brands were some of the reactions. Furthermore, the state government demanded that Nokia pay back the subsidies it had received during the 1990s, claiming that the contractual obligations related to the granting of the subsidies were violated, but Nokia ignored the claim. However, in April 2008, Nokia agreed after negotiations to compensate the workforce and enter into a social plan amounting to €200 million in total, which actually exceeded Nokia's initial offer by around 200 per cent.

Besides, the Romanian press noticed the above-mentioned events. Although the relocation of Nokia's mobile-phone production to Romania in general was welcomed in Romania, the German press coverage and Nokia's initial reactions to the demands created worries among the Romanian public about the company's honesty and not least long-term commitment in the region.

Labour costs constitute a high fraction of production and assembly expenses within the highly price-competitive mobile industry. Thus, the relocation from a high production cost area to a low production cost area – pre-tax salary is approximately six times higher in Germany compared with Romania – was correct from a narrow strategic point of view, as it ensured lower production costs and thereby maintained future competitiveness. However, Nokia completely neglected the interests of key stakeholders, such as employees, unions, and local and federal governments. The lack of awareness about the potential reactions to Nokia's announcement from these stakeholders demonstrated Nokia's shortsightedness.

Thus, corporations should acknowledge that uncertainty prevails and impose the discipline to ask about the important uncertainties that circumscribe the corporate activities and challenge existing views about the future business environment. It is a critical flaw of most predictable surprises that there is a failure to engage in adequate scanning of the internal and external environments either due to insufficient attention or lack of resources necessary to collect information about emerging threats.[27] This might among other things be ascribed to the fact that information gathering in many corporations is tailored to the current business activities through a focus on key performance indicators (KPIs) and other narrowly focused information, which fail to challenge prevailing beliefs. Thus, corporate management should expand their focus and devote more attention and resources to challenge existing preconceptions and raise questions about what they do know, what they think they know and what they know they do not know. This should help to determine areas where the corporation is well informed and not least clarify where major knowledge gaps may exist.[28]

Scenario planning can be a useful tool to evaluate weak signals and challenge rooted beliefs. The analysis of scenarios is adopted in corporate finance as a quantitative analytical approach to evaluate the robustness of projected cash flows and their net present value by estimating the effects of a limited number of different but plausible combinations of underlying assumptions, such as sales growth, operating margin, new products, etc. Scenario analyses can be further

---

[27] Bazerman and Watkins (2004).
[28] Loach, DeMeyer and Pich (2006).

refined by conducting more advanced Monte Carlo simulations as a tool for considering many possible assumptions and variable distributions, thus enabling management to evaluate the projected outcomes.[29]

However, in the strategic risk management field, scenario analysis is adopted as a qualitative analytical tool. First, it is often difficult to estimate many of the strategic risks due to insufficient data. Second, the statistic models backing the quantification of scenarios build on rather restrictive assumptions, such as no regime shifts, stable correlations and the absence of complex probabilistic or 'fat-tailed' behaviours.[30] It is pointed out that the main reason to be hesitant about scenario quantification is that there is a strong tendency for people to focus on numbers at the expense of more important qualitative aspects, such as the value of insights uncovered in the process of investigating the nature of the external environment.[31] Some even go further by pointing out that quantitative analysts with their technically sophisticated risk management models can lull corporate executives and regulators alike into a false sense of security.[32]

On the other hand, some might claim that qualitative scenario analyses are nothing but unfounded guesswork about the future. However, scenarios encourage managers and other employees to think through the diverse pieces of the puzzle, to organize these fragments into a cohesive pattern in the future business environment and discuss the implications they may have on the effectiveness of current strategies while evaluating alternative strategic options. Furthermore, it can help to make blind spots visible and uncover areas where further knowledge and insight are needed.

The scenario planning approach can basically be arranged in five major steps as described below. Each of these steps is illustrated with inserted examples that build on the previous cases applied to the non-life insurance industry. The first step is to identify the key environmental risk factors. These factors can be derived from the external elements identified in a SWOT analysis, risk mapping or influence matrix exercises, with further uncertainties added as required. It should be noted that scenario planning typically deals with external environmental factors exogenous to the firm and thereby outside the direct influence of corporate

---

[29] See, e.g. A. Damodaran (2008). *Strategic Risk Taking – A Framework for Risk Management.* Wharton School Publishing: Pennsylvania, Chs. 6 and 7 for description of scenario analysis, VaR analysis and Monte Carlo simulation techniques.

[30] See, e.g. S. Focardi and C. Jonas (1998). *Risk Management: Framework, Methods, and Practice.* Frank J. Fabozzi Associates: Pennsylvania; R. S. Dembo and A. Freeman (1998). *Seeing Tomorrow: Rewriting the Rules of Risk.* John Wiley & Sons: New York; and Taleb (2007).

[31] R. W. Mills with C. F. Print and S. A. Rowbotham (1999). *Managerial Finance, Shareholder Value and Value Based Management: Linking Business Performance and Value Creation.* Mars Business Associates: London, p. 27.

[32] See, e.g. Taleb (2007) (p. 225) as he criticizes the increasing use of quantitative models in the financial service industry and the proliferation of 'scientists' among the staff handling exposures. He mentions Fanny Mae as a firm that 'seems to be sitting on a barrel of dynamite'. Incidentally, Fanny Mae and many other financial institutions across the world were bailed out by governments or ceased to exist just a year after the book was published. Not to say that the strong dependence on computerized quantitative models was the root cause of the problems (it is obviously more complex than that), but blind reliance on the dominant 'quant-orientation' has been an element conducive to the financial crisis.

management. In contrast, internal environmental factors are endogenous and can in principle be controlled by the corporation (see Box 7.6 – *Key risk factors in non-life insurance* – for an illustration of this).

Box 7.6 Key risk factors in non-life insurance

We can extract three important external risk factors from the analyses of the non-life insurance industry expressed in the influence matrix in Figure 7.4, namely:

1. the emergence of e-insurance practices;
2. new partnerships, including sales through bank branches; and
3. legal restriction on door-to-door selling.

Although operational and technology risks associated with developing e-insurance platforms and building customer relationship systems seem to be important, these factors are typically not considered in the scenario planning approach as they constitute internal endogenous risk factors and consequently can be influenced and managed by the corporation.

The second step is to elaborate some of the major themes that may characterize plausible alternative developments in future competitive market conditions. The elaboration relates to the potential for alternative assumptions that affect the identified external risk factors (see Box 7.7 – *Competitive developments in non-life insurance*).

Box 7.7 Competitive developments in non-life insurance

Three important external risk elements were identified, namely e-insurance, partnerships, including bank-insurance collaboration, and door-to-door selling. These risk factors are influenced by two major environmental trends.

The emergence of e-insurance depends on the penetration of new Internet technology among the customers – this constitutes the first theme, which may be referred to as the 'technology uptake'. The eventual outcome of this theme is quite uncertain.

The other risk factors relate to developments in the 'physical' distribution structure in the industry – this is the second theme, which may be referred to as 'non-e distribution'. It is likely that door-to-door selling will disappear some time in the future. As a consequence, the outcome of this theme may be less uncertain.

The third step is to elaborate on the major themes outlined previously and describe a few environmental scenarios that arise as the consequence of different assumptions about the risk factors and the underpinning themes that are relevant for the corporate strategy (see Box 7.8 – *Competitive scenarios in non-life insurance*).

Box 7.8 Competitive scenarios in non-life insurance

Combining alternative assumptions around the two themes of 'technology uptake' and 'non-e distribution' can be formed into four plausible scenarios as shown below.

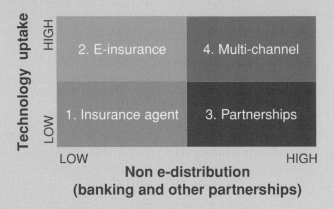

The first scenario (1. Insurance agent) reflects the current business situation, where the distribution to a large extent depends on the insurance agent, i.e. status quo. It is an advantageous situation for the company because a major part of its current sales is carried out by insurance agents. However, it is not a likely scenario in the long run.

In the second scenario (2. E-insurance), the new technology gains a foothold and insurance customers demand e-commerce and availability of on-demand self-service via the Internet. It is an opportunity for the company to develop direct relationships with the customers in an industry characterized by intense price competition and disloyal customers.

In the third scenario (3. Partnerships), access to door-to-door selling is abolished and distribution through partnerships becomes prevalent. It is a major and likely threat to the current focus on agent sales. The insurance companies become sub-suppliers and the element of price competition is likely to be increased.

The fourth scenario (4. Multi-channel) will enable the company to be more selective between use of e-insurance and banking partnerships as the predominant distribution channels. The company can choose between alternative opportunities or pursue both.

The fourth step is to evaluate the consequences of the key strategic risk factors within the themes that shape the alternative scenarios in view of essential strategic concerns and assess the capacity for corporate responsiveness (see Box 7.9 – *Key strategic risk factors in various scenarios*).

Box 7.9 Key strategic risk factors in various scenarios

The key risks identified in the SWOT analysis revealed two major issues of importance with regard to the company's strategic positioning, namely, sales distribution and customer loyalty.

The distribution issue relates to concerns about the vulnerability to abolishment of door-to-door sales, an increase in bank-related insurance and exploiting the e-insurance platform. The customer loyalty issue relates to concerns about how to use 'free space' in the market to establish a distinctive position that bonds with customers and reduces price competition.

These key concerns are important in each of the outlined scenarios, for example, the distribution risk must be addressed in scenarios 2, 3 and 4 and customer loyalty remains an issue in all four scenarios and may be exacerbated in scenario 3 if distribution is handled through bank partnerships where the insurance companies are sub-suppliers.

The current distribution strategy is focused on insurance agents and partnerships across the industry, which is rather narrow in view of the possible future scenarios. This can limit the ability to respond to different outcomes of the possible external market contingencies and reduce the number of available strategic alternatives.

The fifth step is to formulate new strategic alternatives, if required, and evaluate them given the different scenarios. Whether or not the scenarios will occur is after all quite uncertain as, for example, expected trends can unfold quicker or slower than expected or an unexpected inflection point might arise and steer the industry in a completely new direction. Thus, the strategic alternatives should be sufficiently flexible to allow the corporation to react no matter how the future unfolds. One way to ensure this flexibility is to adopt a real options theoretical perspective and reason around the company's strategic alternatives[33] (see Box 7.10 – *Strategic alternatives in various scenarios*).

Box 7.10 Strategic alternatives in various scenarios

The future business scenarios are characterized by external contingencies that are highly uncertain but crucial for the future distribution strategy. Consequently, the chosen distribution channels should be sufficiently flexible to allow adaptation to different outcomes of the external contingencies.

[33] See, e.g. K. D. Miller and H. G. Waller (2003). 'Scenarios, Real Options and Integrated Risk Management'. *Long Range Planning* 36, pp. 93–107, who integrate scenario planning with a qualitative approach of the real option way of thinking.

The alternative strategic options could, for example, comprise:

Development of e-insurance: e-insurance has the ability to reduce the time component of many operations and offer customers access to information and shopping at the time and place of their choice. This distribution platform can also facilitate different third-party services.

Development of call centres (direct selling): a unilateral e-insurance venture is risky as it depends on the technological uptake. Hence, the call-centres solution could be developed to reduce this risk. A strong call centre can also reduce the threat from competing bank-insurance distributors.

Development of bilateral partnerships across the industry: there are two major challenges associated with this option. One is that the quality of underwriting from new partners can be of lower quality. Another is that the company must act as a sub-supplier with a focus on price.

Each of these business opportunities (strategic options) can be broken into a series of smaller investments. That is, the alternative paths can be construed as sequential chains of smaller investments, where each step along the way can contribute with new knowledge and improved understanding of the weak market signals. Hence, it is possible to make a range of small-scale investments in e-insurance, call centres and bilateral partnerships that will provide the basis for collecting new market information as the ventures gradually unfold. This reduces the risk of over-commitment and retains the right to abandon further investment if things turn out to be unfavourable. It also allows for expansion and increased resource commitments if circumstances prove to be advantageous at a future point in time when the environmental uncertainties have been resolved. Hence, the built-in investment flexibilities can increase strategic manoeuvrability under uncertainty.

All in all, even though scenario planning is nothing but plausible stories based on competing assumptions about developments in the future, it can be a powerful analytical tool that helps managers evaluate the robustness of strategic alternatives when operating in an uncertain future business context. It also provides executive decision-makers with the means to think about the need for corporate response capabilities in the face of unexpected events and potentially abrupt and dramatic environmental developments. In scenario planning, the company strategists may focus on how central external environmental factors can frame competitive conditions and thereby affect future corporate performance by applying structured thinking around possible future business scenarios.[34]

---

[34] See, e.g. 'Risk, Uncertainty and Strategy' in J. McGee, H. Thomas and D. Wilson (2005). *Strategy: Analysis and Practice*. McGraw-Hill: Maidenhead, Berkshire, pp. 545–54.

7.3   Adding complexity and uncertainty

The various techniques discussed in the previous sections rest on the assumption that corporations operate in a terrain where it is possible to identify important risk factors at the outset and thereby extrapolate possible future circumstances. With the absence – or only moderate existence – of unpredictable interactions between risk events, the nature of the sample space for analysis can be roughly determined in advance. This situation is used by many corporations to establish a set of key risk indicators (KRIs) and monitor significant deviations, so-called 'residual risks', from the likely outcomes.[35] Appropriate thresholds for the identified KRIs can then be established to represent upper levels that should trigger some form of response. These responses are formalized in many corporations in numerous business contingency plans where pre-planned instructions should be followed when the predetermined contingency situations arise.[36]

However, sometimes the interactions between various risk events are so complex and unpredictable that the outcomes of events are literally unknown. In such an environment, it is naïve to assume that the corporation can design an appropriate and foolproof set of contingency plans, because at least a part of the environment is outside the view of corporate management and therefore cannot be planned for. Or even worse, management can be lulled by the illusion of having robust contingency plans in place. Further, as plans tend to direct attention, interpretation and action towards the expected, contingency plans may lead to ignorance of anything that is considered irrelevant to the existing plans. Thus, in the worst of cases contingency planning can make things worse, as 'a heavy investment in plans restricts sensing to expectations built into plans and restricts responding to actions built into an existing repertoire'.[37] As a result, the corporation becomes unable to sense discrepancies, learn about changing conditions and consequently to take responsive actions to handle unexpected events.

That said, it does not rule out the possibility of foresight and anticipation, but it underpins that planned responses to anticipated risks are insufficient in complex environments. An awareness that all risks cannot be identified at the outset and treated in a pre-programmed way is required. Hence, the organization must possess a capability to handle the unexpected in a flexible manner. Thus, it is an additional requirement under uncertainty and unknown circumstances that

---

[35] The terminology varies. Many companies use key performance indicators (KPIs). However, it is more appropriate to use the term key risk indicator (KRI) in the risk management world, in order to ensure a stringent separation of cause, risk (event) and effect. For example, a KPI could be the customer satisfaction index ($= 85$ per cent), while a KRI could be employee chuck rate ($= 4$ per cent) and the cause could be that main domestic competitors increased their salary package (the underlying KRI could here be the relative attractiveness of the salary package).

[36] While the actions themselves might change, the policies and plans that form the basis for these actions are not changed.

[37] K. E. Weick and K. M. Sutcliffe (2001). *Managing the Unexpected*. Jossey-Bass: San Francisco, p. 81.

members of the organization possess adaptable mindsets and alertness to cope with unexpected events in a timely manner (see Box 7.11 – *Nokia and Ericsson* – for an illustration of the potential importance of contingency planning combined with the right mindset in an environment where the unexpected can arise out of a plausible event – note also that this box extends the analysis of Box 5.10 in Chapter 5 discussing the same risk event).[38]

Box 7.11 Nokia and Ericsson

In March 2000, a lightning bolt hit a power line, which caused a furnace fire in a semiconductor plant in Albuquerque, New Mexico, owned by Philips Electronics NV. The factory supplied ASIC chips to Nokia and L. M. Ericsson. Even though the fire was brought under control in minutes, the event was likely to disrupt supplies to the two competing electronics companies.

It soon became clear that the problem was more serious than assumed initially, making it likely that supplies and any follow-up production would be disrupted for many months (see Box 5.10 in Chapter 5).

L. M. Ericsson eventually lost an estimated €400 million in new product sales as a result of the incident. This was later partially offset by reimbursements from insurance companies. In contrast, Nokia established alternative sourcing channels and, therefore, maintained almost intact production levels. However, what did Nokia and L. M. Ericsson actually do to handle the consequences of this apparent minuscule fire hazard?

Nokia's internal process control systems detected shipment discrepancies within three days. They increased the monitoring of incoming supplies from weekly to daily checks. Nokia engineers flew to Albuquerque, New Mexico, to help out at the Philips production site. However, they realized from self-inspection that it would take many weeks to reinstate production. Consequently, Nokia quickly ascertained the availability of alternative chips to be purchased from Japanese and American suppliers. Nokia's existing relationships with these suppliers made it possible to arrange shipments with only five-day lead times. Yet, two of the parts came from Philips solely. Hence, pressure was brought to bear from the highest executive levels between Nokia and Philips to ensure that all other Philips facilities were committed to use additional capacity to meet Nokia's requirements for these particular parts. Furthermore, a modular manufacturing architecture enabled Nokia to adapt its production so as to use a new chip design that allowed the company to use supplies from elsewhere in the global ASIC market.

---

[38] The insert is based on M. Christopher and H. Peck (2004). 'The Five Principles of Supply Chain Resilience'. *Logistics Europe* 12(1), pp. 16–21; and A. Norrman and U. Jansson (2004). 'Ericsson's Proactive Supply Chain Risk Management Approach after a Serious Sub-Supplier Accident'. *International Journal of Physical Distribution and Logistics Management* 34(5), pp. 434–56.

In contrast, L. M. Ericsson treated the initial call from Philips as 'one technician talking to another' and was content to allow the one-week delay to take its course in the expectation that everything would work out in the end. When L. M. Ericsson eventually realized the potential for catastrophe by early April and then asked Philips for help, Philips was unable to provide it because Nokia had already commandeered all of Philips' spare capacity. Furthermore, all of the available capacity in the global market had also been committed. This left L. M. Ericsson with a serious shortage of essential parts.

Although L. M. Ericsson used single-sourcing of major components contrary to Nokia's multi-sourcing, the case also illustrates the importance of effective information processing, situation analysis, escalation procedures, contingency planning and not least of all an ingrained risk-aware and responsive mindset throughout the organization.

Some authors recommend that the organization develops a general state of 'mindfulness', a capability that corporations can learn from so-called high reliability organizations (HROs).[39] HROs comprise a particular group of organizations where even minor mistakes might result in a fatal outcome and, therefore, these organizations have specific practices in place to prevent this from happening, while retaining sufficient flexibility to deal with unexpected situations. These types of organizations include fire and rescue services, nuclear power plants, nuclear powered submarines, etc. as prime examples. In their studies, Weick and Sutcliffe (2001) have found that HROs compared with traditional organizations are able to sense weak signals and read anomalies to catch the unexpected earlier, comprehend its potential importance and respond strongly to these weak signals. One of the basic guidelines for these kinds of organizations is to impose an attitude of acting mindfully, which in practice means that each staff member should maintain a distinct set of capabilities. These response capabilities are discussed further in Chapter 8.

7.4   Dealing with the unknown

When unforeseeable uncertainties are present and unknowability becomes a predominant phenomenon, the planning-based methods discussed in previous sections are insufficient, simply because it is impossible to plan for something one does not know. Instead of developing a conventional planning template, the identification of important real options, i.e. strategic options, and analyzing the corporate ability to manoeuvre around these may help in assessing the alternative actions available under uncertain environmental conditions. Such

---

[39] 'What Business Can Learn from High Reliability Organizations and a Closer Look at Process and Why Planning Can Make Things Worse' in Weick and Sutcliffe (2001), pp. 1–23 and 51–83.

a real options approach can be a sensible way to analyze corporate actions when strategic exposures are influenced by unknown factors. From this perspective, strategic alternatives will appear as a portfolio of projects or business opportunities where strategy evolves as various projects are selected for execution.

The approach of mapping available real options and analyzing them must, for a good reason, be based on current perceptions of corporate opportunities. However, when acting in an unknown terrain, corporations can experiment in different ways to try to uncover the contours of the environmental context they deal with. Such an experimental approach can be formed as structured experiments where new alternatives are tested systematically through trial-and-error processes that eventually lead to selection of seemingly superior alternatives. Hence, it is pointed out that managing projects effectively under conditions of unforeseeable uncertainties will require an openness to experiment through trial-and-error learning and selectionism.[40] A prerequisite for success here, among other things, is that a corporate culture of never taking things for granted prevails and that all employees are mindful of their surroundings. This project perspective can be extended to dealing with strategic exposures under unknowable conditions as strategy can be conceived as a string of projects or business opportunities developed and executed over time.

In trial-and-error learning, the corporation starts moving towards the best outcome identified at the outset through planning considerations and is then prepared to review and revise the intended course of action during the development process as new information is obtained along the way. This kind of experiential learning resonates with the concept of strategic learning generated through periodic, strategic control processes and corresponds to the cyclical learning models used in development training. The cyclical experiential learning model is also embedded in the total quality control processes, typically incorporating the four stages of Plan-Do-Check-Act (PDCA) in the cycle.[41] However, four key principles apply for the effective design of the PDCA cycle of experiential learning in quality management. First, failures are recognized as sources of the learning opportunity. Second, experiments should be carried out early to gain new information that can inform actions as soon as possible. Third, the firm should organize itself so that frequent, rapid and multiple experiments are carried out and new uncovered information is shared across teams. Fourth, multiple ways of experimenting should be adopted and integrated to create variation and enhance opportunities for learning. Hence, corporate learning can arise from a mixture of formal processes of systematic experimenting tests instigated by a central planning function and initiatives taken by managers at decentralized functional

---

[40] Loach, DeMeyer and Pich (2006).

[41] These ideas are extracted from W. E. Deming (2000). *Out of the Crisis: Quality, Productivity and Competitive Position*. MIT Press: Cambridge, Massachusetts. Deming is widely considered as the father of modern quality control.

entities to try out new product or process enhancements through trial and error (see Box 7.12 *A real options perspective to learning and selectionism*).[42]

Box 7.12 A real options perspective to learning and selectionism

We can distinguish between two distinct ways of creating real options or strategic options: (1) structure pre-planned trials on alternative ways of approaching a strategic challenge, for example, new technologies, product design, etc., where outcomes provide the basis for selecting (*experimentation and selectionism*); and (2) provide sufficient leeways for managers at the operational levels of the organization to take autonomous initiatives in response to evolving events where trial-and-error outcomes eventually determine whether the alternatives will be incorporated into the formal planning process.

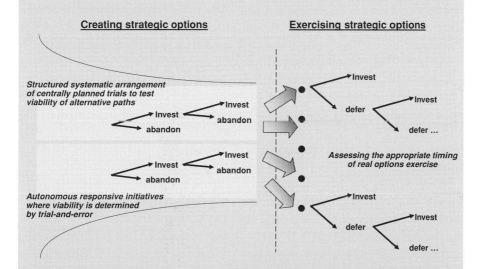

Arranging the planned trials and autonomous experiments in ways that limit the up-front commitments of the firm constitutes abandonment option structure, whereby the potential losses if outcomes are unfavourable are relatively small and the upside potential, at least in principle, is unlimited. Conversely, once the strategic options have been fully developed and are ready for implementation, the issue is to time the exercise appropriately, i.e. to avoid premature irreversible investments and at the same time ensure that excessive delays are avoided, if market conditions turn favourable. This essentially constitutes a series of deferral option structures.

---

[42] Adapted from T. J. Andersen (2000). 'Real Options Analysis in Strategic Decision Making: An Applied Approach in a Dual Options Framework'. *Journal of Applied Management Studies* 9(2), pp. 235–55.

In the planning phase, the corporation can design a series of experiments in a systematic search for products and processes that might work in the unknowable environmental context. All the while, various experiments, including improvisations by members in operational entities, can be carried out in response to changes observed by functional managers. These initiatives are more informal and spontaneous, where individual creativity can play an important role in the development of alternative solutions. The decentralized initiatives are obviously of a rather unsystematic nature responding to unknown events as they emerge, and may not be uncovered for strategic considerations until later after they have proven to be viable business opportunities. Hence, the corporation must arguably find a proper balance between systematic experimentation through the central planning activities and informal responsive improvisations at decentralized decision nodes.[43]

In the process of systematic experimentation and selection, variety is generated through organized independent parallel trials, where a subsequent evaluation determines the most favourable solution. By definition, most of the trials will be abandoned because only one solution is needed or is likely to predominate in the industry. For example, Microsoft was experimenting with several operating systems – Dos, Unix, OS/2 and Windows – during the same time period in the 1980s because it was unclear which of the operating systems would become the most successful. While extensive multiple parallel trials can be expensive and difficult to justify, they can provide the means to create higher flexibility around future options and thus position the corporation better for eventual strategic choices.

When should the corporation choose between selectionism with regard to parallel trials versus cyclical experiential learning? This could be a function of the level of complexity in the competitive environment and the relative costs of the two approaches. If complexity is high and unknown factors predominate, the corporation must choose one of the two approaches, dependent on their relative cost implications. For example, if speed is of the essence, sequential learning may impose high costs of delay. Conversely, running parallel trials over extended periods of time can be very expensive. When complexity is low, the pressure for fast solutions is reduced and sequential learning processes could be more efficient. However, when complexity is more prevalent, the parallel trials should indicate optimal solutions more quickly and thus be relatively more economical.[44] The consequential choice between two approaches is shown in Table 7.5.

---

[43] This perspective corresponds to Burgelman's distinction between 'induced' (centrally planned) and 'autonomous' (initiated decentrally) strategic initiatives where the role of corporate management is to find an appropriate balance between the two. See, e.g. R. A. Burgelman (2005). 'The Role of Strategy Making in Organizational Evolution' in J. L. Bower and C. G. Gilbert (eds.), *From Resource Allocation to Strategy*. Oxford University Press: New York, pp. 38–70.

[44] Costs cannot be estimated at the outset, as the nature of the unknown is invisible. However, over time, the corporation acquires information about implied costs associated with delayed decisions or wrong choices, which can be considered when choosing between the approaches.

Table 7.5 *Approaches in unknown environmental terrains*

		The cost of selecting parallel trials compared to the cost of sequential learning	
		Low	*High*
The complexity and unknowability of terrain	*High*	Selection	Learning
	Low	Selection and learning*	Learning

Note: *Selection and learning is combined.

Source: Adapted from Loach, DeMeyer and Pich (2006), p. 154.

Selection should be favoured when the degree of complexity and unknow-ability of the terrain is high, the cost of learning is relatively high and time is of paramount importance to ensure at least one early success. Thus, speed and cost are emphasized at the expense of learning. For example, the credit card company Capital One developed many ideas, tried them out in the market with the aim of evaluating what worked and what did not work and thereby generated more hits than competitors.[45] Under simple and less complex performance conditions where the cost of learning is low and ex post selection is less consequential, learning will be more appropriate. For example, the Internet browser development in the 1990s made it possible to modify the concept until a short time before launch, which could be ascribed to the fast prototyping of feature changes.[46] During the search for new drugs (cf. the example in Chapter 4 section 4.5), ex post selection can be prohibitively costly because it requires many projects to be carried through to the later development stages. Thus, parallel trials at the sub-experimentation level will often take place with selection performed relatively early, where the early winners will be refined further through learning.

7.5 Handling the different images of risk

The mounting complexity and dynamic nature of business environments mean that foresight is more important than ever, but at the same time it is also very difficult to create accurate foresight. Thus, the corporate ability to scan

[45] Loach, DeMeyer and Pich (2006), p. 147.
[46] Loach, DeMeyer and Pich (2006), p. 148.

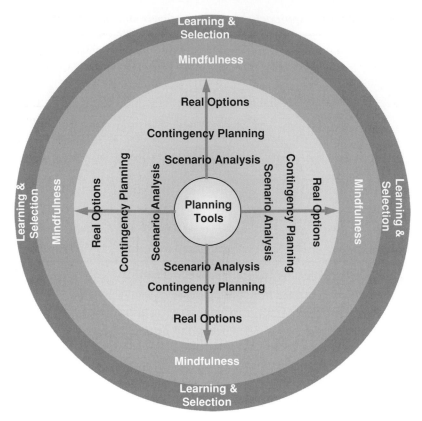

Figure 7.5 *Tools and approaches to handle different images of risk*

the environment for important developments, sense and interpret the many weak signals, and prepare for effective responses to emerging events becomes crucial. The various tools and approaches to scan the environment and handle the different images of risks are plotted in Figure 7.5.

Traditional planning tools, including the PESTEL framework, Porter's five-forces model, value-chain analysis and the like, can be used to assess the external and internal environmental contexts of the corporation. This may also constitute a useful platform to determine initially some of the most important risk factors in the predictable and known business environments to be considered in the corporate risk management process. These analyses can be complemented by scenario planning and real options frameworks to deal with circumstances that are more uncertain and hard to forecast. These approaches may be used to challenge deeply rooted preconceptions, identify and explicate different business opportunities and evaluate alternative strategic paths in uncertain future business contexts. They may also force the senior executives to think about the corporate response capabilities needed in the face of unexpected events and dramatic environmental developments.

The preparation of different business contingency plans can be useful when handling pre-defined risks, imposing appropriate exposure thresholds and planning possible responses. However, such pre-planned response mechanisms can only deal with anticipated events and are insufficient in complex and uncertain environments where outcomes are unknown. Under these circumstances, the organization should try to install operational flexibilities and a portfolio of alternative business opportunities, while staying alert in terms of environmental changes. All organizational members – from the top executives to 'the people on the floor' – should be risk aware and mindful to create a sense of urgency, observance and reaction to environmental changes. This accentuates the importance of a strong corporate risk culture with supportive values, behavioural guidelines and ingrained practices of responsiveness. These practices can include systematic trials to test alternative solutions, as well as exploratory initiatives at the operational levels to test out what may work as the corporation moves into the unknown terrain of the future business environment.

7.6   Conclusion

This chapter has described how different conventional strategic management and planning tools can be complemented by tools from the risk management field and applied to perform extended analyses of the corporate risk landscape beyond hazards and market based risks to consider also operational and strategic risks. However, these tools are rather static in nature as the analyses often lead to one picture of the future ignoring that other alternatives might be relevant. Thus, discussions of extended techniques like contingency plans, scenario planning and real options reasoning to deal with uncertainties and hard-to-forecast developments were carried out. It was argued that extended techniques like scenario planning and real options analysis can help the corporation evaluate the effect of a changing risk landscape and take necessary precautionary measures. It was further argued that practices of experimentation and trial-and-error learning to test out future developments should be encouraged to deal with the unknown.

It was suggested that contingency planning can be useful in dealing with severe deviations in simple and predictable environments. However, such plans are insufficient in complex and uncertain environments where outcomes are unknown. Under these circumstances, the corporation should try to install operational flexibilities and create a portfolio of alternative business opportunities, while staying alert regarding environmental changes. It was finally argued that strong values, behaviour and corporate culture establishing risk awareness and mindfulness to sense, observe and react to environmental changes are paramount.

References

Andersen, T. J., 2000. 'Real Options Analysis in Strategic Decision Making: An Applied Approach in a Dual Options Framework'. *Journal of Applied Management Studies* 9(2), pp. 235–55.

Andrews, K., 1971. *The Concept of Corporate Strategy*. Homewood: Chicago, Illinois.

Barney, J. B., 2002. *Gaining and Sustaining Competitive Advantage*, 2nd edn. Prentice Hall: Upper Saddle River, New Jersey.

Bazerman, M. H. and Watkins, M. D., 2004. *Predictable Surprises – The Disasters You Should Have Seen Coming and How to Prevent Them*. Harvard Business School Press: Boston, Massachusetts.

Brückner, C. and Ciocan, C. G., 2008. 'The Risks of Relocation: Nokia Moving Production from Germany to Romania'. Strategic Risk Management Report, Copenhagen Business School.

Burgelman, R. A., 2005. 'The Role of Strategy Making in Organizational Evolution' in Bower, J. L. and Gilbert, C. G. (eds.), *From Resource Allocation to Strategy*. Oxford University Press: New York.

Choo, C. W., 1999. 'The Art of Scanning the Environment'. *Bulletin of the American Society for Information Science*. February/March, pp. 21–4.

Christopher, M. and Peck, H., 2004. 'The Five Principles of Supply Chain Resilience'. *Logistics Europe* 12(1), pp. 16–21.

COSO, 2004. 'Enterprise Risk Management – Integrated Framework'. Available online at www.coso.org.

Damodaran, A., 2008. *Strategic Risk Taking – A Framework for Risk Management*. Wharton School Publishing: Pennsylvania.

D'Aveni, R., 1994. *Hypercompetition*. Free Press: New York.

Day, G. S. and Schoemaker, P. J. H., 2004. 'Peripheral Vision: Sensing and Acting on Weak Signals'. *Long Range Planning* 37, pp. 117–21.

— 2006. *Peripheral Vision: Detecting the Weak Signals That Will Make or Break Your Company*. Harvard Business School Press: Boston, Massachusetts.

Dembo, R. S. and Freeman, A., 1998. *Seeing Tomorrow: Rewriting the Rules of Risk*. John Wiley & Sons: New York.

Deming, W. E., 2000. *Out of the Crisis: Quality, Productivity and Competitive Position*. MIT Press: Cambridge, Massachusetts.

Eppinger, S. D., Whitney, D. E., Smith, R. P. and Gebala, D. A., 1994. 'A Model-Based Method for Organizing Tasks in Product Development'. *Reseach in Engineering Design* 6, pp. 1–13.

FERMA, 2002. 'A Risk Management Standard'. Available online at www.ferma.eu.tabid/ 195/Default.aspx

Focardi, S. and Jonas, C., 1998. *Risk Management: Framework, Methods, and Practice*. Frank J. Fabozzi Associates: Pennsylvania.

Johnson, G., Scholes, K. and Whittington, R., 2005. *Exploring Corporate Strategy*. Pearson Education: Harlow, United Kingdom.

Kim, W. C. and Mauborgne, R., 2004. 'Blue Ocean Strategy'. *Harward Business Review* 82(10), pp. 76–84.

Kytle, B. and Ruggie, J. G., 2005. *Corporate Social Responsibility as Risk Management: A Model for Multinationals*. Harvard University, John F. Kennedy School of Government.

Laeven, L. and Valencia, F., 2008. 'Systemic Banking Crises: A New Database'. IMF Working Paper, 08/224.

Loach, C. H., DeMeyer, A. and Pich, M. T., 2006. *Managing the Unknown: A New Approach to Managing High Uncertainty and Risk in Projects*. John Wiley & Sons: New York.

McGee, J., Thomas, H. and Wilson, D., 2005. *Strategy: Analysis and Practice*, McGraw-Hill: Maidenhead, Berkshire.

Miller, K. D. and Waller, H. G., 2003. 'Scenarios, Real Options and Integrated Risk Management'. *Long Range Planning* 36, pp. 93–107.

Mills, R. W. with Print, C. F. and Rowbotham, S. A., 1999. *Managerial Finance, Shareholder Value and Value Based Management: Linking Business Performance and Value Creation*. Mars Business Associates: London.

Norrman, A. and Jansson, U., 2004. 'Ericsson's Proactive Supply Chain Risk Management Approach after a Serious Sub-supplier Accident'. *International Journal of Physical Distribution and Logistics Management* 34(5), pp. 434–56.

Porter, M. E., 1980. *Competitive Structure*. Free Press: New York.

1985. *Competitive Advantage*. Free Press: New York.

1990. *The Competitive Advantage of Nations*. Free Press: New York.

Prahalad, C. K. and Hamel, G., 1990. 'The Core Competence of the Corporation'. *Harvard Business Review* 68(3), pp. 79–91.

Slywotzky, A., 1996. *Value Migration: How to Think Several Moves Ahead of the Competition*. Harvard Business School Press: Boston, Massachusetts.

Steward, D. V., 1981. *Systems Analysis and Management: Structure, Strategy and Design*. Petrocelli Books: New York.

Taleb, N. N., 2007. *The Black Swan: The Impact of the Highly Improbable*. Penguin Books: New York.

Walker, S. M., 2001. *Operational Risk Management – Controlling Opportunities and Threats*. Connley Walker Pty Ltd: Melbourne.

Weick, K. E. and Sutcliffe, K. M., 2001. *Managing the Unexpected*. Jossey-Bass: San Francisco.

8 Strategic risk management – amendments to the ERM framework

In this chapter the critique of the existing enterprise-wide risk management approaches is extended with the aim of proposing amendments to the ERM frameworks in ways that take account of unexpected and hard-to-quantify strategic risk events. This outlines a suggestive strategic risk management paradigm that incorporates existing risk management practices into corporate strategy-making processes, while ensuring an appropriate balance between restrictive central management control systems and flexible response capabilities.

8.1 The relationship to corporate strategy

The various ERM frameworks do not establish a convincing link between the proposed formal risk management practices and the dynamic corporate strategy-making processes for framing strategic direction and adjusting operational objectives. The ERM frameworks are preoccupied with various ways in which corporate management can successfully achieve and fulfil predetermined strategic goals.[1] Furthermore, it is common practice in many companies to consider risk management activities and the corporate planning process as two entirely separate management processes. This might be ascribed to the fact that a primary concern of current risk management approaches in many companies is to obtain protection against potential downside effects, while realizing significant cost savings. Accordingly, risk management is typically not perceived as an integral part of strategic management considerations or as part of the creation of new business opportunities, which is a central aim of dynamic strategy-making. Yet, many of the key components within the formal risk management cycle are comparable to central elements of the strategic planning process (Figure 8.1). In either case, the underlying frameworks contain comparable sequential rational analytical steps comprised by: (1) identification, data collection and analysis; (2) evaluations and planning; followed by (3) management actions and monitoring of outcomes. Hence, it should be fairly straightforward to transpose the

[1] See, e.g. P. Henriksen and T. Uhlenfeldt (2006). 'Contemporary Enterprise-Wide Risk Management Frameworks: A Comparative Analysis in a Strategic Perspective' in T. J. Andersen (ed.), *Perspectives on Strategic Risk Management*. CBS Press: Copenhagen, pp. 107–30.

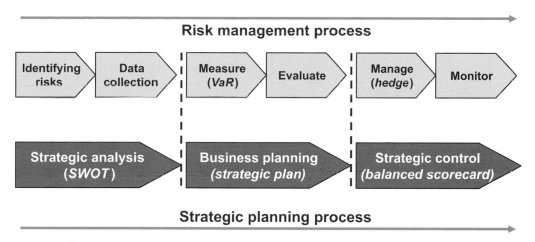

Figure 8.1 *Integrated risk management process*
Source: Adapted from T. J. Andersen (2006), 'Risk in the Strategic Management Process' in Global Derivatives: A Strategic Risk Management *Perspective.* Pearson Education: Harlow, United Kingdom, p. 422.

risk management process embedded in the various ERM frameworks onto the sequential steps of formal strategic planning processes.

The tools applied in the analysis of strategic issues are in many ways similar to the approaches adopted to identify risks in the formal enterprise risk management frameworks, cf. the discussions in Chapter 7. An important element of the strategic planning process as well as the risk management process is to evaluate the robustness of existing and alternative strategies within a changing risk landscape. One of the major critiques of the various ERM frameworks is that they fail to examine the robustness of different strategic alternatives. However, such an evaluation can be incorporated fairly easily into various ERM approaches by adopting the principles of scenario planning discussed in Chapter 7.

When the company has used the scenarios to discuss, reconsider and decide on which strategies to aim for, the subsequent pursuit of these strategies requires that more tactical and operational plans are considered for possible execution. Based on more detailed action plans, phase two of the risk evaluation can be carried out with the aim of supporting an assessment of potential risks for execution failures. These assessments are often related to possibilities for operational disruptions and the probability of environmental hazards. However, use of scenario planning may also turn the focus towards the probable economic effects of failures in the execution of intended strategic plans by using the identification, assessment and evaluation approach. Event tree analysis and cause-consequence analysis may be some of the useful tools that can be applied in the analysis of hazards and operational risks. Once the risks have been identified, different risk mitigation initiatives can be assessed and incorporated into the plans.

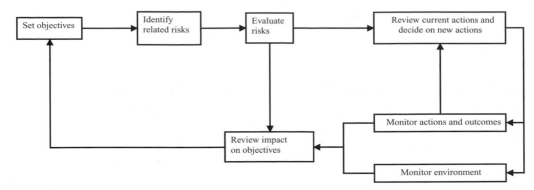

Figure 8.2 *A general strategic risk management process*
Note: This generic framework has been used as the basis for risk assessments within Saxo Bank A/S.

All in all, the strategic planning process and the risk management process can fairly easily be incorporated into the same framework, which means that risk management evaluation can become part of the corporate strategy development process. This could ensure, among other things, that the robustness of various strategic alternatives are evaluated in view of a changing risk landscape, as well as ensuring that risks that might prevent the action plans from being executed appropriately are identified and possibly mitigated in time. The general strategic risk management process resulting from such an integrative approach can be illustrated graphically (Figure 8.2).

8.2   Organizational aspects

The various ERM frameworks implicitly propose a somewhat hierarchical structure across the organization to handle all types of risks in an integrative manner. However, the corporate risk landscape is multifaceted, ranging from simple and predictable events to highly complex and unknowable incidents and chains of events. Thus, it can be discussed whether a uniform way of organizing the various risk management activities throughout the corporation is suitable when execution must handle the multitude of risks faced by the company. Furthermore, it may be questioned whether a centralized decision structure, which is typically implied by a strong monitoring and management control approach, is appropriate for the handling of all types of exposures. Indeed, a hierarchically managed organization is detrimental to flexible and responsive behaviours within the corporation, which poses a challenge on central controls as a universal approach to contain all risks. Incidentally, the imposition of a hierarchical risk management structure might turn out to be incompatible with the existing culture in the company. Hence, the requirement for absolute centralized coordination and control requires an ability to integrate all risks across the entire organization that may be an engrained element of the corporate culture (see Box 8.1 *The challenge of strategic controls*).[2]

Box 8.1 The challenge of strategic controls

The ability to control the fulfilment of strategic goals and organizational actions taken in pursuit of predetermined intentions depends on the degree of uncertainty that prevails in the environmental context under which the company operates. If the stipulated goals and outcomes can be measured with a high degree of precision, i.e. uncertainty is low, then it is viable to use results controls to monitor ongoing performance and manage corporate activities. Similarly, if the ability to predict the outcomes from stipulated actions with a high degree of precision, i.e. uncertainty is low, then action control is a useful way to monitor and manage organizational activities (see figure below).

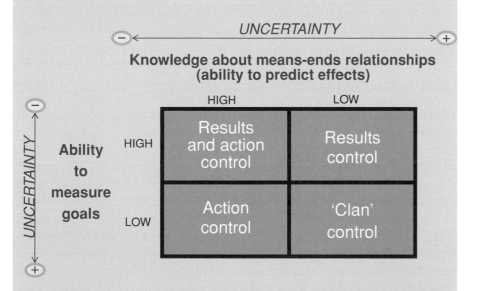

Consequently, when an organization is operating in relatively certain, stable and predictable internal and external environments with a high ability to measure outcomes and goals and to predict the effects of corporate actions, a combination of results and action controls will be sufficient for effective management.

However, the problem arises when the level of uncertainty increases and it becomes impossible to measure relevant outcomes and goals because the

2 The issues discussed in this insert draw from M. Goold and J. J. Quinn (1990). 'The Paradox of Strategic Controls'. *Strategic Management Journal* 11, pp. 43–57.

competitive environment is continuously changing and it also becomes impossible to know the exact effects of different actions taken because the firm operates in unknown territory. In this situation, both results control and action control will fall short and become incomplete as management tools. Goold and Quinn (1990) argue that clan control constitutes the possible answer. Clan control is basically a social organizational structure where actions are driven by common values and accepted behavioural practices, i.e. corporate culture.

This does not mean that managerial accounting and internal control systems should be abolished altogether under uncertainty, but it means that they are insufficient as effective managerial approaches. That is, something else is needed to complement our standardized management tools, such as a supportive corporate culture.

The general urge for integration that often seems to permeate risk management recommendations is partly inspired by the value-at-risk concept developed to address the multitude of market-related risks faced by large financial institutions. However, the need for complete coordination across all types of risk can be questioned because integration only matters for the truly interrelated risk factors. The economic impact of non-correlated risks can be aggregated when assessing the overall corporate exposure and can, therefore, also be managed separately without any pressing need to contain them as an integral part of a corporate-risk-response portfolio. Therefore, while it makes sense to have a corporate function in charge of developing a better understanding of the corporate risk profile, this does not necessarily imply that this unit should also control all risk management activities across the organization. This is particularly prevalent if major risk factors show limited interrelation and require highly specialized expertise to handle. In this case, we may conceive of a central risk management office that mainly tries to create an overview of the corporate risk profile for the benefit of top management, while leaving the specific risk management interventions to specialized functions that maintain the competencies needed to do this professionally. This obviously does not preclude the risk management office from issuing general guidelines to specialized entities or from engaging actively in the supervision of other parts of the organization where there may be a need for general risk management support.

Generally speaking, this means that corporations faced with multifaceted risk landscapes should organize their risk management activities in a way that is tailored to the specific exposures they are facing and the particular risk management needs required by these exposures. Hence, some exposures are handled most appropriately from a central location, while others are more appropriately handled decentrally by specialized functional entities and focused operational units. The higher the interaction between different risk factors, the higher the need to coordinate the risk responses from a centralized function that can take these

		Degree of complexity and unpredictability	
		Low	High
Degree of interaction across the value chain	High	I: Centrally	IV: Neither centrally nor decentrally is sufficient
	Low	II: Centrally or decentrally	III: Decentrally

Figure 8.3 *Risk management organization as a function of complexity and interaction*
Source: Inspired by K. K. Jeppesen (2006). 'Risk and Complexity in Social Systems: The Case of the Business Risk Audit' in T. J. Andersen (ed.), Perspectives on Strategic Risk Management. *CBS Press: Copenhagen, pp. 89–106.*

interrelationships into account. Conversely, the more complex the risk landscape and the higher the need for specialized risk management expertise, the higher the requirements for decentralized risk management engagements.

All the while, a high degree of uncertainty that enforces the unpredictability of risk events and outcomes will further increase the need for decentralization to facilitate faster and more tailored responses to specific incidents as they arise. Figure 8.3 indicates how the risk management activities should be organized depending on the characteristics of the particular exposures in question. That is, interdependent risks with a high ability to forecast and little need for specialized expertise (low complexity and good predictability) should be handled by a centralized function (quadrant I in Figure 8.3). If there is low uncertainty and complexity with little interaction across the value chain, risk management can be handled either by decentralized entities or by a centralized function (quadrant II in Figure 8.3). Risks that are hard to forecast/foresee and require specialized responses (high complexity and unpredictability) while showing little interdependence should be handled by decentralized functions (quadrant III in Figure 8.3). Finally, risks that are hard to forecast and require specialized responses (high complexity and unpredictability) while also showing a high degree of interdependencies need a combination of centralized and decentralized risk management functions (quadrant IV in Figure 8.3), i.e. neither of the two approaches are sufficient by themselves.

The various ERM frameworks typically propose highly centralized processes within rather hierarchical risk management structures, but, as discussed, this is only appropriate in those instances where the company deals with risk situations that are predictable, generic and interdependent (quadrant I). Yet, it may also possibly work in the case of risks that show little interaction (quadrant II). It is exactly in those instances where it is possible to determine the key risks and implement appropriate risk mitigation strategies, including appropriate controls, while imposing relevant key performance (or risk) indicators in the monitoring process. Controlling market-related, credit extension and many operational risks observed within the banking industry may be categorized as such risks with a high degree of measurability, predictability and interrelatedness. Hence, the ERM frameworks seem particularly suited to handle these types of exposures.

Some common risk management approaches include imposition of upper threshold limits on exposures to various types of market and credit risks as well as implementing control procedures and internal audits of key risks associated with operational processes. Similarly, the Sarbanes–Oxley Act, with the aim of strengthening financial controls and reporting transparency in the organization, illustrates how a more formal control framework may be adopted in a predictable risk environment. Many risks within the corporate value chains can be classified on a similar basis within this risk category,[3] cf. the extended Nokia-Ericsson situation described in Chapter 7 as a classical case example of supply chain risk management.

Conversely, operational failures that are hard to predict and only affect selected parts of the value chain in isolation when they occur are most appropriately handled within the respective part of the value chain, i.e. decentrally (quadrant III in Figure 8.3). However, neither centralized nor decentralized risk handling is sufficient on its own in dealing with risks that are unpredictable and highly complex if they affect other parts of the value chain. This is because a high degree of interaction between risk events calls for a centralized coordination of exposure assessments, whereas unpredictability by itself speaks for an ability to react decentrally where things are happening (quadrant IV in Figure 8.3). Consequently, these kinds of risks are more difficult to manage through a formalized organization of the corporate risk management activities and hence other approaches are required in these situations. The attack on the World Trade Center on 11 September 2001 is an example of an unpredictable event that had unprecedented consequences for the ability to conduct business in many of the exposed companies.[4] The reason for the severe economic impact was partly caused by the direct losses imposed by the destruction of fixed assets, information systems and

---

[3] It is predictable in the sense that it should be quite conceivable that parts of the value chain can break down when it is exposed to different types of pressures and extreme events. Even though specific causes may be difficult to foresee with any degree of precision, such events should not take the organization by surprise.

[4] Incidentally, the event was foreseeable and had been discussed by various sources years in advance, but was just deemed too extreme to ever happen in reality.

Is implementation of an unmodified ERM framework viable?		Risk management process	
		Formal	*Informal*
Decision-making	*Centralized*	Yes	Probably not
	Decentralized	Probably yes	No

Figure 8.4 *Decision-making and risk management processes*

human capital, but also related to the interdependency among firms operating within the same value system.

In short, a uniform organization of the corporate risk management activities across the entire organization is generally not a suitable way to approach effective handling of highly diverse exposures. Furthermore, an existing organizational structure might simply not be compatible with the tight reporting structure imposed by a strictly enforced ERM framework. For example, while tight reporting may be legitimate and fairly easy to implement in formal and centralized organizations, it seems unlikely and inappropriate to implement in network-oriented organizations with involved decision-making processes and high autonomy. Similarly, it will require extraordinary efforts to implement such a structure in organizations where the decision-making process is decidedly informal but centralized or where it is decentralized but formal (Figure 8.4). According to some surveys,[5] the call for a high degree of centralization and control is often the key reason why ERM is not being implemented, because it is resisted by managers in the corporate business units.

Various financial market prices and economic variables affect the corporate business activities directly through transaction and operating exposures, as well as subsequently by adaptations in market demand, competitive postures, etc., cf. the discussions in Chapter 3. Thus, the interaction between such variables should be taken into consideration and coordinated at the corporate level when deciding on financial and business strategies, as they represent strategic parameters that have complementary effects. For example, financial market exposures can often

---

[5] See, e.g. S. Gates (2006). 'Incorporating Strategic Risk into Enterprise Risk Management: A Survey of Current Corporate Practice'. *Journal of Applied Corporate Finance* 18(4), pp. 81–90; CFO Research Services (2002). *Strategic Risk Management: New Disciplines, New Opportunities.* CFO Publishing: London; and P. W. Schrøder (2006). 'Impediments to Effective Risk Management' in T. J. Andersen (ed.), *Perspectives on Strategic Risk Management.* CBS Press: Copenhagen, pp. 65–87.

be hedged or diversified through use of financial instruments for shorter time periods, whereas geographic dispersion might be the only viable alternative to diversify the exposure over longer periods of time. On the other hand, not all risks are correlated, and to the extent that this is the case, they can be managed separately without consideration of other risk factors. From this perspective, the challenge is to decide on how the various key risks should be managed across the corporation, i.e. the extent of integration needed to coordinate handling of related risks while maintaining an ability to handle unforeseeable risks decentralized to increase speed and responsiveness.

A main argument for the desire to integrate all risks is that the consideration of all risks as a portfolio may allow a corporation to diversify the exposures much in tune with the principles guiding modern portfolio theory. However, not all of the corporate exposures are interrelated, which speaks for only handling those risks that are interrelated from an integrated management perspective, while the other risks can be handled individually. Since risk management from a portfolio perspective means that risks should be monitored centrally, this approach is mainly related to predictable risks that can be managed through central coordination, as discussed above.

At the strategic level, the company should try to create an overview of the corporate risk landscape and develop a sense for how risks may interact to achieve the best possible foundation for decision-making. This foundational understanding of the corporate risk situation can help to determine both the pursuit of mitigation efforts as well as business innovations aimed to exploit new market opportunities.[6] These decentralized autonomous initiatives may eventually affect the corporation's strategic direction. The more predictable exposures arising around more conventional business activities are incorporated in the strategic planning process and managed centrally. The more unpredictable risks that also may give rise to develop new market opportunities should be managed decentrally to achieve a high degree of flexibility and responsiveness. All the while, decentralized responses should be conditioned by corporate policies so that exposures are retained within the strategic confines of the corporation. This obviously does not preclude lively reporting and informal communication between decentralized business entities and a central coordinating function with open information exchanges that can update environmental reconnaissance and monitor current developments.

In conclusion, the corporation should try to assess all of the key risks at the strategic and tactical levels to obtain a reasonable overview of the corporate risk profile. On the other hand, the extent of integration at the operational level must depend on the characteristics of the key risks identified by the corporation where predictable and interrelated risks might be handled centrally, whereas unpredictable and unrelated risks are better handled decentrally. In situations where

---

[6] See, e.g. R. A. Burgelman (2005), 'The Role of Strategy Making in Organizational Evolution' in J. L. Bower and C. G. Gilbert (eds.), *From Resource Allocation to Strategy*. Oxford University Press: New York.

the risk events are unpredictable and yet interdependent, which may characterize many strategic risks, there is a need to combine both the centralized and the decentralized risk management approaches.

8.3   Organizational involvement and cultural aspects

The preceding discussion has demonstrated that a uniform way of organizing the company's risk management activities across the entire corporation generally is insufficient to handle multiple and diverse risks effectively. Particularly the management of more unpredictable and unknowable risk elements is challenging and requires a combination of risk management approaches. Central control frameworks are appropriate in more predictable risk environments where the aim is to enhance forecasts and thereby avoid material adverse effects from major risk events. For firms operating in more unpredictable risk environments, creating a risk awareness culture aiming at enhancing the observance of emerging events and facilitating internal responsiveness to such developments is essential to effective risk handling. This does not imply that a centrally monitored risk management process is not important in conjunction with strategic response capabilities; cf. the Nokia-Ericsson case discussed in Chapter 7. When Nokia observed the risk signals from the formal monitoring process, they reacted promptly in the field on the signals they observed, involving a number of functional managers and eventually using corporate executives as a lever to bring the necessary contingency solutions into place.

Hence, in the face of unpredictable events where dependencies exist across the value chain, the combination of central control systems and the ability to react fast on the spot becomes crucial. However, this response capability can probably only develop within corporate cultures that emphasize and reward observant behaviours and involvement in responsive actions as and when they are needed. In risk environments where unknowable strategic risk factors predominate, the absence of precise measurable indicators monitored in a central control system increases the need to engage organizational members in the scanning of environmental changes and thereby enhances the ability to sense emerging threats and opportunities.

A study of mass fatality and general reputation crises points out the clear advantage of having the right risk-awareness culture in place.[7] This study investigated the impact of corporate catastrophes on shareholder value. It found that companies could fall into one of two relatively distinct groups of 'recoverers' and 'non-recoverers' (Figure 8.5). The primary axis in Figure 8.5 represents one calendar year following the observed crises, where the day of each crisis has been aligned to the event day as 0. The secondary axis shows a modelled share price

---

[7] Oxford Metrica, 'Protecting Value in the Face of Mass Fatality Events'. Available online at www.Oxfordmetrica.com.

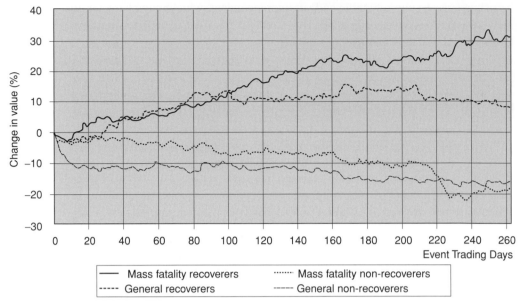

Figure 8.5 *Value reaction to corporate crises*
Source: Oxford Metrica (Oxfordmetrica.com)

reaction where general market influences are eliminated and returns have been risk-adjusted. As a result, the value reaction should provide a fair indication of the impact from a sudden and unexpected event on the share price.[8]

Figure 8.5 illustrates two important patterns. First, the impact of mass fatality events is greater than general reputation crises, as the difference between recoverers and non-recoverers is around 50 per cent in the former case, compared to 25 per cent in the latter case. Consequently, a corporate ability to manage mass fatality crises seems more important to investors than reputation crisis management in general. Second, the divergence in performance between recoverers and non-recoverers emerges more slowly but consistently after mass fatality events than after reputation crises. The authors attribute the amplified value impact to the fact that it is not always immediately clear whether the company is responsible for the event, such as acts of terrorism and natural catastrophes, and, therefore, the verdict of managerial responsibility is generally made later than for reputation crises. This could persuade some corporate managers to postpone proactive actions until such a time where the risk event has been legally determined as a corporate responsibility.

The general conclusion from the study is that the way in which corporate management handles a disaster situation is a much more important determinant for economic recovery than the direct economic losses imposed by the risk events. Similar conclusions are discerned from other risk events in quite different

---

[8] The value reaction construct is registered as an official trade mark (ValueReaction[TM]).

situations (see Box 8.2 *Recovery from tsunami emergency*).[9] A key determinant in the process of recovering the market value of the firm was 'related to the ability of senior management to demonstrate strong leadership and to communicate at all times with honesty and transparency'.[10] Furthermore, it was found that for mass fatality events in particular, the logistical care and efficiency with which engaged response teams carried out their work was paramount. The study further concluded that: 'beyond the obvious moral rationale for good executive risk management behaviour, it is clear that the markets respond positively to firms that demonstrate essential human qualities: sensitivity, compassion, honesty and courage. The managerial awareness of what is required, and the courage to act accordingly, sends a strong signal of skill to investors.'

Box 8.2 Recovery from tsunami emergency

The Merlin Beach Hotel in Phuket, Thailand suffered severe damages from the tsunami that hit the South China Sea in late 2004. However, in contrast to many other hotels in the region that were waiting for government support, international relief and insurance compensation, the Merling Beach Hotel was one of the first to begin the recovery process.

It was paramount for the general management to act quickly and be first with good transactions for local construction companies and show commitment to the hotel personnel that the hotel would remain in business as usual in the future. Hence, the hotel re-opened for tourists only three months after the tsunami and was applauded for its speedy return to business. All employees were offered a role in the recovery process and, therefore, none was laid off as a consequence of the disaster. More than half of the original staff stayed on and were retained in the continuing business organization.

With hindsight, the general management believed that their prompt actions were driven by the overarching values and objectives established for the hotel as a part of its planning process to maintain satisfied clients and achieve superior performance compared to peers in the industry. This realization subsequently urged management to develop contingency plans and install recovery systems for dealing with similar emergency situations in the future.

The reported research results and case examples also illustrate the importance of installing a general risk awareness sentiment across the corporation, while engaging organizational members in the responsive actions needed to circumvent

---

[9] This example is extracted from B. Butler (2007). 'Crisis Management and Security: Strategize versus Improvise in a Turbulent Environment'. Working Paper, Curtin Business School: Perth, Australia.

[10] The market value of the firm in principle reflects the net present value of the future expected cash flows from corporate activities as perceived by market traders and as such should capture the ability of corporate management to safeguard or recover the future earnings potential of the company.

repercussions from major risk events. Indeed, this may be one of the most important executive roles in the risk management process. All of these 'soft' managerial issues that ensure the involvement of employees at all levels in the risk management concerns are captured by the term 'culture', and the right corporate culture is important to make risk management work.[11] However, cognitive biases of the human mind make this a challenging task. Research shows a variety of cognitive biases working against a balanced judgment and decision-making, and indicates further that these biases can lead to predictable surprises.[12]

First, we tend to have *positive illusions*, which mean that we have unrealistic expectations about the future, but not least that we tend to ignore or undervalue signals that contradict our preconceptions. Second, we tend to *interpret events in an egocentric manner*, which means that we tend to take a disproportionately large share of the credit for success, while accepting too little responsibility for failures. Going beyond this 'self-assessment', it further implies that we tend to interpret events in a self-serving and biased way. Further, we might cherry pick information that supports our preconceived beliefs. Third, we *exaggeratedly discount the future* in favour of immediate concerns. Thus, instead of evaluating various long-term options, we tend to focus on short-term considerations. Fourth, we tend to *maintain the status quo*, as we are reluctant to make changes. Interrelated to this, we prefer to do nothing instead of causing (a small amount of) harm to prevent a situation of potentially greater harm. Fifth, we do not want to invest in preventing a problem that we have not personally experienced or witnessed through *vivid* data. In other words, we fail to take action before it is too late – namely, when the disaster materializes and becomes vivid. In addition to personal biases, the fact that sense making occurs in a social environment where people are not just sensitive to what is being said but also who is saying it means that most organizations are prone to adopt a uniform mindset and engage in group-thinking.[13] The question is how companies can eliminate these biases from individual behaviours and attitudes and develop a more rational approach to judgment in decisions and thereby create a more risk-aware culture.

Very often, essential knowledge already exists within the organization, but it is just not located in the heads of those who formulate the corporate strategies – rather in the heads of operational managers positioned at lower hierarchical levels in the organization.[14] Hence, failure to access and involve dispersed but existing

---

[11] While the 'cultural' issues are often considered 'soft' managerial levers, they actually appear to demonstrate significant influences on performance outcomes and in that sense arguably constitute some of the 'hard' managerial concerns.

[12] Predictable surprises are abrupt risk events that could have been foreseen if the organization has been sufficiently alert to central environmental changes. See M. H. Bazerman and M. D. Watkins (2004). 'Cognitive Roots – The Role of Human Biases' in *Predictable Surprises: The Disasters You Should Have Seen Coming, and How to Prevent Them*. Harvard Business School Press: Boston, Massachusetts.

[13] See 'Interpreting: What the Data Mean' in G. S. Day and P. J. H. Schoemaker (2006). *Peripheral Vision: Detecting the Weak Signals That Will Make or Break Your Company*. Harvard Business School Press: Boston, Massachusetts.

[14] Day and Schoemaker (2006).

knowledge within the organization is one of the culprits of predictable surprises.[15] Thus, leaders should actively seek out multiple and constructive conflicting inside (and outside) views aimed to challenge existing faith in current assumptions to create new ways of interpreting the environment.[16]

However, it is quite common not to disseminate local information because it is deemed too sensitive to share across the organization. But it is in fact the failure to put disparate pieces of information located in various parts of the organization together that often leads to predictable surprises.[17] Thus, knowledge sharing and engaging in informal information exchanges as the need arises should be more prominent as people engage in open dialogue to ensure that the disparate pieces of the puzzle can be brought together.

The ability to extract the lessons from prior experiences and disseminate these insights to other relevant parts in the organization may enhance organizational learning and support continuous improvement efforts. Many organizations benchmark their activities against best practices among other firms to emulate what appears to be successful, but active endeavours to learn from own failures and the mistakes of others are rare. Thus, corporations could become collectors of worst practices and use them to seek clues for potential causes to problems and risk incidents.[18] At the same time, corporations should create an internal environment that will permit employees to learn from past mistakes and use them as learning experiences.[19] While corporate leaders may participate in task forces to uncover the circumstances of highly visible failures after the fact, they rarely attend to internal problems as they emerge at an early stage, which, if addressed quickly, could help to avoid crises arising in the first place. Thus, corporate managers should give more attention to the weak signals of smaller failures that often require only minor changes in existing strategies, compared to highly visible failures that will call for major strategic changes, which are much more difficult to execute successfully.

Whereas engagements in responsive actions are often prevalent in the advent of environmental hazards that can impose direct economic losses on productive assets, the same risk management perspective can be applied to strategic risk factors. For example, an emerging threat that is being observed may also represent a new business opportunity that can be exploited if the organization possesses the appropriate strategic response capabilities (see Box 8.3 *Creating an opportunity-aware culture*).[20]

---

[15] 'Organizational Roots – The Role of Institutional Failures' in Bazerman and Watkins (2004).

[16] Day and Schoemaker (2006).

[17] 'Organizational Roots – The Role of Institutional Failures' in Bazerman and Watkins (2004).

[18] J. Baum (2005). 'The Value of a Failing Grade' in R. Mitchell and R. Mattu (eds.), *FT Mastering Risk*. FT Partnership Publications: London, pp. 28–32.

[19] See, e.g. K. Blacker (2003). 'People Risk and Organisational Culture: A Case Study'. Discussion Paper, Henley Management College.

[20] For a discussion of this event see, e.g. 'Building a Culture of Flexibility' in Y. Sheffi (2007). *The Resilient Enterprise: Overcoming Vulnerability for Competitive Advantage*. MIT Press: Cambridge, Massachusetts, pp. 243–65.

> **Box 8.3 Creating an opportunity-aware culture**
>
> When Southwest Airlines was rejected with short notice as a subscriber to UAL, the flight reservation system managed jointly by the two competitors, Continental and Delta Airline, the company was facing an unpleasant strategic situation that had to be resolved quickly if the firm wanted to remain in business. Hence, the company was effectively brought into a position where it was unable to sell its products to the customers.
>
> As senior management grappled with the new challenge and involved the organization in developing possible solutions to the dilemma, it turned out that engaged employees within the company had already used their own initiative to consider ways in which to streamline operations and make the organization more effective and competitive.
>
> To this end, they had already experimented with a ticketless booking system whereby customers could order their flights online on the company website via the Internet and thereby avoid a costly and time-consuming ticketing process. Conventional sales were based on issuance of physical paper tickets that first had to be ordered by phone, then issued and subsequently mailed to the customers, etc., and often got lost in the process.
>
> Hence, this internal attempt to make the airline more competitive in effect provided the innovative solution that could circumvent the unexpected strategic events and that allowed the company to respond fast at a time when there was an urgent need to deal with an acute strategic risk event.
>
> Eventually, the ticketless system provided Southwest with an upside potential that became a competitive advantage for the company as the convenience of ticketless sales became popular, while providing the firm with significant cost advantages.

The discussion about risk awareness and the importance of subtle cultural artefacts in the companies may gain further inspiration from various studies performed on high reliability organizations (HROs). One of the basic guidelines for these kinds of organizations is to have a determined attitude to act mindfully, which includes the following elements:[21]

- a well-developed situational awareness;
- an ability to see significant meaning in weak signals;
- giving strong responses to weak signals;
- being reluctant to accept simplifications; and
- articulating mistakes and organizing to handle them.

[21] 'What Business Can Learn from High Reliability Organizations' and 'A Closer Look at Process and Why Planning Can Make Things Worse' in K. E. Weick and K. M. Sutcliffe (2001). *Managing the Unexpected*. Jossey-Bass: San Francisco, pp. 1–23 and 51–83 respectively.

First and foremost, the managerial mindset is crucial in establishing such an environment, as expressed in the following passage: 'Managers in HRO regard successful fire fighting as evidence that they are resilient and able to contain the unexpected. Most managers in business regard successful fire fighting as evidence that they are distracted by daily nuisances and unable to do their "real work".'[22] Well-developed situational awareness means that managers and employees in general have a pronounced ability to make sense of ambiguous situations in highly uncertain and complex environments. They are aware of what they know as well as what they do not know, but not least they are worried about the unexpected and expect to be surprised. Thus, they are fostered to be sceptical, suspicious and sensitive towards weak signals and faulty assumptions. Further, they are encouraged to be honest about mistakes, raise questions and challenge each other's actions.

Training can be an important way to create a capacity to see the significant meaning in weak signals. Employees can engage in discussions about how their actions may affect the organization in different ways – upstream as well as downstream – and competencies needed to identify and handle mistakes can be developed further. Completing drills and simulations around worst-case scenarios can be useful in uncovering required behaviours in case of abrupt and unexpected events. In conjunction with formal training sessions, recording of all incidents and near misses within the organization and open sharing of this information can facilitate learning about how to avoid major incidents and keep the margins for error low.[23] Good risk management is preoccupied with failure, refrains from being blinded from prior success and avoids the temptation of complacency. It reflects a habit of constantly being on the lookout for small things happening that are out of the norm and that later could spiral into large failures. Any lapse or near miss is seen as a signal of possible weakness in the system that calls for instant adjustments to existing routines to prevent errors from accumulating and evolving into major risk events. Every signal is treated as though it is novel and is probed further to provide a more complete and nuanced picture of the context in which it occurs.

There is a strong deference to expertise where diversity is actively cultivated and exploited. When people come across an anomaly, they seek other viewpoints in an effort to obtain a deeper understanding of what that anomaly means. By involving people with different views, current preconceptions and dominant logics are challenged, thereby avoiding everyone being blinded by the same things. Shifting of leadership roles is pronounced. Many good risk managers have a hierarchical structure, but they have a built-in operational dynamic that enables them to shift command mode when required. This is achieved by combining

---

[22] Weick and Sutcliffe (2001), p. 70.
[23] The aim is not necessarily to be faultless, but rather to be conscious that errors are part of the ability to learn and advance.

a hierarchical decision structure with a specialist decision structure that allows expertise at the bottom of the organization to migrate upwards when needed. This means that decision authority moves towards the expertise, so those organizational members who are closest to the problem are empowered to make important decisions. Hence, imposing overly hierarchical structures may eliminate some of these built-in flexibilities and a dominating management style might cause ignorance around detailed information from within the organization that later may turn out to be essential. For a thought-provoking account of this, see Box 8.4 *Columbia's final mission*.[24]

Box 8.4 Columbia's final mission

The space shuttle Columbia re-entered the atmosphere over the Pacific Ocean early on Saturday morning, 1 February 2003 in completion of a sixteen-day research mission. The communication with Columbia was lost at Mission Control in Houston around 9 a.m. after registering high temperature readings on the orbiter's left wing. The shuttle and its seven-member crew vanished and close to 84,000 pieces of debris were later collected over a stretch across the US South East towards the planned landing site in Florida. The Columbia Accident Investigation Board (CAIB) later declared that the physical cause of the catastrophe was a breach in the thermal protection system on the edge of the left wing. When the shuttle took off on Thursday, 16 January 2003, a large part of the insulating foam from the external tank hit the shuttle's left wing and penetrated the reinforced carbon-carbon panels that constitute the temperature-resistant protective layer underneath the shuttle. A team of National Aeronautics and Space Administration (NASA) engineers detected the incidence the morning after the initial take-off from the Kennedy Space Center in Florida when reviewing the imagery from various tracking cameras.

The foam problem was not new to NASA. In fact, it had occurred in most of the preceding shuttle lift-offs. However, since nothing of serious consequence had occurred during any of these flights, the phenomenon gradually became perceived as an acceptable risk, even though the underlying reasons for it never were determined and hence not corrected for. Indeed, the circumstances around the NASA space shuttle programme enforced organizational behaviours that downplayed and even ignored the potential disastrous consequences of these unexplained incidences.

NASA had been created in 1958 to promote US space exploration efforts in view of an early lead by the Soviet Union. President Kennedy launched the ambitious goal of landing astronauts on the moon before the end of the

---

[24] The insert is based on various contributions in W. Starbuck and M. Farjoun (eds.) (2005). *Organization at the Limit: Lessons from the Columbia Disaster*. Blackwell Publishing: Malden, Massachusetts.

decade, leading to the first human moon walk by Neil Armstrong on 20 July 1969 in the eleventh Apollo mission. The Apollo missions were not without inherent risks, as evidenced by a fire during take-off in 1967, where three crew members died, and when an oxygen tank burst during the moon landing of Apollo 13 in 1970 that was barely circumvented through the intense involvement of an emergency team created to handle the crisis.

The Space Shuttle programme arose in the aftermath of the successful Apollo programmes, but faced tougher budgetary constraints that required more economic justifications for the programme efforts, which also explains the rationale for deploying reusable shuttles as connecting vehicles to permanent space stations. The first take-off was scheduled for 1978, but the project faced obstacles and Columbia was not launched until 12 April 1981 as the first shuttle mission. On 28 January 1986, the Challenger shuttle exploded 73 seconds after take-off. The Rogers Commission – the investigative task force appointed by President Reagan – found that the incidence was caused by problems with the rubber O-rings used to seal the rocket boosters and prevent leakage of the explosive gases during take-off. Despite the possible malfunction of the O-rings below a temperature of 40° Fahrenheit, a warning about the potentially devastating effect of an unfavourably cold weather forecast was dismissed because the engineers were unable to document the risk. In view of this, the commission noted an organizational tendency among managers to downgrade the risk factors even though the engineers had not resolved the underlying technical problems. Hence, some of the organizational shortcomings observed in connection with the Columbia disaster had already been pointed out seventeen years earlier.

The CAIB concluded that the catastrophe was not an inevitable accident, but occurred in an organization with internal communication barriers that stifled the flow of mission-critical information. This structural issue arose in an organizational setting where actions seemingly were driven by budgetary considerations, thus motivating mission management to downplay inherent technological risks and push deadlines to retain the economics of scheduled flight programmes.

The lessons from the NASA Columbia disaster show the potentially devastating consequences of over-reliance on ambitious deadlines as a coordinating mechanism with a supportive culture that reinforces their validity.[25] This may lead to a tendency to focus solely on plan-supported scenarios as opposed to

---

[25] See, e.g. S. Blount, M. Waller and S. Leroy (2005). 'Coping with Temporal Uncertainty: When Rigid, Ambitious Deadlines Don't Make Sense' in Starbuck and Farjoun (2005), pp. 122–39.

consultations with relevant organizational experiences from past mistakes, where employees are better able to foresee potentially adverse outcomes of complex interdependent activities. The imposition of tighter budgetary constraints caused the Shuttle programme to impose a more centralized management structure and more time pressures with less search and internal information processing than would otherwise be the case. Time stress caused a more singular focus on pre-determined solutions and less probing for alternative actions where some organizational slack, openness to change, informal communication and a general willingness to learn from mistakes would have made for a more conducive risk management culture.

These risk management approaches emphasize the importance of involving key employees and functional managers in the observance of potential and emerging threats, the open communication about weak signals that may reveal them and spontaneity in organizing appropriate teams to develop effective responsive actions. However, this emphasis does not preclude a central focus on the consideration for and development of various contingency plans to deal with potential emergency events. In fact, conscious consideration of contingencies for potential emergency situations and some involvement in the business contingency planning process might complement and reinforce the decentralized risk awareness. Formal contingency planning to deal with potential crisis situations will typically include a number of sequential steps:[26]

- conduct a crisis audit to determine the company's vulnerability to, for example, product defects, hazards, key managers, employees, customers, partners, etc.;
- set up a crises organization and determine who within the chain of command is in charge in a crisis situation and distribute roles and responsibilities;
- prepare monitoring processes and recovery plans to enhance preparedness;
- develop alert systems in order to determine when it is appropriate to react;
- anticipate potential emergency responses in order to prepare how to react;
- identify the key stakeholders, including journalists and media, and elaborate how they should be informed; and
- rehearse for effective action.

To the extent that potential threats can be identified in advance, it may also be useful to install risk-preparedness programmes that formalize how observed environmental changes are communicated and reacted to in the organization (see Box 8.5 *Nike risk monitoring – detecting market reputation risk*).[27] The installation of risk-preparedness programmes should ensure that potential crises situations are detected in a timely manner and that corporate resources are directed towards the handling of potential threats in an appropriate way.

---

[26] See, e.g. D. Turpin (2006). 'When Disaster Strikes: Communicating in a Crisis'. *European Business Forum* 25, pp. 50–5.

[27] The comment on Nike's risk approach is drawn from a presentation on 'Corporate Risk Management' by Geoff Taylor, Director of Risk Management, Nike EMEA Region, and financial data have been extracted from Yahoo! Finance.

Box 8.5 Nike risk monitoring – detecting market reputation risk

The June 1996 issue of *LIFE Magazine* featured an article about child labour in Pakistan implicating Nike's involvement in unethical manufacturing practices. A photograph showed a twelve-year-old boy working with pieces for Nike soccer balls. The picture was soon used by activists confronting North American Nike stores. Nike would suffer a damaged reputation and consumer boycotts that decreased the value of its global sports brand (see charts of the stock price development in 1996).

As appears from the development in the adjusted stock price during 1996, the positive trend faded out and market prices became considerably more erratic during the latter half of the period, reflecting an increase in unsystematic firm-specific risk. Such a development should contribute to increase the required rate of return on the stock, thereby resulting in a higher weighted average cost of capital (WACC) for the firm.

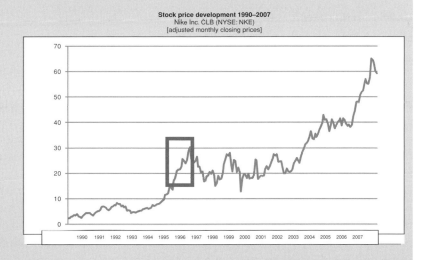

Stock price development 1990–2007
Nike Inc. CLB (NYSE: NKE)
[adjusted monthly closing prices]

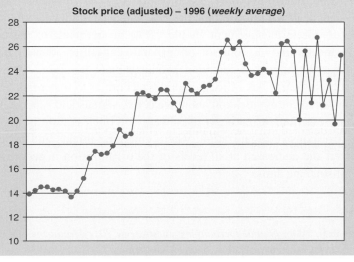

Stock price (adjusted) – 1996 (*weekly average*)

According to the US constitution, child labour is illegal and US companies adhering to these practices can be prosecuted. Pakistan also has laws against child labour, but it has been difficult to impose effective actions to enforce them. Hence, Nike faced an issue associated with the monitoring of external suppliers as manufacturing activities were outsourced to low-cost producers outside the home country.

While Nike acknowledged having received a shipment of soccer balls from Pakistan, the company subsequently imposed more stringent ethical rules and established a formal warning system to detect and monitor potential market reputation risks. The basic principles of this warning system include increased risk awareness in corporate sub-units and formal reporting of emerging risks when they are seen to escalate corporate exposures.

8.4   Conclusion

The various ERM frameworks do not establish a direct link between the company's risk management process and its strategy planning process. However, the key components of the risk management process and the strategic planning process are conducted in very similar ways. Consequently, it should be relatively easy to incorporate risk management analyses into the strategic planning process and modify the ERM frameworks accordingly. This could ensure that risk management concerns become an integral part of the corporate strategy-framing and objective-setting processes. However, the various ERM frameworks propose a uniform structure across the organization to handle all risks, which is insufficient when the corporate risk landscapes are complex and unpredictable. A multifaceted risk landscape implies that the risk management process should be tailored to the specific risks that expose different parts of the organization, with some risks coordinated centrally, while others are handled decentrally and yet other risks are dealt with in combined central and decentralized approaches.

Hence, corporate management should create an overview of the prevailing risk landscape, outline the contours of corporate exposures, identify interacting risks and handle them in a central risk management function. All the while, there must be sufficient flexibility in operational entities to foster risk awareness, enhance informal communication about weak risk signals and support initiatives for responsive actions. Creating a risk-aware corporate culture is important to facilitate a responsive organization, where emerging threats and opportunities are observed and addressed at all levels of the organization in accordance with the general strategic aims.

References

Andersen, T. J., 2006. *Global Derivatives: A Strategic Risk Management Perspective.* Pearson Education: Harlow, United Kingdom.

Baum, J., 2005. 'The Value of a Failing Grade' in Mitchell, R. and Mattu, R. (eds.), *FT Mastering Risk*. FT Partnership Publications: London, pp. 28–32.

Bazerman, M. H. and Watkins, M. D., 2004. *Predictable Surprises – The Disasters You Should Have Seen Coming, and How to Prevent Them*. Harvard Business School Press: Boston, Massachusetts.

Blacker, K., 2003. 'People Risk and Organisational Culture: A Case Study'. Discussion Paper, Henley Management College.

Blount, S., Waller, M. and Leroy, S., 2005. 'Coping with Temporal Uncertainty: When Rigid, Ambitious Deadlines Don't Make Sense' in Starbuck, W. and Farjoun, M. (eds.), *Organization at the Limit: Lesson from the Columbia Disaster*. Blackwells Publishers: Malden, Massachusetts, pp. 122–39.

Burgelman, R. A., 2005. 'The Role of Strategy Making in Organizational Evolution' in Bower, J. L. and Gilbert, C. G. (eds.), *From Resource Allocation to Strategy*. Oxford University Press: New York.

Butler, B., 2007. 'Crisis Management and Security: Strategize versus Improvise in a Turbulent Environment'. Working Paper, Curtin Business School: Perth, Australia.

CFO Research Services, 2002. *Strategic Risk Management: New Disciplines, New Opportunities*. CFO Publishing: London.

Day, G. S. and Schoemaker, P. J. H., 2006. *Peripheral Vision: Detecting the Weak Signals That Will Make or Break Your Company*. Harvard Business School Press: Boston, Massachusetts.

Gates, S., 2006. 'Incorporating Strategic Risk into Enterprise Risk Management: A Survey of Current Corporate Practice'. *Journal of Applied Corporate Finance* 18(1), pp. 81–90.

Goold, M. and Quinn, J. J., 1990. 'The Paradox of Strategic Controls'. *Strategic Management Journal* 11, pp. 43–57.

Henriksen, P. and Uhlenfeldt, T., 2006. 'Contemporary Enterprise-Wide Risk Management Frameworks: A Comparative Analysis in a Strategic Perspective' in Andersen, T. J. (ed.), *Perspectives on Strategic Risk Management*. CBS Press: Copenhagen, pp. 107–30.

Jeppesen, K. K., 2006. 'Risk and Complexity in Social Systems: The Case of the Business Risk Audit' in Andersen, T. J. (ed.), *Perspectives on Strategic Risk Management*. CBS Press: Copenhagen, pp. 89–106.

Oxford Metrica. 'Protecting Value in the Face of Mass Fatality Events'. Available online at www.Oxfordmetrica.com.

Schrøder, P. W., 2006. 'Impediments to Effective Risk Management' in Andersen, T. J. (ed.), *Perspectives on Strategic Risk Management*. CBS Press: Copenhagen, pp. 65–87.

Sheffi, Y., 2007. *The Resilient Enterprise: Overcoming Vulnerability for Competitive Advantage*. MIT Press: Cambridge, Massachusetts.

Starbuck, W. and Farjoun, M. (eds.), 2005. *Organization at the Limit: Lessons from the Columbia Disaster*. Blackwell Publishing: Malden, Massachusetts.

Turpin, D., 2006. 'When Disaster Strikes: Communicating in a Crisis'. *European Business Forum* 25, pp. 50–5.

Weick, K. E. and Sutcliffe, K. M., 2001. *Managing the Unexpected*. Jossey-Bass: San Francisco.

9   Strategic risk management

In the preceding chapters, we have looked into the many ways in which the corporation can manage the adverse economic influences caused by a variety of risk factors. These risks include environmental hazards and market volatilities that can be recorded and thereby have a basis for quantification and instrumentation to diversify and hedge exposures. They comprise operational disruptions from irregular internal processes, errors, fraud, etc. where exact exposures are difficult to determine and are often managed by imposing exposure limits and internal controls. They also count various strategic risks that not only may be hard to quantify, but also difficult to foresee and thus require firm-specific response capabilities to observe subtle environmental changes and enable the organization to reconfigure and adapt. The effective handling of such diverse, complex and partially interacting risks must include a combination of different risk management approaches rather than adopting a single unified enterprise-wide framework.

Drawing on the previous discussions, it seems clear that effective risk management requires an amalgam of centralized risk monitoring and coordinating processes supported by specialized risk functions in combination with a general ability to respond decentrally where new risk events arise. In the following, we will discuss further how these integrated risk management processes may be organized and how they can accomplish the commonly stated purpose in risk management of avoiding downside losses and at the same time exploiting upside potentials. We will subsequently use the outcomes from these analyses to outline the contours of a set of effective risk management practices.

9.1   Organizing the risk management activities

There is clearly a need for specialized risk management capabilities at the functional level to manage specific risks and access professional risk transfer markets, for example, in areas like insurance contracting, financial hedging, internal auditing, legal concerns, regulatory compliance, etc. At the same time, the firm must be able to integrate risk assessments at the corporate level to the extent that risk factors are significantly interrelated. These dual needs for risk management expertise dispersed at functional entities and centralized risk management coordination and reporting is to a large extent related to identifiable and quantifiable exposures. However, as we move more towards long-term economic and strategic exposures, the more we deal with uncertainty and hard-to-quantify exposures that impose special risk management requirements on the organization. To this end, we may need to conduct analytical evaluations of developments in the corporate environment that could be anchored within a top-management-driven strategic planning process.

However, we also need flexible processes that involve managers operating at different hierarchical levels throughout the organization as operational entities are closer to and thus have the best insights about specific market conditions. While corporate executives may possess a good overview of corporate activities and their strategic interplays, lower level operational managers have more direct information and insights about the specific environmental context where many new risk events can arise. The combination of integrative central planning and flexible decentralized decision processes could conceivably be organized to coincide with the corporate risk management processes. This kind of enterprise-wide approach would serve to increase general risk awareness across all organizational entities, as well as support interventions from risk managers in a central risk management office.

Operational managers should be involved in the formal risk management and strategic planning processes to support the identification of important current and emerging risk factors that need attention and where risk observations from the field feeds into the strategic planning considerations. The engagement of operational managers in these central corporate processes serves to uncover important insights from within the organization that may need reporting to senior executives and that otherwise might be left unnoticed. At the same time, the corporation can provide sufficient autonomy for operating entities to take some responsive initiatives when environmental conditions suddenly change and thereby probe for effective responses that might turn out to be new important business opportunities. These probing activities require an active engagement by middle- and line-managers as the liaisons between operational level managers and corporate executives. Their roles would be to ensure that responsive initiatives are reasonably aligned with corporate intentions supported by the top management team and the board and to ensure the economic viability of new responsive initiatives (Figure 9.1).

Hence, we may see the contours of a simplified three-layered set of managerial roles in the strategic risk management process evolving around three hierarchical management levels that oversee different parts of the corporation. In the outer management layer overseeing the entire enterprise, top management is setting the overarching direction and aspirations of the corporate activities based on comprehensive environmental analyses. This may typically be expressed in general business policies on corporate practices. In the middle layer overseeing specific geographical and/or functional areas, line management participates in the strategic thinking exercises in and around the corporate planning process and acts as liaison between the corporate intent imposed by top management and the

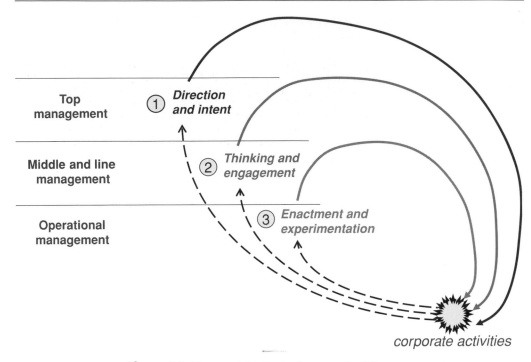

Figure 9.1 *Managerial roles in the strategic risk management process*

enactment of intentions by operational management as they take initiatives in response to observed changes. In the inner layer of functional specialists, operational management tries to enact the intended business activities as effectively as possible, while experimenting with new adaptations as they observe changes in the environment. Ideally, this set-up combines the strategic planning and risk management processes, where managers at all levels across the corporation are engaged within their areas of expertise and apply their specific business insights. The planning and analytical activities will most likely take place within regular time intervals where the outcomes from ongoing business activities can feed back and inform periodic reassessments of the surrounding risk landscape and corporate policies.

9.2 The integrative strategic risk management process

Risk management and strategic management coincide in the way both processes refer to a sequential analytical chain of activities comprising identification of environmental conditions, assessment of the potential consequences of those conditions, formulation of corporate actions to achieve strategic aims within reasonable risk boundaries, and follow-up activities to monitor and evaluate corporate performance and environmental developments. Both of these processes

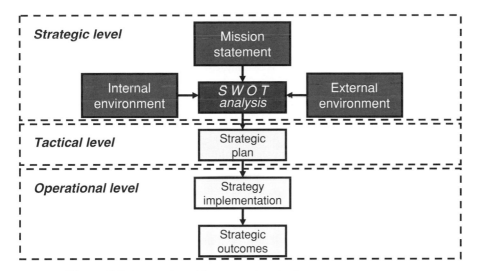

Figure 9.2 *Integrating risk perspectives in the strategy process*

should involve key constituents in the organization to draw on the insights of operational managers that are located closer to the real actions and by engaging people widely in the organization with the relevant insights and knowledge. In this sense, both processes operate across different organizational levels and, therefore, the integration of the two processes should also take place across all hierarchical levels in the corporation.

In addition to promoting the active involvement of managers in different parts of the organization, the various elements of the risk management and strategic management processes also relate to similar elements of the process (Figure 9.2). Hence, the initial part of the strategic management process comprising the development of mission statement, analyses of external and internal environmental conditions, and the outlining of a strategic intent, for example, based on extensive SWOT analyses, all operate at the *strategic level* aimed at providing a common understanding of the strategic position of the corporation and outlining the overarching aspirations for future corporate activities. This level of process activity corresponds to the initial identification of important environmental risk factors and efforts to determine the contours of the corporate risk landscape. The subsequent development of a strategic plan with related business plans at operational entities takes place at the *tactical level*, where concrete steps that could be taken to achieve the intended outcomes are outlined. This corresponds to the pursuit of concrete risk management objectives and the enforcement of exposure limits on operational entities. Finally, the strategic plans require that actions are taken in the operational entities in line with the long-term strategic aspirations, which then takes place at the *operational level*. This implies subsequent actions where middle- and line-managers take charge and engage the organization in the business execution needed to reach outcomes in line with the overarching strategic intentions. In the risk management process, this corresponds to the conduct of daily business activities across organizational entities, while operating within the established corporate risk objectives.

It seems obvious that the initial risk analyses and assessments in the risk management process will be complementary to the environmental analyses pursued in the strategic management process and that these complementary processes both provide the basis for policy guidelines applied at the tactical and operational levels. Similarly, the experiences gained through ongoing activities of execution at the tactical and operational levels should feed back to inform the risk and environmental analyses pursued in the next planning cycle. This perspective also implies that the different levels of activities have different time horizons. That is, the guidelines deriving from the analyses performed at the strategic level typically have longer-term durability. Furthermore, since they constitute rather comprehensive processes, they will only be pursued within certain time intervals, say once a year or perhaps every second or fifth year (in the case of five-year plans). The actual frequency of the strategic considerations might depend on how dynamically the environment is changing. That is, firms operating in highly dynamic industries with frequent and abrupt changes may pursue their planning considerations and strategic thinking exercises with shorter time intervals. Conversely, firms operating in more stable industries may conduct the analytical planning considerations with a lower frequency.

Compared to the strategic planning analyses, the activities at the tactical level are conducted more frequently – typically at least once a year in conjunction with the annual budgeting exercise, possibly with shorter-term follow-up sessions, say quarterly or monthly, to track realized performance, monitor key risk indicators and incorporate ongoing adjustments to the corporate action plans. The activities at the operational level are fairly continuous and constitute day-to-day activities as well as more prolonged initiatives aimed at responding to more immediate environmental requirements.

In this context, the timing aspect of different risk factors should be taken into account when prioritizing and allocating responsibility to monitor and manage the identified exposures. Some risk factors need immediate and ongoing treatment with high-frequency monitoring, such as mitigation initiatives and process improvements. This would normally be handled at the tactical and operational levels of the organization. Other important risk concerns may have longer-term potential effects, as reflected in environmental trends and gradually emerging phenomena sometimes referred to as 'phantom' risks. These types of risk may require regular monitoring, but less frequent reporting, that will generally be handled by entities at the tactical and strategic levels of the organization.

The strategic level issues are typically of a longer-term nature, where the risk management aims are more focused on creating better insights and developing an understanding about major developments in the competitive environment. Top management will try to develop a good and comprehensive overview of the corporate risk landscape and create a sense for how different risk areas are interrelated. More detailed activity planning may try to support the good foundation for ongoing strategic decisions, while the development of a corporate mission, aspirations, long-term goals and core values may support responsive initiatives arising as a consequence of abrupt environmental changes that are hard to foresee and plan for.

The tactical level issues would typically have a medium-term focus supported by specific analyses in support of action plans, development of concrete business plans, performance follow-ups and management control activities. The more pre-dictable exposures arising from conventional business activities can be managed centrally and incorporated in the strategic planning process, whereas exposures characterized by high uncertainty are much harder to manage in a central planning function.

The operational level risk issues are typically short-term or day-to-day con-cerns dealing with ongoing operational issues, execution of strategic initia-tives and engagements in more immediate response initiatives. Hence, the more unpredictable risks should be handled decentrally by managers located in the operational entities to achieve the highest possible responsiveness. These more autonomous responsive actions at the operational level will be conditioned by common corporate policies that should keep exposures and strategic initiatives in line with the overarching direction of the corporation as supervised by line management.

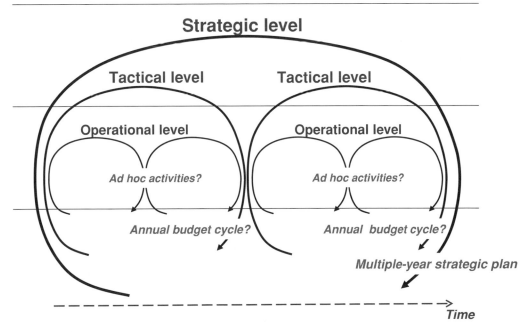

Figure 9.3 *The time horizon of strategic risk management activities*

As discussed above, the timing of risk management and strategic response initiatives at different organizational levels will follow different time horizons (Figure 9.3). At the strategic level, considerations may typically cover one- to five-year time spans. At the tactical level, activities are normally planned for shorter time periods, say within a twelve-month time horizon, and possibly coinciding with the common annual budgeting cycle. At the operational level, activities are organized to gain short-term effects, possibly in response to current events that need more immediate responses.

Hence, we suggest that effective risk management and strategic management processes should incorporate central integrative capabilities combined with an ability to facilitate and engage in decentralized response initiatives at the operational level. This approach instils the comfort of general guidelines that provide direction and aspiration to let corporate entities operate in accordance with overarching corporate aims, while allowing autonomous actions to arise in response to changing environmental conditions (see Box 9.1 *Risk management effects of the dual strategy process*).[1]

Box 9.1 Risk management effects of the dual strategy process

The interrelatedness of risk factors and the degree of unknown events occurring are two important aspects of the environmental context that can facilitate our understanding of how to handle and respond to corporate risk effectively. In environments where risk events are intertwined and affect each other, risk relatedness is very high. These circumstances require a central function to analyze the aggregate exposures and devise appropriate corporate responses to deal with these risks. In environments where risk factors are difficult to identify, measure and foresee, the degree of unknowns is very high. These circumstances require a decentralized capability that can identify emerging events and respond to these occurrences (see graphic below – 'Central risk handling and decentralized responses').

However, contemporary business environments are often characterized by very complex and tightly coupled business systems, i.e. high on both dimensions (section IV in the graphic), which will result in interacting and highly unpredictable risk effects. Under these circumstances, the previous logic suggests that effective risk management will require a combination of central coordination and decentralized responsiveness at the same time.

---

[1] This insert draws on information developed in a previous research project. For a more detailed discussion of how the business entities were identified and how the constructs of central planning, decentralization and economic performance were measured, see T. J. Andersen (2004). 'Integrating Decentralized Strategy Making and Strategic Planning Processes in Dynamic Environments'. *Journal of Management Studies* 41, pp. 1271–99.

Central risk handling and decentralized responses

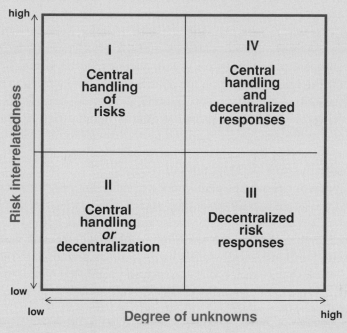

Source: Based on C. Perrow (1999). *Normal Accidents: Living with High-Risk Technologies.*

Integrated analysis and coordination of corporate business systems is typically achieved through central planning activities aimed at assessing the corporate risk landscape and stipulates appropriate responses to deal with identified threats and opportunities. Local observance and responsiveness to emerging risk events is typically achieved through decentralization, whereby managers are allowed to take actions in view of changing conditions within their areas of operation. In an empirical study of 185 business entities operating in different manufacturing industries, data was obtained on the extent to which the entities adhered to central planning and decentralization respectively, combined with information about their market growth and profitability. Hence, this data set can provide a basis for testing whether simultaneous adherence to central planning and decentralization actually reflects the kind of risk management effectiveness effects proposed by the 'interrelatedness-unknowns' framework.

A simple way to pursue this analysis is to split the sample into four segments, as suggested by the 'interrelatedness-unknowns' framework. We can do that by identifying the entities with above and below median values on the central planning dimension and the entities with above and below median values on the decentralization dimension. This approach to splitting the sample into four groups of low-low, high-low, low-high and high-high entities will produce four sub-samples with approximately an equal number of firms in each group. Once the sample split is completed, we can calculate the average level of economic performance across each of the four sub-groups as well as determine the standard deviation in performance outcomes as a rough indicator of the level of risk associated with each of the sub-groups (see graphic below – 'Risk management outcomes').

To clarify the resulting effect on the relationship between risk and return, the analysis calculates a Sharp ratio, indicating the return obtained per unit of underlying risk. The ratio is referred to as an R/R indicator (R/R ind.) determined as the average standardized performance (Return) for the sub-group divided by the standard deviation in the standardized performance measure (Risk) for the sub-group.

As is apparent, the average performance is significantly higher in the high-high sub-group of business entities, which at the same time displays the lowest standard deviation in performance outcomes. That is, the sub-group of business entities that has the ability to combine central coordination with decentralized responsiveness reaches higher average performance outcomes with lower risk characteristics. This is displayed in an R/R indicator for the high-high sub-group of 0.79, which is significantly above the indicators in all of the other sub-groups (0.14, −0.28 and −0.40).

Risk management outcomes

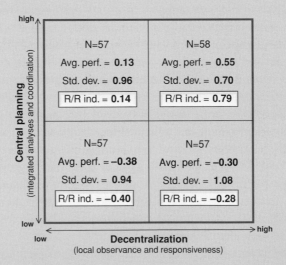

Source: Andersen (2004). 'Integrating Decentralized Strategy Making and Strategic Planning Processes in Dynamic Environments'.

This simple study provides some empirical support for the proposition that effective risk management capabilities comprise combinations of central coordination and decentralized responsiveness.

With appropriate communication channels in the formal risk management and strategic management processes, combined with informal internal communication networks, the central integrative function and the decentralized initiatives at the operational entities should provide fruitful informational feedback over time (Figure 9.4). Since resource-committing decisions are taken at different levels of the organization, the corporate communication and feedback systems will become

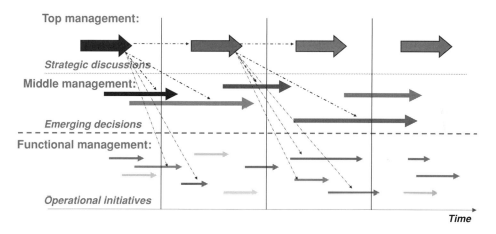

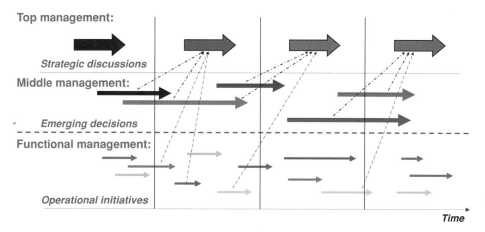

Figure 9.4 *The dual aspects of integrative strategic management (a, b)*
Source: The illustration is adapted from T. J. Andersen (2002). 'Reconciling the Strategic Management Dilemma'. European Business Forum *9(1), pp. 32–5.*

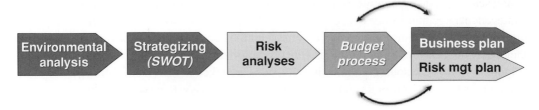

Figure 9.5 *Integrating the strategic management and risk management processes*
Source: Adapted from T. J. Andersen (2006). Global Derivatives: A Strategic Risk Management Perspective. *Pearson Education*: Harlow, United Kingdom.

of central importance.[2] Hence, the directive guidelines and overarching mission statement influenced by strategic discussions at the top management level provide input to important organizational decisions among the middle- and functional-managers at the tactical and operational levels of the corporation as strategic activities are executed throughout the organization (Figure 9.4a). Similarly, the ongoing experiences gained among functional managers from the actions taken at the operational levels can provide important insights and thus inspire discussions in subsequent planning considerations at the strategic level (Figure 9.4b). In this way, the risk management and strategic management processes at different organizational levels may interact and provide useful feedback over time to inform ongoing business development activities.

While general involvement in strategic planning activities and related feedback processes may be very important to uncover effectively new initiatives and modify planned activities, the implied analyses and reports should not be excessive. The formal analytical and reporting requirements should be geared to the specific needs of the particular managerial level. While top management might need relatively comprehensive oversight reports, the associated work at the operational level should not be too complicated and work intensive. That is, the reporting should not become a bureaucratic burden or an end in itself. It is essential to keep things simple, effective and relevant to ensure that the implied risk management process is not over-bureaucratized. This may also imply that a large part of the associated risk management communication within management levels and across managerial hierarchies can be rather informal and conducted on an as-needed basis.

In this context, it is opportune to see the risk management and strategic management processes as conjoint activities interacting with internal budgeting and resource allocation considerations (Figure 9.5). Hence, a formal risk analysis can benefit from a wider risk scope associated with environmental and scenario

---

[2] For a current discussion of this perspective, see e.g. J. L. Bower, Y. Doz and C. G. Gilbert (2005). 'Linking Resource Allocation to Strategy' in J. L. Bower and C. G. Gilbert (eds.), *From Resource Allocation to Strategy*. Oxford University Press: New York, pp. 3–25.

analyses in the strategic management process. Together, these analytical antecedents can provide the basis for developing business plans at the corporate level and risk management plans geared for operational level activities. As the execution of planned activities typically requires resources, the planning considerations would typically be intertwined with parallel concerns revealed in the budget process and might lead to mutual revisions of plans and budgets. While the formal planning cycle deals with intended activities, the handling of emerging risk events is linked to ad hoc procedures related to revisions of short-term action plans and periodic budget follow-up exercises.

9.3   Organizational structure and risk management

Imposing a centralized formal control apparatus as a way to respond to the risk management challenge may jeopardize the ability to facilitate the need for autonomous responses as conducive for effective risk management. There is arguably a need to centralize some aspects of the risk management process to create a general overview of the corporate risk landscape and integrate the handling of interrelated exposures. It may also be argued that there is a need to coordinate responsive actions across corporate entities and that this must be facilitated by some headquarter intervention, as well as by the imposition of some controls to enable central monitoring. However, imposing a rigid and joint risk management structure to handle all exposures may come at an expense because it will make it more difficult to nurture specialized risk management capabilities located at the functional entities, while jeopardizing the ability to react spontaneously to emerging risks as they arise in the field away from the corporate headquarter. In observing how contemporary companies go about implementing new enterprise-wide risk management systems, it does indeed appear as if they adopt these types of central-decentralized hybrid approaches to risk management (see Box 9.2 *Enterprise risk management at Stora Enso*).[3]

Box 9.2 Enterprise risk management at Stora Enso

Two graduate students at the Copenhagen Business School conducted a study of risk management at Stora Enso – a major player in the global paper industry. The motivation behind this study was to provide initial insights as to how organizations deal with uncertainty becoming an increasingly important element of the global risk landscape. Subsequently, the aim was to explore whether the integration of risk management and strategic planning processes can improve the ability to handle uncertainty in the

---

[3] This case example draws from F. S. Montero and C. Bruun (2008). 'Managing Risk in an Uncertain Business Environment – An Exploratory Study of Risk Management and Strategic Planning'. Master Thesis, Copenhagen Business School: Copenhagen.

surrounding business environment. Stora Enso was used as the basis for an exploratory case study to validate and extend underlying theoretical rationales. It operates in a dynamic global industry characterized by very volatile market prices and ongoing competitive and technological developments. In short, the company is a highly relevant candidate for a study of effective handling of environmental risk and uncertainty.

The study builds on the conceptualization of two parallel risk management (RM) and strategic planning (SP) processes that follow the same underlying sequential logic of 'identification' through environmental analyses, 'assessment' through measurement and evaluation, and 'treatment and monitoring' through management information and strategic control systems (see graphic below). While these process elements can be seen as parallel in sequential time, they are likely to take place at different levels of the organization, with risk management more focused on operational issues geared to functional concerns and strategic planning concerned with corporate issues in view of developments in the competitive market environment.

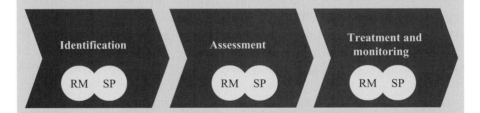

Using this theoretical understanding as a starting point, together with a plethora of related risk management and planning approaches, the study was conducted to uncover the organization of and interaction between the various elements of the integrative risk management framework. As it turned out, Stora Enso, being a foresightful organization, had established a sizeable risk management department within the last five years, but also employed a very significant number of risk-handling specialists in various parts of the organization. The risk specialists were located within the areas of treasury, insurance, compliance, safety, environment and IT. At the same time, the company had established a number of focused task groups to deal with potential crisis situations, including fires, kidnapping, etc. with a view to ensure appropriate communication, continuity and recovery processes. The risk management department reports to the deputy CEO with an aim of making risk management a part of the strategic planning process.

While this description simplifies what is a somewhat complex set of specialized and interactive functions, the study uncovered the dual processes of risk identification and evaluation taking place at two levels, namely the corporate level and the functional level. The corporate level deals with the 'big' risks often associated with strategic and economic concerns; the functional level deals with more specific risks associated with operational issues and particular market exposures. The role of the risk management department in this context was to support corporate level risk analyses and report on aggregate exposures, while providing needed support to the functional entities in the risk management activities and possibly instigating workshops where functional risk management ideas and experiences could be shared. That is, the risk management department did not emerge as a central control function per se, but more as a 'service' entity supporting a centralized risk management perspective by aggregating risk information from the business units and supporting the executive management team by analyzing the 'big risks' (see graphic below).

Centralized risk management

Decentralized risk management

Hence, the study uncovered the contours of two rather distinct risk management processes – one centralized at the corporate level and another decentralized at the business unit level, with the risk management department acting as a kind of liaison function between the processes. The two risk management processes are also furnished by informal approaches and communication lines as an ingrained part of the company culture. That is, risk management is not just imposed by corporate policies, guidelines and formal systems, but is also supported by the conscious behaviours of all employees.

In a completely stable and unchanging world, there is no urgent need for comprehensive risk management processes. In somewhat dynamic yet relatively stable industry environments, where changes do happen but are less frequent and abrupt, a centralized risk management structure as suggested by a stringent ERM framework may work quite well because there is no direct requirement for ongoing adaptive behaviours. However, in highly dynamic, complex and uncertain environmental settings, where business conditions are in constant flux, such a rigid risk management structure may impose restrictions on the corporate ability to react as and when operating managers are faced with new risk situations. Hence, implementation of a rigid ERM framework may be most ideally suited in the less dynamic industry settings of yesteryear as opposed to the hypercompetitive conditions that seem to be the reality for most contemporary companies (Figure 9.6).

A strictly hierarchical organization can be detrimental to retain flexible and responsive behaviours throughout the corporation. In essence, this poses a fundamental challenge on all centrally managed control systems and thereby puts a limit on their candidacy as the universal panacea to deal with all important exposures. The implementation of ERM is frequently seen as a complementary tool to contain the operational risks imposed by conscious pursuit of lean efforts aiming for increased economic efficiencies in a more tightly coupled value chain. However, as our previous discussions have uncovered, this is not a task that can be adequately accomplished by ERM alone if the corporation is faced with dynamic and complex environmental conditions. ERM in its conventional form is unable to handle the complexity associated with intertwined risk scenarios characterized by high uncertainty. This also requires an ability to engage in decentralized

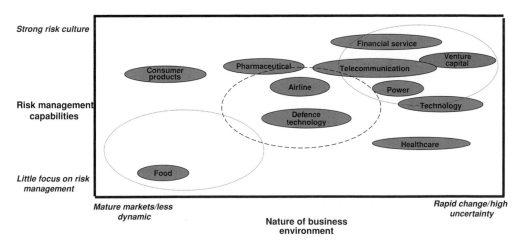

Figure 9.6 *The appropriateness of a centralized risk management process*
Source: The illustration is adapted from C. J. Clarke and S. Varma (1999).
'Strategic Risk Management: The New Competitive Edge'. Long Range
Planning *32(4), pp. 414–24.*

responsive behaviours. The managerial challenge then becomes how to modify the ERM framework, or extend it, so as to accommodate the necessary risk management capabilities in combined central control and decentralized response approaches.

Executives are under much pressure to heed the advice from proponents of standardized enterprise-wide risk management frameworks in a world characterized by increasing regulatory and quasi-governmental demands. Yet, as the previous discussions conclude, the choice of simple one-off solutions may provide legal and compliance comfort, while they in reality augment the corporation's exposure to future turbulent change. Hence, the real executive challenge is to devise effective integrative risk management approaches that combine elements of central control with decentralized abilities to react to change. There is no simple solution to this challenge, and every organization must find the solution that is right for them.

The following section describes a Scandinavian company where an executive initiative introduced a new risk management department to implement what turned out to be a quite successful set of risk management practices that seem to live up to the multiple requirements discussed throughout the book. While we cannot provide final answers on how exactly to introduce the perfect strategic risk management system, we suggest that this case study can serve as a relevant example for assessing how risk management effectively can become an integral part of the strategic management process.

9.4   Risk management at If P&C Insurance

The following description is an example of how effective risk management can be implemented in practice with a central risk management function acting as integrator, coordinator and facilitator of corporate strategies and decentralized risk initiatives. The example is the property and casualty insurance company If P&C Insurance (IF), where risk management was successfully established over a relatively short period of time from initial starts in 2002. The risk management practices implemented at IF integrated the risk management and strategic planning processes, while emphasising a corporate risk culture with a proactive attitude of responding to environmental changes. The practices introduced in IF are described below, based on discussions with then General Risk Manager Ulf Rönndahl, who was in charge of the development and implementation of the new risk management practices at IF by executive order.[4] The approach developed at IF considered all of the intricacies proposed by the ERM framework, but also

---

[4] Ulf Rönndahl is presently Chief Risk Officer at Telenor Sweden, a Norwegian company providing mobile communication services around the world with more than 160 million mobile subscriptions, revenues of NOK 97.2 billion and over 38,000 employees in 2008.

emphasized pragmatic, practical and low bureaucracy solutions. Ulf Rönndahl's stated aim was to create a risk-sensitive culture among all employees that ideally would make the risk management department superfluous within a period of five years.

IF was a leading property and casualty insurance company in the Nordic region, conducting its operations on a pan-Nordic basis within private, commercial and industrial business areas, with approximately 3.6 million customers in the Nordic and Baltic countries.[5] Gross premiums amounted to SEK 37 billion in 2006 handled by some 6,600 employees. The company had maintained a presence in the Russian market since 2007 through subsidiary company CJSC If Insurance.

There was a general realization that IF faced a changing business environment imposing new exposures on the company and leading to intensified market competition. In this context, IF saw risk management as an important function to protect the corporate reputation and brand value by bringing stability and security to the company's business activities, while enabling the identification and exploitation of new opportunities. The overall goal for IF's risk management initiative was to avoid surprises for the top management team and the board of directors, i.e. steer clear of material threats and avoid missing major opportunities.

Hence, IF's risk management charter was not limited to traditional risk practices, but took a broader view of the risk management challenge encompassing all corporate business units and operational support functions. In this context, IF emphasized the importance of creating the right risk attitudes across the organization. Furthermore, a key objective of the risk management function was to create an organization where all employees shared a common view on risk. Another objective was to create awareness about what was going on outside the company and sensitize employees to emerging risks, while creating a sense that risk should also be seen in terms of future business opportunities.

As proposed by many risk management frameworks, IF also saw risk management as an opportunity to create new business potential for the company. Accordingly, the identification and management of risk became an integral part of IF's strategic planning process. Hence, in the annual planning and budgeting activities, the traditional questions, such as *Where are we heading?* and *What are our targets?* were supplemented with questions such as *What risks are on the way? What risks can my department/our company turn into new business opportunities? What risks should the company accept?* and *Does the company have the right processes in place to manage these risks?* The IF risk management model ensured a broad coverage of different types of risk, where each risk type also received particular focus and specialist treatment, and the model included all legal entities and business activities across the corporate value chain (see the risk management governance model in Figure 9.7).

---

[5] IF was a wholly owned Swedish subsidiary of the Finnish stock exchange listed company Sampo plc.

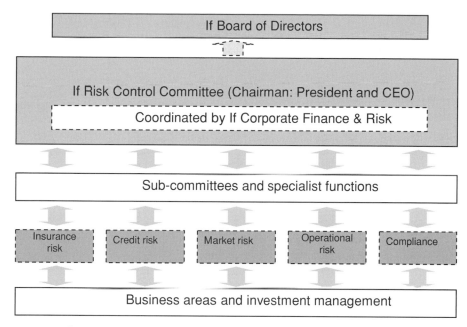

Figure 9.7 *Risk management governance model at If P&C Insurance*
Source: Ulf Rönndahl, If P&C Insurance.

The introduction of a new risk management function within IF was an important change management process that required considerable effort and involvement from top management as well as functional managers to ensure appropriate organizational anchoring. Furthermore, key elements behind the successful implementation of the new risk paradigm at IF included the ability to involve staff actively in the process. This delegated responsibility for specific risk management initiatives and tried to demonstrate the added value of the new risk management efforts.

The risk management function at IF was established as a central organizational entity that engaged in decentralized activities across functional units, business areas and subsidiaries to provide an overarching picture of the risks in the IF group as a whole. The main responsibility of the risk management function was to facilitate the process by helping the line organization identify and manage exposures and new business opportunities to achieve corporate objectives. Furthermore, the entity ensured that management and the line organization obtained objective, reliable and continuously updated environmental information to ensure that business decisions were made on a sound basis.

The risk management function was responsible for conducting general environmental analyses, including the business activities as the central elements of the strategy planning process in IF. All the while, the risk management function engaged actively with decentralized business entities and functional units

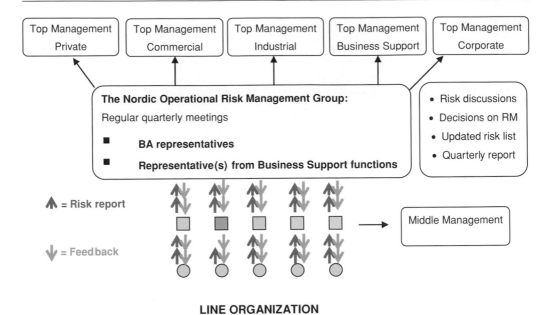

LINE ORGANIZATION

Figure 9.8 *The daily operational risk handling at If P&C Insurance*
Source: Ulf Rönndahl, If P&C Insurance.

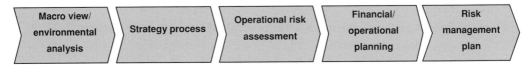

Figure 9.9 *The overall strategy and risk management process at If P&C Insurance*
Source: Ulf Rönndahl, If P&C Insurance.

to assist them in the process of uncovering risks and opportunities that, in turn, could be reported back to top management in a condensed format. Hence, in many respects the risk management entity was operating in a *liaison role* supporting business units conducting risk analyses and developing business initiatives while carrying out the general environmental risk analyses at the corporate level. All of these activities were subjected to the scrutiny of a Risk Control Committee (the operational structure of the risk handling activities is shown in Figure 9.8).

The sequential and interrelated nature of the corporate strategy and risk management activities is shown in Figure 9.9 and illustrates the close link between the strategic planning and risk management processes in the company.

The sequencing and specific timetable for the risk management activities at IF during the calendar year 2007 is shown in Figure 9.10.

Ulf Rönndahl emphasizes the importance of the environmental macro analysis and the continuous looking out for environmental changes, which is an integral part of creating a company-wide risk-awareness culture. As allegedly stated by the

2006	2007											
Dec.	Jan.	Feb.	March	April	May	June	July	Aug.	Sept.	Oct.	Nov.
Environmental macro analysis	Risk assessment interviews				Risk assess-ment workshops	Report			Approved risk lists updated		
		Risk Committee meetings				Risk Committee meetings			Risk Committee meetings		
✓ Incident analysis. Reported by RM quarterly. ✓ Environmental watch. Reported by RM on demand. ✓ Key risk indicators. Reported by RM quarterly. ✓ Process-based risk assessments according to plan.											

Figure 9.10 *Timetable for risk management activities at If P&C Insurance in 2007*

Source: Based on information from Ulf Rönndahl, If P & C Insurance.

famous Canadian ice hockey player Wayne Gretsky: 'The key to winning the game is getting first to where the puck is going next.' The overall environmental analyses and macro perspectives are conceived as four elements: (1) the macroeconomic environment and market conditions; (2) the short-term opportunities and threats; (3) the long-term trends; and (4) the emerging risks and opportunities (Figure 9.11). The environmental analyses foster three basic concerns: (1) the potential short-term and longer-term effects of environmental incidents on IF's businesses; (2) the economic impact of the environmental incidents on IF's future business potential; and (3) the timing of environmental incidents and business effects. The environmental macro analysis would feed directly into the formal strategic planning process, where the robustness of the strategy is being evaluated based on a scenario planning approach.

The process starts by appointing representatives from the central departments of sales, marketing, legal, HR, underwriting, claims, etc., as well as the different business units. The various support function and business area (BA) representatives bring qualified views on what is happening both within and outside their own areas of responsibility. They provide a written report to the other members for prior study in preparation for the first workshop. The risk management function would then take a lead in the workshop and manage a general discussion or brain-storming session challenging all participants with relevant questions.

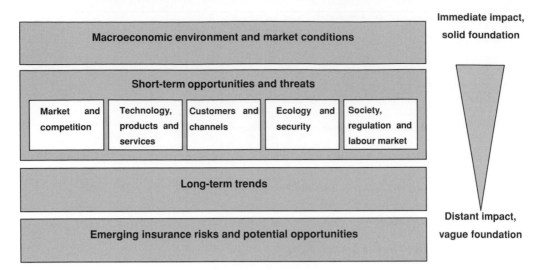

Figure 9.11 *The environmental analysis and the continuous lookout at If P&C Insurance*
Source: Ulf Rönndahl, If P&C Insurance.

Some of these questions might include the following:

Relevancy

- How relevant is this environmental incident for our business?
- Think 'around the corner' ... what does this incident mean in a longer-term perspective?

Degree of influence

- How much will this environmental incident influence our business?

Timetable

- When will this environmental incident become a significant factor for our business?

The different environmental incidents that arise from this process, including evolving trends and weak signals on new developments, would be registered. Each incident would then be assessed, with scores assigned on the dimensions of 'potential economic impact' and 'expected time horizon' for these effects. This exercise is conducted across the various business units and functional areas to uncover all incidents of potential significance to the corporation. The scores would

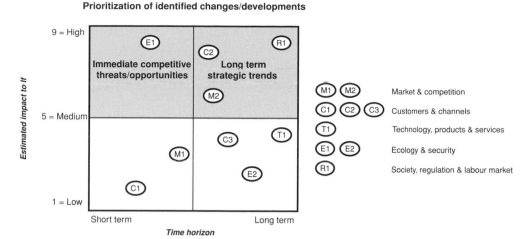

Figure 9.12 *Assessing expected impact and timing of risk events*
Source: Ulf Rönndahl, If P&C Insurance.

then be mapped on an impact-time matrix for further analyses and discussions (Figure 9.12).

All information from the brain-storming session would be collected in a report entitled 'Threats and opportunities in an environmental perspective' to document the key discussion points from the session. This document then forms the beginning of the corporate strategy or strategic planning process. Hence, this approach very much constitutes a bottom-up process, where line managers and functional specialists bring forward information and insights from their diverse business perspectives. However, the process is also top-driven in the sense that top management initiates and encourages these initial activities. All of the emerging insurance risks and potential opportunities identified and prioritized as being sufficiently important for the company will then be appointed to a 'risk owner'. This person will be in charge of tracking the risks and opportunities on an ongoing basis and report on new relevant developments every quarter to the risk management department.

At the same time, the macro environment is also scanned on an ongoing basis by members of the central risk management function. Their role is to monitor both internal and external environmental developments and major events from various sources, including the company incident reporting systems and different news agents, etc. Furthermore, the risk management function is informed about crises and serious incidents that may occur in different IF entities. They also observe risk incidents in other firms that are thought to have relevance for IF as suitable case examples for learning and improving. Thus, IF is not just focused on its own internal incidents, but also scans for events among other organizations

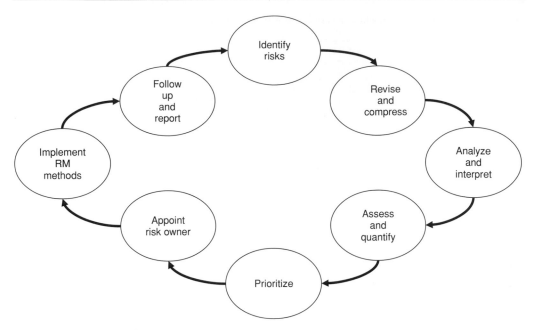

Figure 9.13 *The operational risk management process at If P&C Insurance*
Source: Based on information from Ulf Rönndahl, If P&C Insurance.

to learn from their deeds. Thus, the organization's attitude is that it can learn much from the successes and failures experienced by other organizations.

Once the formal strategic intent has been outlined, an 'operational' risk assessment is carried out to ensure that risks that might interfere with the realization of the intended strategy would be identified and somehow mitigated. The outcomes of these risk assessment activities at the functional level are then channelled back into the strategic planning process where the risk assessments might require changes to the initial outline of the corporate strategy. This operational risk management cycle is shown in Figure 9.13.

The identified risks would then be determined and evaluated using various methods, such as executive interviews, and questionnaires to top, middle and functional managers including key personnel and staff in the line organization. In addition, workshops are held within each of the business areas and functional units. Furthermore, processes would be selected across different parts of the organization and exposed to thorough internal scrutiny to identify risks and areas for improvement. These common exercises also serve to ensure that definitions of various risk areas are tailored and understood by everyone in the organization.

Although IF is trying to quantify exposures as much as possible, it is quite aware that not everything that counts can be counted. Therefore, a very important task for the risk management function would be to develop and train staff to become their own risk managers. That was done in a simple and uncomplicated way from the outset by raising questions such as:

- Which are the five greatest risks in the business that prevent us from achieving set targets?
- What is happening outside IF that might affect the business?
- Where should I turn when I identify a risk that I cannot handle myself?
- Where should I turn if incidents occur in the business?
- What vital and critical processes are the risks interrelated with?
- Which controls are in place to monitor and manage the risk?

These training sessions are further supported by simulation runs and exercises around contingency plans.

However, training is not enough. The organization must be able to develop a corporate culture that engages all employees around the importance of risk awareness to avoid severe losses and develop new business opportunities. Based on the experience of risk management at IF, Ulf Rönndahl has listed what he believes are some of the key components to ensure that all members of staff develop the right attitude to risk:

(1) Support from the top:
  - the right scope from top management;
  - a statement from the CEO on the intranet;
  - mention by the CEO in the weekly letter;
  - a message from the CEO to top management that the process is vital for the company.
(2) A process that adds value:
  - the employees develop an understanding of why the process was introduced into the organization;
  - the employees can see the value created from the process and the benefits to the organization;
  - the value for the individual employee is made visible in a clear and unambiguous manner.
(3) The employees are able to exert their influence on the process.
(4) The company is prepared to adjust, adapt and change the process.

9.5 Conclusion

In this chapter we have discussed how the treatment of hazards and market-based risks in conventional risk management practices can be linked with the corporate strategic management process. The risk management and strategic planning cycles are largely corresponding and thus should make it possible to coordinate and integrate the activities of the two processes. Thereby, top management concerns about overarching strategic issues can frame a general direction for the risk management activities, while decentralized risk considerations can provide useful inputs from the field to the central strategy concerns.

It is argued that the introduction of conjoint and complementary processes of central integrative planning approaches and the ability to take decentralized responsive initiatives to changing conditions and experiment with effective solutions can lead to superior risk outcomes. The potential benefits of combined central risk integration and the ability to respond with autonomous initiatives is analyzed based on empirical evidence and provides support for this proposition. That is, we round off the discussion of effective risk management practices by demonstrating that central controls may be a necessary prerequisite, but are insufficient by themselves to manage contemporary risk environments characterized by uncertainty, unpredictability and unknowability. In contrast, it seems like combinations of central integrative risk management competencies with decentralized responsive risk initiatives generally lead to the best risk–return performance outcomes.

These general observations are illustrated in a concrete case of an organization that recently and successfully introduced a set of risk management practices based on integrative risk and strategic management processes. The basic success factors in this venture include support from top executives, use of effective processes dismissing bureaucracy, inviting engagement and providing influence, adopting suggestions for change, getting everyone onboard and demonstrating the potential benefits to the business.

References

Andersen, T. J., 2002. 'Reconciling the Strategic Management Dilemma'. *European Business Forum* 9(1), pp. 32–5.

2004. 'Integrating Decentralized Strategy Making and Strategic Planning Processes in Dynamic Environments'. *Journal of Management Studies* 41, pp. 1271–99.

2006. *Global Derivatives: A Strategic Risk Management Perspective*. Pearson Education: Harlow, United Kingdom.

Bower, J. L., Doz, Y. and Gilbert, C. G., 2005. 'Linking Resource Allocation to Strategy' in Bower, J. L. and Gilbert, C. G. (eds.), *From Resource Allocation to Strategy*. Oxford University Press: New York, pp. 3–25.

Bower, J. L. and Gilbert, C. G. (eds.), 2005. *From Resource Allocation to Strategy*. Oxford University Press: New York.

Clarke, C. J. and Varma, S., 1999. 'Strategic Risk Management: The New Competitive Edge'. *Long Range Planning* 32(4), pp. 414–24.

Montero, F. S. and Bruun, C., 2008. 'Managing Risk in an Uncertain Business Environment – An Exploratory Study of Risk Management and Strategic Planning'. Master Thesis, Copenhagen Business School: Copenhagen.

Perrow, C., 1999. *Normal Accidents: Living with High-Risk Technologies*. Princeton University Press: New Jersey.

10 Postscriptum

The preceding nine chapters have covered many aspects of risk management, ranging from highly developed techniques dealing with different financial market volatilities and insurable risk phenomena to newer enterprise-wide approaches that also try to incorporate operational and strategic exposures. The discussion throughout these chapters has revealed a number of technical and rather sophisticated approaches to dealing with specific types of risk in highly professionalized market contexts. This clearly illustrates that a high degree of specialization is needed if organizations want to take advantage of the wide possibilities to obtain covers for and hedge against different exposures. These professional risk markets continue to evolve and introduce new opportunities to diversify excess exposures. At the same time, the discussions uncover a need to consider how different risks may interact and thereby show potential conjoint effects on aggregate corporate exposures. To the extent that the corporation is faced with positive or negative co-variations between some of the essential risk factors, there is a need to assess corporate exposures on an enterprise-wide basis. This overarching concern has obviously been an essential motivator for the introduction of different enterprise risk management frameworks that try to embrace all types of corporate exposures. As appears, the concerns for different sets of professional risk expertise and integrative considerations of corporate exposures point towards the simultaneous needs for professional skills dispersed within the organization and centralized analytical competencies.

While various enterprise-wide risk management approaches are aiming to satisfy these contemporaneous requirements, the need for integration, coordination and central controls seem to drive many of these approaches[1] and thereby challenge the corporate ability to deal effectively with uncertain events that are hard to forecast. Hence, the conventional enterprise risk management frameworks are deemed insufficient in dealing with the new risk landscape characterized by higher uncertainty and a large component of *unknowability* about future developments and events. That is, the major risk management problems seem to arise when the environmental context evolves, and sometimes quite abruptly, in entirely new and unexpected directions, where the records of past events no longer serve as a viable

---

[1] E.g. the Committee of Sponsoring Organizations of the Treadway Commission (COSO) initially introduced an open standard for internal controls more than ten years ago, which was subsequently extended into an open standard for risk management referred to as enterprise risk management (ERM).

basis for predictions about the future. This goes for situations of financial market crisis, operational disruptions caused by environmental hazards and internal misconduct as well as competitive moves, technology leaps, paradigmatic shifts in industry structure, major socio-political developments, etc. Hence, effective risk management is increasingly being challenged by a corporate ability to respond to sudden and unexpected circumstances. This constitutes an entirely new aspect of the risk management challenge that needs to be incorporated into the current ERM frameworks.

The analyses presented in this book suggest that effective responses require a more complex organizational set-up that leaves room for both specialized professional risk management entities and a centralized analytical risk management function, combined with the ability to engage in decentralized risk initiatives in the operational entities. In fact, a singular focus on centralized controls within a very tight ERM framework can be detrimental to an organization's ability to respond to unforeseeable events because it tends to keep the organization operating along a predetermined track that may become increasingly inappropriate as environmental conditions change. To accommodate the multifaceted risk management requirements of the contemporary risk landscape, we suggest that the central risk management department takes on the special role of a facilitating liaison function with a range of tasks to oversee. The risk management department should ensure that:

- sufficient risk management expertise is handled by internal professional units;
- major risk areas are managed professionally;
- operational entities receive encouragement and support in hands-on risk management handling;
- strategic risk policies are outlined and communicated;
- dispersed risk identification and response initiatives are noted, monitored and reported; and
- the overarching multifaceted corporate risk landscape and current developments in it are brought to the attention of top management and the corporate board.

Incidentally, these multiple tasks may very conveniently be integrated as coinciding elements of various parts of the corporate planning process comprising extensive environmental analysis and consideration about possible strategic options for dealing with significant corporate exposures.

All of this appears quite convincing and appealing. Yet, the astute manager may ask him- or herself whether this idealized state of affairs is attainable and, if so, how it can be achieved. To this effect, the book presents a practical example that constitutes a quite pragmatic approach to effective risk management practices. For organizations that have never thought in terms of risk or concepts that may resemble risk awareness and strategic responsiveness, the introduction of a risk management system may be challenging. Indeed, it may represent a major change in the management process. The effective risk management model comprises an amalgam of risk practices handled by specialized units, decentralized operational risk initiatives and a central liaising risk management function. A formal risk management system can be described in terms of types of reports, contents, reporting frequencies, regular committee meetings, locations, timing, process cycles, etc. However, given the requirement for specialized risk professionals and decentralized risk respondents, there is also a need for informal processes and communication channels that allow a free flow of risk information to pass between individuals located in different functional entities and management levels on an as-need basis. Many of these informal activities are embedded in the ingrained beliefs, values and behaviours of employees at all levels of the organization. The features of such a predominant corporate culture matter significantly for potential success when new risk management practices are imposed on the organization.[2]

While we recognize that the introduction of a new risk management approach can constitute a major managerial challenge, change management is not the central theme of the book. Yet, we feel compelled to pinpoint a number of resemblances between the proposed effective risk management model and some of the leading change management propositions. Before getting to this it may be worthwhile to re-emphasize that when we relate to the need for a particular set of risk management practices, it does not operate in the context of a conventional planning-directing-implementing framework.[3] Rather the proposed risk management practices operate from the assumption that an important part of the executive risk management role is to provide a foundation for all members of the organization to act and interact in ways that are conducive to generate effective risk management outcomes.[4] In other words, while top management tries to outline general directions for the organization in view of all the things that happen in and around it, top management should also be very cognizant about what happens in the periphery of the corporation. This means that some leeway is left to organizational members to act in response to emerging risks within their particular areas of responsibility.[5] Ideally, this will allow the organization to engage in ongoing adjustments to operating processes, technology adaption, and product and service developments and may serve to align the corporation with

---

[2] According to Schein (2004), corporate culture involves common sharing of beliefs, attitudes, values and assumptions that distinguish corporate members from other groups. To change the way in which an organization operates, these shared assumptions must be challenged to unfreeze existing commonalities and open up for new interpretations, e.g. by introducing new disturbing data that create discomfort and anxiety. This could, for example, comprise identification of serious new risks that must be handled for continued survival, etc. See E. H. Schein (2004). *Organizational Culture and Leadership* (3rd edn). Jossey-Bass: San Francisco.

[3] By comparison, the major ERM frameworks, including COSO, link the risk management to formal control processes around fulfilment of predetermined strategic and operational goals, which is consistent with the conventional strategic planning model. However, such an approach runs the risk of ignoring the need for adaptive strategic moves as environmental conditions change, particularly if these risk management practices are strictly enforced.

[4] In principle, the organizational members comprise directors, executives, managers, specialists, employees and all of the other people who work around the organization to make it tick.

[5] In many ways this resonates with Jeffrey Pfeffer's ideas about 'people-centered strategies' as organizational members manage essential stakeholder relationships and engage in experimentation around organizational relationships in response to emerging circumstances. See, e.g. J. Pfeffer (2007). *What Were They Thinking? Unconventional Wisdom About Management*. Harvard Business School Press: Boston, Massachusetts.

changing environmental conditions. In the absence of these response capabilities, the organization may become increasingly misaligned with effective processes and new technologies, while gradually getting out of tune with changing customer demands. If this kind of creeping misalignment is allowed to develop excessively, the corporation will eventually end in a situation that requires major and dramatic organizational changes for it to survive.

This view of corporate risk leadership and organizational risk management activities resonates with some of the key points emphasized by pre-eminent change management scholars. For example, John Kotter impresses on management that in addition to creating a sense of urgency and engaging key constituents in the process of change, it is essential to create a common understanding or vision about the need and potential advantages of effective risk management practices.[6] This should be communicated clearly and repeatedly throughout the organization, while constantly circumventing potential obstacles along the way. That is, there is a need for an active top management role, but it is inductive and persuasive rather than operational in nature. It is a leadership function to develop general direction, align common interests and motivate all organizational members to engage in the process. Once the road for change is prepared by instilling a commonly accepted risk management vision, Kotter recommends that employees be empowered for broad-based action. This means that any structural and managerial barriers must be eliminated to allow employees to pursue risk initiatives possibly in collaboration with employees in other functional entities as may be deemed relevant – that is, opening up for the development of new ideas and taking initiatives to test things out through new actions while engaging everyone in risk-aware behaviours that may both foresee major risks and identify areas for operational improvement and new business development. The latter parts of Kotter's change model emphasize the need to sequence the process and show sequential gains, consolidating those gains and imprinting the very risk management practices into the way all organizational members think about risk management – that is, anchoring the risk management thinking as a part of the corporate culture.

Hence, the change management process itself arguably contains the core elements of the effective risk management model by combining general direction with leeway for decentralized responsive actions, while a central function tries to keep track of ongoing activities and consolidate them for corporate use. Kotter relates good leadership to lifelong learning and that is exactly what strategic risk management can open up. This is also echoed by John Hayes, who argues that managers plan detailed action steps and allocate resources to achieve specified goals, whereas leaders set general direction and create strategic aspirations that engage organizational members in doing the right things as threats and opportunities emerge.[7] Ideally, the model becomes a vehicle for creating awareness to

---

[6] J. P. Kotter (1996). *Leading Change*. Harvard Business School Press: Boston, Massachusetts.

[7] See J. Hayes (2007). 'The Role of Leadership in Change Management' in *The Theory and Practice of Change Management* (2nd edn). Palgrave Macmillan: Houndmills, Basingstoke, Hampshire, pp. 168–75.

environmental changes of all types as identified in specialist risk units, various operational entities and a central analytical function around the top management team. This awareness should create a permanent sense of urgency that encourages employees in the field to stay alert and take appropriate responsive actions, while top management steers the corporation towards more attractive shores and the risk management function liaises between these efforts.

While we believe the discussions conducted throughout the preceding nine chapters of the book are helpful in outlining the contours of a more effective risk management model, we make no claim that this constitutes a final answer to the complex risk management challenge. Our aspirations are more humble, as we consider this an ongoing quest that requires continuous development. Hence, it is our hope that this book contributes genuine and well-founded ideas about how strategic risk management practices should be conducted. The book may fail in the attempt to find a panacea to the complex risk management challenge, but hopefully it constitutes a valuable stepping stone in the search for better ways to manage the current environmental challenges. As the book has extended the corporate risk landscape to consider all types of risk, encompassing more traditional hazards and economic risks, as well as operational risks and hard-to-quantify and sometimes unforeseeable strategic risks, the practices needed to achieve effective risk management outcomes obviously make for a more complicated puzzle. To some extent, it could be argued that *strategic risk management* boils down to imposing effective strategy-making processes or simply to instituting good management practices. However, we claim that the risk management perspective can prove useful in dealing with the complexity of the associated management challenge by providing fairly hands-on suggestions for how to deal with the contemporaneous needs for central integration, specialized risk expertise and decentralized responsiveness. We hope that this is indeed the case, but as expressed by one of our favoured (and anonymous) reviewers: 'the proof will be in the pudding'.

References

Hayes, J., 2007. 'The Role of Leadership in Change Management' in *The Theory and Practice of Change Management* (2nd edn). Palgrave Macmillan: Houndmills, Basingstoke, Hampshire, pp. 168–75.

Kotter, J. P., 1996. *Leading Change*. Harvard Business School Press: Boston, Massachusetts.

Pfeffer, J., 2007. *What Were They Thinking? Unconventional Wisdom About Management.* Harvard Business School Press: Boston, Massachusetts.

Schein, E. H., 2004. *Organizational Culture and Leadership* (3rd edn). Jossey-Bass: San Francisco.

Appendices

Appendix 1
A strategic responsiveness model

If we make the basic assumption that performance is a function of the extent to which the firm is able to create a better fit with current environmental conditions, for example, by adapting to the changing needs of customers, and firms have different adaptive abilities, then we will observe the inverse risk–return relationship: (see equation below)[1]

$$P_{t,i} = K - b|c - d_{t,i}|^a$$

$P_{t,i}$ is the performance of firm i during period t
K is an optimal performance indicator (the efficient frontier)
a, b are functional coefficients that affect the risk–return relationship
c can be interpreted as a universal environmental parameter
$d_{t,i}$ is the position of firm i in period t with regard to the environmental parameter

The adaptive capacity of an organization may comprise multiple capabilities, including financial hedging, economic exposure management, internal control systems, decentralized responsiveness and formal integrative risk management functions, which altogether may serve to accommodate effective adaptive behaviours. Such a comprehensive and balanced set of risk management processes may provide more systematic control of recurring risk events, while allowing observance and assessment of new emerging risks. This should allow the firm to avoid downside losses, while at the same time being able to exploit upside gains from new business opportunities.

The maximum return at a certain point in time (t) is K, which is determined by the current state of business competencies in the economy at large. However, the firm will gain higher returns when it is able to adapt and move the organization ($d_{t,i}$) closer towards the prevailing environment (c). The maximum level of performance (K) is achieved when the firm is completely adapted to the current environmental condition (this happens when $c = d_{t,i}$). High values of the

---

[1] Upside potentials can be achieved when the organization is able to position itself better to meet new market requirements regarding customer taste, operational structure, process configuration, technology adaptation, etc. The inverse risk–return relationship can also be reproduced from time sequential simulations where the firm adapts to environmental conditions observed during a previous period, i.e. $P_{t,i} = K - b|c - d_{t-1,i}|^a$. For a discussion of this, see T. J. Andersen and R. A. Bettis (2006), 'The Risk Return Effects of Strategic Responsiveness: A Simulation Analysis' in T. J. Andersen (ed.), *Perspectives on Strategic Risk Management*. CBS Press: Copenhagen, pp. 47–64.

coefficients a and b mean that the firm will experience higher penalties (in the form of lower performance) if it is falling off from responding to the current environmental condition.[2] Hence, with a more positive b and an a significantly above 1, the model describes a hostile competitive dynamic where firms are more severely punished for being off market. This will also lead to more dramatic inverse risk–return outcomes as reflective of hypercompetitive market conditions.

The basic principles of the model will also hold if K and c change over time and whether this change happens stochastically, in large jumps or along trend lines. That is, the underlying premises for the inverse risk–return relationship appear rather robust. The model can also be extended to incorporate an entire string (or vector) of different environmental characteristics (c's) and a comparable number of organizational positions ($d_{t,i}$'s). In that case, the inverse risk–return outcomes would still hold. This assumes that a risk management perspective implies that the environmental characteristics (the c's) can incorporate all of the significant risk management parameters (or risk factors).

The model then considers the effect of the firm being able to adapt towards the current environmental conditions, for example, by adapting inventory to current demand, fulfilling customer needs, adopting optimal technology, assuming appropriate operating processes, etc. If we interpret the risk factors widely to include also threats and opportunities identified in strategic risk analyses, then this approach may provide the firm with an ability to create foresight on major emerging risks, with a potential to exploit new business opportunities. This more comprehensive view corresponds to good risk management practice where the firm can avoid excessive downside losses as well as exploit upside business potentials, which is often implied, but rarely discussed explicitly in conventional ERM frameworks.

---

[2] The coefficient b determines the linear performance effect, whereas the coefficient a affects the performance function exponentially.

Appendix 2
Determining the premium on a call option

A call option gives the holder the right to buy the underlying asset before final maturity at a predetermined price. If the call option is in-the-money, the premium must exceed the difference between the current market price of the asset and the exercise price, otherwise the option can be exercised at a profit right after purchase.

Call option premium $\geq$ (Market price of asset – Exercise price) ≥ 0

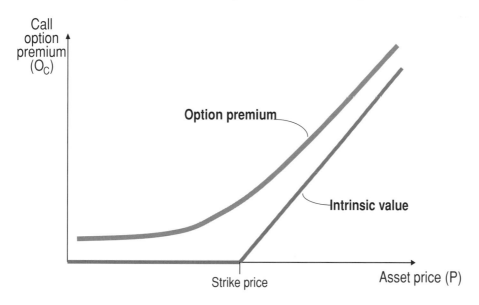

The option premium (O) will depend on the following factors:

- the market price of the underlying asset (P);
- the option strike or exercise price (S);
- the time to expiration date (t) [days/360];
- the volatility of market price or returns (v) – annualized standard deviation of returns;
- the risk-free rate (r); and
- the present value of dividend payments (D) [(div)e^{-rt}].

Whereby $O = g(P, S, t, v, r) - D$

The option price relationship to these factors was formalized by Black and Scholes as they developed a formula to approximate the call option premium (O_c) under simplifying assumptions:

- there are no transaction costs or taxes;
- the price of the asset follows a lognormal distribution (the compounded return is normally distributed);
- the volatility on the price movements is constant;
- the interest rate level is unchanged;
- there is continuous trading in the underlying asset; and
- in the case of stock options, no dividends are paid out before the maturity date.

In most cases, all of these assumptions will not be fulfilled. However, the theoretical option premium still provides a useful benchmark for the assessment of option premiums.

The call option premium is then determined by the following formula:

$$O_c = P[N(d1)] - S[N(d2)]e^{-rt}$$

Where:

$(d1) = (\ln(P/S) + (r + v2/2)t)/(v\sqrt{t})$
$(d2) = (\ln(P/S) + (r - v2/2)t)/(v\sqrt{t}) = d1 - v\sqrt{t}$
$N(\bullet) = $ Cumulative normal density function
$e = 2.71828$

Example: Assume the following market conditions: the market price of the asset is currently $41, the volatility of the price development is determined as 0.20 (20 per cent) and the risk-free rate is 5 per cent. The theoretical option premium of a call option (O_c) can then be determined on the underlying asset with strike price of $42, i.e. the option is slightly out-of-the-money, and with 90 days to final maturity, i.e. $t = 0.25$. To determine the premium of the call option, we perform the following calculations:

$$d1 = (\ln(41/42) + (0.05 + 0.22/2)0.25)/(0.2\sqrt{0.25})$$
$$= (-0.0241 + 0.07 \times 0.25)/0.1 = -0.066$$

$$d2 = -0.066 - 0.1 = -0.166$$

$$N(d1) = N(-0.066) = 0.4745$$

$$N(d2) = N(-0.166) = 0.4351$$

Whereby:

$$O_c = P[N(d1)] - S[N(d2)]e^{-rt}$$
$$= 41 \times 0.4745 - 42 \times 0.4351 \times e^{-0.05(0.25)}$$
$$= (19.45 - 18.05) = 1.40$$

That is, the theoretical premium of a call option giving the right to buy one entity of the asset at a price of $42 amounts to $1.40.

Appendix 3
Determining the value of a real option

A real option constitutes a right, but not an obligation, to carry out a particular action, such as a concrete business project, at some point in the future. All resource-committing decisions in an organization can be construed as such real options and when they exert significant influence on the future business of the corporation they may be referred to as strategic options. Real options give additional value to the corporation because they can be exercised under favourable conditions and left alone if conditions turn out to be unfavourable. Hence, the more environmental change envisaged around the payoff from a resource-committing action, the higher the incremental value of the associated options, because they represent opportunities to execute investments under particularly favourable conditions.

Evaluating a real option entails an assessment of the value potential associated with the environmental dynamics surrounding the business opportunity. Whereas financial options valuation is based on the price development of an underlying asset, real options valuation is typically based on the investment value of the underlying project.

A major difference between financial options and real options is that financial options are based on assets that are traded in transparent markets, while real options are based on investment opportunities that are idiosyncratic to the corporation itself and often remain undisclosed to the market until the time of implementation. Financial options are written into legally binding contracts, while real options relate to the identification and planning of corporate investment opportunities. Hence, the strike price of a financial option is the predetermined price level of the underlying asset specified in the contract, while the strike price of a real option corresponds to the investment required to effectuate the business opportunity and realize the underlying investment value.

Example: The investment needed to engage in a business venture is determined to be €1,000,000 (strike price) and the investment value of the venture is determined as €1,050,000 (market price), representing a positive net present value of €50,000. The development of the investment value is highly uncertain and is assumed to follow a log-normal distribution with a volatility of 35 per cent. The underlying investment opportunity is expected to be valid for some time, but must be executed within the next two years to utilize a superior technological capability. Hence, this project has an embedded option to defer the investment for two years (time

Comparing a financial option with a real option

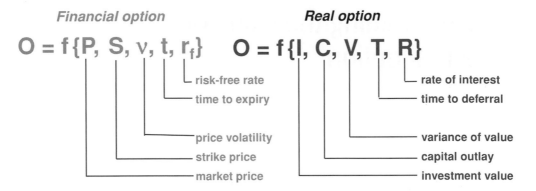

Financial option   **Real option**

$$O = f\{P, S, v, t, r_f\} \quad O = f\{I, C, V, T, R\}$$

- risk-free rate
- time to expiry
- price volatility
- strike price
- market price

- rate of interest
- time to deferral
- variance of value
- capital outlay
- investment value

The 'intrinsic value' of the option corresponds to the NPV of the underlying project, i.e. (I – C)

to maturity). Since the deferral corresponds to a future opportunity to exploit the project, it can be formalized as a call option with the value determined using the Black-Scholes formula:

$O_c = P[N(d1)] - S[N(d2)]e^{-rt}$, where
(d1) = $(\ln(P/S) + (r + v2/2)t)/(v\sqrt{t})$
(d2) = $\ln(P/S) + (r - v2/2)t)/(v\sqrt{t}) = d1 - v\sqrt{t}$
P = Market price
N(•) = Cumulative normal density function
S = Strike or exercise price
e = 2.71828
r = risk-free rate
t = time to maturity [days/360]
v = volatility − annualized standard deviation of returns

The real option premium (Oc) can then be determined on the basis of a strike price of 1,000 corresponding to the initial investment, two years to final maturity, i.e. t = 2.00, an assumed volatility of the underlying investment value of 35 per cent (= 0.35) and a risk-free rate of 5 per cent. Then:

$$d1 = (\ln(1050/1000) + (0.05 + 0.35^2/2)2)/(0.35\sqrt{2})$$
$$= (0.0488 + 0.1113 \times 2)/0.495 = 0.5481$$
$$d2 = 0.5481 - 0.4950 = 0.0531$$
$$N(d1) = N(0.5481) = 0.7082 \text{ and } N(d2) = N(0.0531) = 0.5211$$
Whereby $O_c = P[N(d1)] - S[N(d2)]e^{-rt}$
$$= 1050 \times 0.7082 - 1000 \times 0.5211 \times e^{-0.05}_{(2.00)}$$
$$= (743.61 - 471.51) = 272.1$$

That is, the real option is worth approximately €272,100 under the given assumptions.

Index